Contemporary industrialization

Contemporary Industrialization:

Spatial analysis and regional development

edited by **F. E. Ian Hamilton**

Longman
London and New York

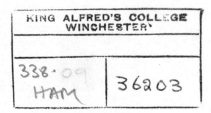
Longman Group Limited London

*Associated companies, branches and representatives
throughout the world*

*Published in the United States of America
by Longman Inc., New York*

© Longman Group Limited 1978

First published 1978

ISBN 0 582 48592 4

Library of Congress Cataloging in Publication Data
Main entry under title:

Contemporary industrialization.

Includes index.
1. Industries, Location of—Addresses, essays, lectures.
2. Industrialization—Addresses, essays, lectures.
3. Regional economics—Addresses, essays, lectures.
I. Hamilton, F. E. Ian.
HC79.D5C66   338'.09   77-13205
ISBN 0-582-48592-4

Typeset in Great Britain by The Pitman Press, Bath and printed by
Richard Clay (The Chaucer Press) Ltd., Bungay, Suffolk

Contents

Contributors

MARK K. BANDMAN — Institute of the Economics and the Organization of Industrial Production, Siberian Branch of The Soviet Academy of Sciences, Novosibirsk, USSR

BRENTON M. BARR — University of Calgary, Alberta, Canada

SERGIO BOISIER — United Nations Latin American Institute for Economic and Social Planning, Santiago, Chile

JOHN N. H. BRITTON — University of Toronto, Ontario, Canada

KENNETH J. FAIRBAIRN — University of Alberta, Edmonton, Alberta, Canada

JOHN B. GODDARD — University of Newcastle-upon-Tyne, England

F. E. IAN HAMILTON — London School of Economics & Political Science and School of Slavonic Studies, University of London, England

KARL H. HOTTES — Ruhr University, Bochum, North Rhine-Westphalia, Federal German Republic

GERALD J. KARASKA — Clark University, Worcester, Massachusetts, USA

ANTONI R. KUKLINSKI — Committee for Space Economy, Polish Academy of Sciences, Warsaw, Poland

ROGER LEIGH — Middlesex Polytechnic, Enfield, London, England

KIYOJI MURATA — Chuo University, Tokyo, Japan

DAVID J. NORTH — Middlesex Polytechnic, Enfield, London, England

ANETTE REENBERG — Copenhagen University, Denmark

MICHAEL J. TAYLOR — University of Auckland, New Zealand

GUNNAR TÖRNQVIST — Lund University, Sweden

Acknowledgements

We are grateful to the following for permission to reproduce copyright material: Institut de Sciences Mathématiques et Économiques Appliquées for the article 'Organizational information flows and the urban system', from *Revue Économie Appliquée*.

Preface

An examination of contemporary trends and problems in world industrialization and its locational analysis reveals that the initiatives taken by the International Geographical Union (I.G.U.) at its 22nd Congress in Montreal, Canada, in 1972 in establishing the Working Group on Industrial Geography were both timely and essential. In the majority of the world's states, which are seeking to move along the path of modernization, industrialization is perceived or is treated by governments as the key tool of policies for economic development, the catalyst for social change. In the older, most advanced nations, industrial policies must be adapted to take cognizance of the changed and changing role of industry in an emergent 'post-industrial' society while also reckoning with the impact on their industrial structures of industrialization in developing countries.

The implications are far-reaching for all countries in a wide range of related phenomena: patterns of resource use, regional development, employment structures, urbanization, provision of transport and social infrastructure, as well as for political and social behaviour. And increasingly these phenomena are coming under the more direct, as well as greater indirect, influence of government policymakers at all levels – national, regional and urban. Above all, however, contemporary industrial processes and their technological, organizational, economic and structural components are of great actual or potential significance in generating dynamic changes in the functional interrelationships *between places* at the local, urban, regional, national and international scales. Yet if the policies for industrial development, modernization and adaption – or even to create the right environmental conditions for such development – are to produce the desired economic, social, cultural and spatial results, then far more needs to be learned and understood by policymakers about the existence, functioning, dynamism and potential manipulation of industry as a tool for human betterment.

It is part of the task of the Working Group to contribute to this wider awareness of the processes operating in the real industrial world by: reviewing the current state of industrial location analysis; by identifying those questions and methods which, hitherto, have been inadequately investigated; and by initiating national studies of industrialization stages, processes, structures and their spatial manifestation to improve and, above all, to internationalize the theoretical, conceptual and practical attributes of modern spatial industrial research.

Such an enormous task cannot be more than initiated in one book. The chapters that follow, therefore, represent one small step on the long road towards these goals. The majority of chapters were specially prepared for, or were discussed as a result of, the first conference of the I.G.U. Working Group on Industrial Geography that was held at the London School of Economics and

Political Science, London, England, in September 1974. All are thus original essays.

Broadly the book sets out some of the issues that confront politicians and planners in shaping policies for spatial management at the national, regional or urban levels. A variety of ideas, approaches and experience is presented from a range of countries at different stages of development and with different environments for industrialization. The objective is to confront policy-makers with analytical issues which they appear to have neglected. Nevertheless, the path towards achieving this very objective is fraught with difficulties which are somewhat analogous to Myrdal's concept of 'circular' or 'cumulative causation'. For very extensive gaps remain in our knowledge and understanding of the scale, structure, organization, behaviour and functioning of industrial systems, however small or large, and of their socio-economic impact in geographic space, largely because policy-makers, planners or governments are often insufficiently aware of the complex ramifications of change in such systems – and so do not use their positions of power to collect enough of the necessary data – or they fear the use of collected data by internal pressure groups and opposition forces or by foreign agents against them; and so they suppress the publication or dissemination of information. In this way, therefore, they inhibit scientific study and understanding, stifling the quest for 'truth', and ultimately this has a feedback or 'backwash' effect upon the effectiveness of their own policies.

In this book members of the I.G.U. Working Group on Industrial Geography from Denmark, the Federal German Republic, Japan, Poland, the Soviet Union, the United Kingdom and the United States examine in broad terms the increasingly complex interrelationships between industrialization, organizations, location decisions, regional development and agglomeration, urbanization, technological change, site considerations and the growing awareness of environmental costs. This discussion paves the way for more detailed examination of challenges posed to policy-making by current trends in business organization: the expansion of non-manufacturing functions within industrial or industry-related organizations; and the increased importance of face-to-face contacts. Examples are drawn from experience in Sweden, the United Kingdom and the USA. Three papers focus upon the linkage behaviour and entrepreneurial perception of spatial economic opportunity among industrial firms in contrasting regions of the New World: the Albertan oil province in Canada, 'metropolitan' Ontario and New Zealand. While in a sense a more 'traditional' field of enquiry in industrial location studies, these chapters break new ground in their methods, in their investigation of service as well as manufacturing linkages and in their concern for the impact on behaviour or organizational structures, particularly of local *v.* non-local or 'national' *v.* 'foreign' ownership. The final two chapters examine new fields of industrial research which have major implications for regional development and urban economic structure: acquisitions or takeovers studied in selected British industries and spatial variations in industrial productivity and wages in a developing Latin American state, Brazil.

F. E. Ian Hamilton
Chairman, I.G.U. Working
Group on Industrial Geography

Chapter 1

The changing milieu of spatial industrial research

F. E. Ian Hamilton

The spatial study of human endeavour — whether that be economic, political or social and conducted on the urban, regional or global systematic plane — has entered an exciting period of envigoured debate, of searching enquiry, of re-evaluation. Geographical interest and involvement in policy-formulation for improving the quality and the spatial pattern of the living and working environment is not at all new. Yet there is a parallel need for change on the applied side of spatial sciences as well as for the reappraisal of theory, concepts and techniques. In the twentieth century a tardy process of scientific modernization in economic geography has gradually replaced descriptive analysis by the application of neo-classical economic theories which, after the Second World War, were supported by quantitative techniques of spatial analysis. While these proved valuable in measuring *pattern*, limitations in their utility for analysing *process* have spawned behavioural studies. Recently, however, neo-classical economic theory, quantitative analysis and behavioural studies have collectively come under increasing attack from those calling for a more dialectic or structural approach to spatial problems (Massey, 1974; Olsson, 1975).

A neglect of political economy in location analysis

Until the early 1960s, the spatial patterns of industrial activity in the mixed or capitalist societies of the western world were interpreted through the manufacturers' responses to dominantly economic variables. Utilization of material-resource and energy inputs, employment of labour, distribution of products to markets, tapping external 'agglomeration' economies of scale were explained by the rational, mechanistic response of entrepreneurs, mainly to costs, in the quest for profit maximization. Despite a growing interest both in internal economies of scale and in locational inertia, attention was focussed primarily upon the impact of the external economic environment on the firm's locational behaviour — an environment over which, it was supposed, the individual entrepreneur had little or no influence. The assumption of an isotropic plain with insignificant spatial variation in resources or population and of fixed production or market situations channelled analysis towards the dominant spatial influence of transport costs upon locational choice. Such an approach was very deeply rooted in classical and neo-classical economic theory and its spatial expression (Launhardt, 1882; Lösch, 1954; Weber, 1909).

Persistence of this approach has been strong. The process of modernizing industrial location analysis under the conditions of capitalism has been very slow.

1

So much spatial economic theory – even more so economic geography with its primary concern for location factors – has neglected the questions of the ownership and the management of the factors of production. Implicitly, analysts have assumed, by intent or by default, that the 'firm' is a static or 'given' organizational element and of no spatial consequence. By so doing, they supposed that individual firms continued to be small and numerous enough not to influence the prices or demand and supply conditions of material inputs, labour recruitment, transport services and markets, flows of capital and information or diffusion of technological and other innovations.

By accepting the same idealistic misconceptions of 'perfect' economic and information environments assumed by the neo-classical economists, many authors committed the error of being attracted by the sophisticated but academic rigours of the micro-economic theory of the firm and related marginal analysis: studies by Hyson & Hyson (1950), Mills & Lav (1964), Smith (1966) and Dean, Leahy and McKee (1970). By stimulating abstract and equilibrium analysis, it stifled conceptual and empirical study of the *realities* of industrial organization in capitalist societies. These could be summarized as follows:

1. the persistent growth, in relative importance as a result of great absolute expansion, of large corporations;
2. markets dominantly characterized by the highly imperfectly competitive conditions of oligopoly and monopoly, restricting consumer sovereignty;
3. business decisions which are the product of corporate strategy towards sets of objectives and only partially reflect the responses of corporations to an external environment which they can partly manipulate;
4. those same decisions are based on imperfect information and hence reflect varying degrees of uncertainty;
5. corporations rationalize such decisions – whether these are implicitly or explicitly spatial – according to their own corporate non-spatial objectives and criteria without concern for the spatial socio-economic or environmental consequences of their actions.

Multi-locational, multi-functional firms owning and operating many constituent productive units in vertically, horizontally or diagonally-integrated fields of economic endeavour were shaping forms of monopolistic or oligopolistic competition long before publication of Weber's work in 1909. Monopolies – 'probably as old as commercial civilization' (Letwin, 1968) – were fed and nurtured by aristocratic medieval and autocratic mercantilist governments through grants of privileges, especially in central Europe. Patent systems combined with floods of technological innovations in the eighteenth and nineteenth centuries, and the spatial and economic extension of empires by Western European states and Russia or of developing territory in North America, to generate large-scale enterprise gaining initial advantages. The same process, however, also produced severe competition and cyclical depression in the late nineteenth century. In response, firms combined into cartels, and adopted devious pricing tactics resembling the Pittsburgh-plus system. Such activities clearly expressed the attempts of corporations themselves to create – through the dominance and manipulation of capital, labour, product and transport markets – the economic environmental conditions both nationally and internationally, for both their survival and growth. One eloquent example is that the 187 *currently* largest American-controlled multinational industrial corporations owned 83 subsidiary firms in Europe *already by 1900* and that by 1939 these same corporations had 335, and, by 1967, over 1400 subsidiaries, in Europe (Vaupal & Curhan, 1969; Vernon, 1973).

The rise of monopolistic competition did not go unheeded by economists (Hamilton, 1967): leading examples are works by Chamberlain (1933), Fetter (1931), Piotrowski (1933), E. A. G. Robinson (1941), J. Robinson (1933), Bain (1956), Fellner (1949), Kaplan (1954), Machlup (1952), Stocking and Watkins (1948), and Stocking and Watkins (1951). Despite contributions by Hotelling (1929), Smithies (1941) and much later, Isard (1956) and Greenhut (1956), there was little attempt to incorporate theories of monopolistic competition in location analysis. Certainly the complexity involved in extending spatial analysis at the macro-economic and macro-geographic levels required made this technically difficult. More might have been achieved had fewer scientists with philosophical and quantitative expertise turned in the 1960s from economic geography towards the more 'fashionable' fields of urban studies and regional science.

Yet these are secondary problems. More basic is the neglect of political economy by spatial analysts in explaining why recognition of the force of large-scale organizations in shaping spatial economic and patterns and functioning has been so belated. Political economy integrates the study of economic behaviour with the study of the state, including institutions (and hence corporations) which are responsible for that behaviour. Among the most compelling economic theories are those emanating from the powerful socialist thinking embodied in the writings of Marx and Lenin. Because of their strong political overtones, predicting and charting the ultimate collapse of capitalism, their economic ideas have been large-ly ignored by western location theorists. The latter erect, in effect, their own ideological and political barriers against the introduction of Marxist–Leninist thinking because they perceived it to be unacceptable on two grounds: first, it con-flicts with their conservative views, vested interests or acclaimed national ideals; and second, they identify the translation of Marxist–Leninism into practice with the 'siege situation' of the Soviet Union during its phase of 'socialism in one country'.

Nevertheless it was Marx who, as early as 1848, sowed the seeds of the idea that capitalism embodies a process for creating ever larger industrial enterprises (Hamilton, 1967, pp. 369, 381, 403) which in time become also multinational enterprises, diffusing their multi-functional activities throughout the world:

The bourgeoisie cannot exist without constantly revolutionizing the instruments of production, and thereby the relations of production . . . . The need of a constantly expanding market for its products chases the bourgeoisie over the whole face of the globe. It must nestle everywhere, settle everywhere, establish connections everywhere. The bourgeoisie has, through its exploitations of the world mar-ket, given a cosmopolitan character the production and consumption in every country . . . . Industries no longer work with indigenous raw material but draw raw material from the remotest regions, industries whose products are consumed not only at home, but in every quarter of the globe . . . . In place of the old . . . national self-sufficiency we have . . . a universal interdependence of nations. (Marx, 1848; *see also* Mendel, 1961.)

Later, in *Das Kapital*, Marx vividly portrays how increased efficiency sharpens competition, creates periodic over-production crises, puts smaller capitalists out of business and so concentrates business even more: 'Their factories are absorbed by the sturdier, bigger enterprises, and . . . in the wake of each crisis, ever-increasing number of workers find themselves concentrated in these continually expanding industrial centres.' (Mendel, 1961, p. 8.)

It requires little conceptual effort either to link the strands of *The Communist Manifesto* and *Capital* together or to extend the principles involved in the process of the capitalist takeover of smaller, 'available' or less efficient firms to the conditions of economic growth, when Marx's term 'crisis' can be identified for individual firms with 'stress conditions' (Hamilton, 1974, p. 15).

Early in the twentieth century, Lenin conclusively sealed the identity of the capitalist corporation as a real and very powerful international force, the purveyor of a new, very subtle and more complex imperialism. By so doing, he not only extended the economic theories of Marx and Engels, but defined the building of empires by the subjugation and exploitation of colonial territories as the 'old' form of imperialism. In 1916, in *Imperialism, The Highest Stage of Capitalism*, he wrote:

Monopolist capitalism combines — cartels, syndicates, trusts — divide among themselves, first of all, the whole internal market of a country, and impose their control, more or less completely, upon the industry of that country. But under capitalism the home market is inevitably bound up with the foreign market. Capitalism long ago created a world market. As the export of capital and as the foreign and colonial relations increases and extends the 'spheres of influences' of the big monopolist combines, things tended 'naturally' toward an international agreement among these combines and toward the formation of international cartels . . .. But, concentration in Europe is part of a process of concentration in America . . .. The epoch of modern capitalism shows us that certain relations are established between capitalist alliances, based on the economic partition of the world; while parallel to this fact and connected with it, certain relations are established between political alliances, between states, on the basis of the territorial division of the world, of the struggle for colonies, of the 'struggle for economic territory'. (Lenin, 1916, *also see* Christman, 1966, pp. 219–21, 226.)

Lenin cites innumerable examples drawn from official, statistical, corporate or other published sources to substantiate his argument. Significantly, most relate to American and German industrial and finance corporations, though contemporary British and French concerns do not escape examination. A penetrating analysis demonstrates the processes of concentration within, and agreement between, the American and German electrical corporations, creating '*two* "Great Powers" . . . (G.E.C. and A.E.G.) . . . from which, no other electrical firm in the world is completely independent . . . and spawning subsidiaries in "new" countries and in other branches of industry' (Christman, 1966, pp. 221–2). Many other examples are presented, particularly from the oil, steel, mining and automobile industries. As Christman states (1966, p. 178): 'Of particular interest . . . is Lenin's attention to the history of American industry and finance . . . and his striking predictions concerning the development and role of the modern corporation.'

Yet Lenin had no delusions that 'leading bourgeois politicians fully appreciated the connection between . . . the purely economic and the politico-social roots of modern imperialism'. He quotes Cecil Rhodes (whom he described as 'a somewhat more honest social-chauvinist') as saying, after attending a meeting of the starving unemployed in London's East End, in 1895: '. . . to save the United Kingdom from a bloody civil war, we colonial statesmen must acquire new lands for settling surplus population, to provide new markets for the goods produced in the factories and mines. The Empire, as I have always said, is a bread and butter question.' (Christman, 1966, p. 229.)

Thus implicit in Marxist–Leninist thinking are the following. First, the notion that capitalism, through its multinational industrial and other business corporations and the spatial arrangement and functioning of their activities, perpetuates division of the world into 'rich' and 'poor' areas. Second, this operates through a 'core-periphery' relationship within corporations, both individually and in aggregate, which may be respectively identified spatially with the political empires of respective 'mother' countries – the homes of the corporations (cores) – but which may spread outside it into 'economic territory' (the periphery). Third, as a result of the quest for profit through greater efficiency and concentration, the capitalist process in effect forges a 'nested hierarchy' of 'cores' undergoing development and ringed by 'peripheries' experiencing under-development processes. The hierarchy comprises four 'orders':

1. Developed nations house corporate 'cores', whereas the periphery of under-developed nations lacks significant indigenous firms.
2. Irrespective of their very different stages of national development, within each country are found relatively advanced regions, nodes or metropolitan areas ('cores') where corporations localize their activities. In the 'home' developed country this comprises a complex web of head and divisional offices, manufacturing plants, warehouses, transport depots and subsidiaries while in the 'core' of the developing 'foreign' nation only smaller branch plants or subsidiaries and market outlets exist. The remainder of each country is made up of relatively 'backward' regions without corporate facilities, except in the most advanced countries where branches may be located in such regions.
3. Within each region are similar highly 'advanced' cities with corporate activities contrasting sharply with 'backward' rural hinterlands subservient in labour and other input supplies to the needs of corporate-dominated cities.
4. By logical extension there is a fourth and lowest spatial order: the contrast between the affluent zones inhabited by corporation shareholders and managers and the more extensive and relatively poverty-stricken zones or shanty towns inhabited by the workers (the proletariat) dependent either directly or indirectly upon those corporations.

Six decades have elapsed since Lenin wrote *Imperialism: The Highest Stage of Capitalism* and almost thirteen decades since publication of *The Communist Manifesto*. One may ask, quite legitimately, why Alfred Weber did not incorporate at least the significance of capitalist industrial organization in his location theory. After all, the writings of Marx and Engels, and many of the published sources used by Lenin, were available in Weber's native German language before 1900. Moreover, the spirit of the period throughout all Europe (including Germany) was one of socialist enlightenment, if not of socialist revolution. The likely answer to this question lies in the ideological barrier: Alfred Weber was much influenced by his renowned brother, Max Weber, whose conservative view of political economy strongly opposed the Marxist school. And, while there were more legitimate linguistic barriers to the diffusion of German theories, including Weber's, to the English-speaking world, it would appear that politics has been the chief obstacle even to the *examination* for relevance – which does not necessarily mean adoption – of Marxist–Leninist ideas.

The spatial significance of large-scale industrial organizations

The gravitational 'centre' of the Weberian school of research located in Europe in the late nineteenth and early twentieth century, and expressed in the works of Launhardt (1882), Weber (1909), Chisholm (1910, 1914) and Palander (1935) had moved by the mid-twentieth century to North America where it underwent extension and refinement into a neo-Weberian school through the writings of Hoover (1937, 1948), Greenhut (1952, 1956) and Isard (1956). This shift reflected as much a time-lag in the translation, diffusion, adoption and modification of theories published in the German language as also the geographical shift in the dominant centre of capitalist enterprise.

A new climate of thinking in industrial location analysis began to emerge in the 1960s and, since then, has constantly warmed the winds of change, altering their course with increasing force. The importance of organization is now fully recognized (Hamilton, 1974), although there are critics, mainly on grounds that geographers might become preoccupied in case studies with 'process' rather than with 'pattern' or with descriptive behaviouralism rather than behavioural theory. Significantly, the trend began in North America, the very environment in which geographers had for so long and so vehemently followed the neo-classical economic trail.

Indeed, most research into the spatial implications of organization pertains to, and is localized geographically in, Anglo-America, though recently it has begun to proliferate more generally within the English-speaking world (Wadley, 1975). This is hardly surprising: a high proportion of the non-socialist world's business is conducted by American, British and Canadian corporations. For example, the 187 largest US industrial corporations accounted for about two-fifths of *all* sales and assets of manufacturing in the US in 1966 *as well as* for the following percentage ranges of sales of leading manufacturers elsewhere: between 25 and 100 per cent in Canada; 8–40 per cent in Latin America; and 3–40 per cent in Western Europe. Expectedly, therefore, research interest in multinationals is growing within these areas too, as, for example, in Europe (Keuning, 1960; de Smit, 1966; Hamilton, forthcoming 1978).

Through its sheer scale dimensions (Loitard-Vogt, 1973; Pryor, 1972), multinational enterprise, as an extension of the problem of the geography of the corporation or of multi-locational organizations in general, brings into sharp focus the need for a modern approach to the location problem. The traditionally-viewed issue of selecting a location must be seen not in isolation but in the context of interrelationships of existing sets of production and service units and management objectives within the corporation. It raises questions regarding the nature and intensity of spatial interrelationships between those units within and across national frontiers (Ch. 10). Analysis thus hinges upon the spatial forms and consequences of the growth of multi-locational enterprises and hence upon the decision-making processes and motivations that corporations employ in formulating locational strategies. Moreover, long-term evolution and continued survival of any corporation can only be successful through pervasive influence in, or sensitive adaptation to, changing economic, social and political environments.

Geographers must examine the ways in which corporations alter the use, size and number of facilities under their control to attain corporate goals. A further field of enquiry, brought very much to the fore by multinational enterprise, is the need to compare the spatial behaviour and 'spatial adaptability' of: (1) firms with different organizations and scales operating in the same environments; and (2) identical organizations or, indeed, simply one organization, operating in contrasting environments.

The rise of large corporations has embodied two contrary long-term spatial tendencies. First, the increased concentration of capital, decision-making and administrative control leading to a diminution in the numbers of firms and hence also of decision control centres in operation in each industry. Concentration occurs at headquarters of decisions and services for the entire corporation, i.e. of those which have a high threshold and so demand intense, high-level, horizontal communication and personal contacts. (The analogy for the state is central government.) Greater concentration of production may result, too, from rationalization and increased scale economies through organizational or technological change. Second, the increased dispersion or decentralization of production, services, marketing and, to a lesser degree, decision-making. This contrary tendency results from corporate expansion and its concomitant creation or acquisition of branches or subsidiaries and franchised outlets and from functional diversification or product differentiation. These processes have generated new and higher thresholds to support greater division of labour within corporations (Richardson, 1972). An increased number of more specialized production, service or decision-making units becomes feasible, with an attendant increase in the scale and complexity of linkages or spatial interdependences among them.

In the medium- or short-term, there are cyclical shifts or oscillation between greater spatial concentration and greater spatial dispersion of administration, production and services (Hamilton, 1974). Undoubtedly such shifts reflect changes in corporate strategy and functional evolution, most probably related to the overall pattern of product life cycles of its outputs (including both goods and services). That pattern combines the four stages (Polli and Cook, 1969) of initiation, exponential growth or spread, maturation or slowdown, and decline for each component of the product-and-service mix. Shifts also result from responses to other external environmental changes.

Jansen (1974) generalizes corporate growth patterns in an analogue model of Myrdal's cyclical regional development process of cumulative causation (concentration) facilitating spread effects (dispersion). This notion acquires special significance when the spatial organization of all corporations is seen to comprise broadly a 'core' and a 'periphery' (Hamilton, 1974). At the scale of the multinational corporation such spatial organization frequently becomes identifiable in terms of a 'mother country' (the core) and the semi-colonial or colonial territories (the periphery) in Lenin's politico-economic sense.

Overall, growth and diversification strategies reflect a 'push–pull' corporate response to two types of perceived corporate need: (1) to counteract threats from competitors by entering or strengthening the share of, and control over, attractive and expanding, or necessary but contracting, markets; and (2) to reduce uncertainties by forward integration into markets to combat competition or economic recession, by backward integration into input supplies of materials and information and by general adaptation to technological, political or other changes.

In a broad world environment of economic expansion, political and psychological optimism since the Second World War, it has been natural to emphasize growth. Of course, without such growth opportunities corporations would not be as large as they are. Currently it is well to recall the hyper-inflation of the 1920s and early 1970s, the economic depression of the 1930s, the First and Second

World Wars, the 'cold war' years, and the more radical long-term changes – particularly 'decolonization' – of the past two decades. One should underline the crucial importance, therefore *uncertainty* and risk, especially resulting from political trends, in the decision-making balance sheet of the corporation.

In practice the 'psychic' cost-savings or benefits of uncertainty restriction that accrue from very large scale operations, market dominance and diversification make significant market entry difficult for new competitors and cushion the destructive effects of weakness in one product sector, so ensuring stability. Real production and service cost savings accrue from specialization of constituent functional units within the corporation, though a study of the three largest corporations operating in each of twelve industrial sectors in West Germany, France, the UK, Sweden, Canada and the USA concludes that greater savings realizable in transport costs encourage dispersed production to a greater extent than scale economies encourage concentrated production (Scherer, 1974). Control over 'middle' profits is achieved through backward and forward integration so reducing 'leakage' in the form of the higher profits normally required by contractors. All these savings more than offset higher real costs (Bannock, 1973) created by the substantial inefficiencies in huge corporate administrative bureaucracies.

Concern for the spatial aspects of business organization removes a fundamental error committed by location analysts in the past in isolating the choice of a location for long-term and short-term management decisions. Unquestionably *all* business decisions have geographical implications. From the spatial viewpoint, however, it is useful to distinguish between two broad types of decision. The first comprises decisions which involve an *explicit* or *direct* locational choice: *the establishment of a new, or the closure of an existing, plant or other facility.* The overwhelming focus of location analysis on this type of decision since Weber's time has largely obscured the great, often very much greater, importance of the second type of decision. This embraces those decisions which involve an *implicit* or *indirect* locational choice: *the alteration of the scale (a quantitative change) or of the functions (a qualitative change), or often both, in existing plants and other facilities.* Such a form of words is preferred to use of the terms 'explicit location decision' because the majority of business decisions are primarily taken with non-spatial objectives in mind and their 'locational' dimension is thus a consequential but not necessarily intentional 'by-product' of some overriding corporate economic or political strategy (Ch. 13).

The problem of small enterprise

Nevertheless, while study of the multi-locational organization brings these questions into prominence, it should not eclipse investigation of small-scale, single-facility enterprises. Frequently these are significant, and even dominate, in shaping the spatial socio-economic structure and prosperity of specific environments and areas (Barreyre, 1975). Often they remain important in the 'industry-related' environment of large-scale organizations by providing ancilliary or auxiliary industrial products and services through sub-contracting, especially in metropolitan regions. Even in urban or regional economies where a few major lead firms exhibit rapid growth and dominance, that very process of growth can 'spawn' a relatively high birth and survival rate of small firms.

Such businesses in aggregate can be very significant specifically in the economic and social fabric of 'inner city' zones. Their importance for research becomes more critical as larger-scale, or rapidly expanding smaller-scale, industrial organizations progressively leave the inner city to escape the disadvantages of the congested, ill-adapted built environment and to settle on 'greener sites', offering greater and new advantages in or beyond the suburban zone. Whether such movement results from 'spontaneous' economic and technological innovations of the industrial environment which encourage larger-scale operation on larger sites (Ch. 5), or whether it is hastened by government urban and regional planning policies, rarely is it paralleled by more than limited migration of the inner-city labour force. Small scale activities which remain, or new firms which are born and occupy vacated premises, can sometimes employ the industrial labour so released in the inner zones of cities.

But the survival of small manufacturing firms is threatened in the long term. Rising land values, emanating as inflationary 'tides' from the urban business centre, create pressures on industrial firms through rising rents and other costs and through the demand by commercial developers to construct more 'lucrative' and 'intensive' functions or of councils to build housing on their land. Automation of production processes and the impact on markets of competitors from overseas with significant labour-cost advantages can lead to the loss of highly-skilled jobs in, or closure of, traditional 'craft' industries. Relocation of larger or growing industries 'out-of-town' may result in the evaporation of the local market for the products of small firms which, if their management or labour is poorly adaptable to change, will also shut. Once significant breaks are made in a chain or network of linkages in such traditional industrial 'quarters', the process of manufacturing decay in inner urban zones may be rapid. Changing economic circumstances – local urban or wider market conditions – are not only explanations of such breaks. 'Death' of firms results, too, from the retirement of entrepreneurs or the passing away of entrepreneurial families, so causing 'holes' in entrepreneurial-level inter-personal contact networks and chains which are the very stuff of inner-city linkage patterns.

Many questions remain unanswered regarding the present and potential future role of small industrial enterprise, especially in cities. Increased concern for individual and aggregate entrepreneurial behaviour has revived interest in the study of births and deaths of firms which was examined long ago by Beesley (1955). Much needs still to be learned about the spatial importance and character of these processes, despite recent references by Lever (1975) and Singh and Whittington (1975). Even less appears to be known about the extent and nature of the survival of small firms through their adaption to altered conditions resulting from changes further along the line of either backward or forward industrial and service linkages. (The 'death' of firms frequently expresses their inability to adapt.) Most authors stress the key role of close personal contact in facilitating adaptation by small business to rapid alterations in market taste and fashion in the design of final products. But few can demonstrate the implied extension of their argument to the successive 'markets' in a chain or network of linkages: the latest work by Steed (1976) is an exception.

What is the process of adaptation as innovation and its feedback effects ebb and flow through the chain? To what extent do existing firms adapt successfully even to the problems created by the disappearance of 'old product' markets by innovating new manufactures or by moving 'up the chain', 'down the chain' or 'across chains and networks' of linkages into other products or components manufacture or into service activities? Do firms in 'traditional craft industries' – like precision optics, custom-made furniture, luxury goods or in those industries sub-contracting to larger manufacturers nearby – alter their output profiles as markets decline and adapt to producing or to servicing the expanding office and service requirements of city centres? Or do these firms die, leaving the new markets open to new enterprise, to newly-born firms or to in-migrating firms from elsewhere which occupy the premises vacated by 'dead' firms? No doubt the aggregate process results from some combination of births, deaths, in-migration and adaptation by surviving firms. But does it vary significantly from one type of industrial field to another within the same city, and from city to city, from one ethnic entrepreneurial group to another, from nation to nation, or not?

Greater understanding of these processes of industrial change within cities and metropolitan areas is required for very practical reasons. First the need to coordinate and to match evolving industrial situations both with projected or necessary renewal in the built environment which invariably involves a highly complex weave of interrelated changes serving potentially conflicting objectives: land-use redistribution for more and better housing and open space, the provision of new shopping and service centres, the construction of better roads and transport access; and changes in social relationships involving community cohesion, local job provision and access to jobs and services in other areas of the city. Second, it underlines the need to examine not only changes in the quantity of jobs available in, or accessible to, the inner city but also the ranges and degrees of labour *quality* of the remaining population, how these match or mismatch with new job provision and what measures are required to bridge the skill gaps. Certainly in Britain the long-term decline in inner-city industries, outmoded transport and associated warehousing facilities has focussed political and economic attention on quantitative employment situations. Far more information is required about the relationships between the supply from the inner-city labour pool (taking account of trends, which may be radical, in the socio-economic and ethnic composition of that population) and the demand by new local or central-city functions for various skills, aptitudes and adaptabilities. Above all, the role of small enterprise in preserving, or in achieving the right transition to, the 'best' inner-city living and working environments needs identification. Not least this demands a realistic assessment of the future place of small industries in the adaptation, development and evolution of regional and national economic systems.

This latter study has wide international significance. First, the problems of the out-movement or adaptation of small industries in inner areas of major cities repeat themselves across the industrialized world, whether this be New York, London (Martin, 1966; Hall, 1976), Paris (Bastié, 1975; Thompson, 1973), Moscow (Hamilton, 1976a) or Sydney (Logan, 1966; Lonsdale, 1972); it also occurs in large cities of the developing world as, for example, in São Paulo (Costa Santos, 1961). Second and at least as important, small-scale industrial enterprise plays a key role in the entire spatial economic structure of developed nations which have small populations and limited home market thresholds, such as in Norway, Denmark or New Zealand. Their presence should not be underestimated either in large countries which are 'compartmentalized' into essentially separate and restricted market areas by state regulations, as in Australia (Linge, in Hamilton, forthcoming, 1978). Third, far more significant, is the actual or potential role of small industries in the evolution of the urban structure and particularly in the modernization of the rural space economy of the vastly extensive and populous developing world. Not infrequently that role assumes more than just local or just economic importance: continued and successful operation of small industries in such countries becomes a key issue in the sheer survival, let alone the fostering, of indigenous entrepreneurship, capital ownership and traditional skills in the face of increased penetration by larger-scale, foreign-owned enterprises. Careful examination is required of the place that indigenous industrial enterprise can play in African, Asian and Latin American countries not only in achieving industrialization but, more important, in launching 'indigenous' or 'autonomous' industrialization which can counteract the long-term negative consequences of external economic control. The latter is indisputable: Bertin (1973) and Muller and Morgenstern (1974) show, from data collected in Latin America for 1966-9, that multinational enterprises 'bleed' developing countries by their pricing behaviour of marking-up prices of imports of equipment, components or materials to, and by marking down prices of products exported from, their branches and subsidiaries in those countries. Studies by Chaudhuri on India and Onyemelukwe on Nigeria (Hamilton, forthcoming, 1978) provide a starting point for studying industrial trends in developing countries. Yet they also indicate the existence of severe data limitations on such study.

Other changes in the industrial milieu

The shift from the pervasive influence of many small-scale enterprises to control by a limited number of large-scale organizations is not the only alteration that has occurred in the environment of industrial location analysis. Other rapid and radical economic, political, social and technological changes have occurred, mainly since the Second World War, though their origins frequently date back to the quarter of a century preceding the First World War.

Technological progress, innovating mass-production, and bulk transport, has demanded large-scale capitalization beyond the resources of all but the largest firms or of the State. Until recent inflationary processes began to alter the situation potentially, that progress also greatly lowered per unit material production (including energy) and transport costs, substantially reducing – but not eliminating – their locational importance. Technological and product innovation have continually lengthened the chain, and increased the complexity, of manufacturing, putting an increased premium on the frequency, the reliability and the quality of material and information input-supplies, labour supplies, on research and development. Automation of production processes is progressively reducing the relative – even the absolute – importance of manufacturing while, simultaneously, the scale and range of demand for non-manufacturing (services, maintenance, administration, information) has greatly increased *within* industrial systems. The spatial significance for policy-making of these trends is elaborated by Goddard and Törnqvist (Chs. 8 and 9). Contributing to the further expansion of organizational scale, this tendency has stimulated the rapid growth of multifunctional organizations, becoming integrated backwards, forwards and horizontally into primary, other secondary, tertiary and quaternary economic activities. The acquisition activity discussed by Leigh and North (Ch. 13) and the significance of linkage patterns examined by Britton, Barr and Fairbairn, and Taylor (Chs. 10–12) expound on these issues.

Parallel with these trends, complex changes have altered the world environment. Independent states have proliferated and new groupings and balances have been formed in the international political arena.

The role of the State as economic entrepreneur and arbiter and as a force formative of national and regional socio-economic environments has been strengthened (see Hamilton, forthcoming, 1978). Changing international trading environments (tariffs, quotas, agreements, economic unions, currency and price fluctuations) have very strongly influenced the spatial pattern of international flows of industrial capital, technical assistance, input supplies, labour and the shape and size of market areas and remain to be investigated. Political and economic forces have thus altered significantly the world geography of industry during the past four decades.

Greater complexity and increased dynamism of the political, economic and technological environments has increased the overall uncertainty facing the long-term, even medium-term, investment and operational programmes of industrial organizations whether these be private and corporate capitalist or state-owned. This has two major consequences, among many others: first, organizations are further encouraged to diversify their functions by acquiring ownership of, and franchises in, or cooperating with, organizations managing material and energy supply sources, transport services, market outlets, servicing and research. Second, greater importance is attached to obtaining, collecting, processing and applying information on pertinent matters both internal and external to the organization. Both assist in reducing, but do not eliminate, uncertainty.

The scientific environment for industrial location research has been no less dynamic, particularly during the past decade. Relationships between and methodologies in economics and other social and behavioural sciences have changed significantly. With respect to industrial location, micro-analysis and economic-deterministic approaches are beginning to be dislodged from their former positions of dominance and cast within a macro-analytical or general-systems framework which rightly takes into account the varied human dimensions – economic, social, political and psychological – that truly affect the motivations for, and the processes of, industrial development and change.

This trend, however, demands research into many problems at different scales. First, it encourages the macro-scale investigation of the spatial functioning and adaptation of entire industrial systems and of their place within urban, regional, national and international economic systems. Second, it necessitates greater study of spatial industrial change including migration and structural shifts at each of these levels (Hamilton, forthcoming, 1978). Third, it requires analysis of the evolution, structure, adjustment and goals of organizations engaged in industrial activities to establish how these elements affect perception of the spatial variable in location decisions of any kind and how that spatial dimension has a feedback effect upon organizational structures and their functioning. Fourth, it demands far deeper understanding at the micro-scale and their evaluation at the macro-scale of issues which, hitherto, have been recognized but inadequately examined: investment decision-making processes; market areas; spatial and functional linkages; and urban and regional economic attributes (Ch. 14). Far more needs to be understood about these facets since they apparently cast a socio-political, managerial, public administrative and psychological framework within which decision-maker perception of the more traditional economic forces, costs and benefits, operates.

Given the data, such research can bring into true prominence the importance in industrial systems of expansions, contractions and changes in functions of existing units and facilities as also the nature, scale and direction of diffusion of change (innovations, growth, decline, incomes or job-generation) among the units in each organization and in the total urban, regional, national and even the international system.

Some reflections on recent research

Analysis of these problems has already begun. Emergence of behavioural studies has been a key feature of the social sciences and geography in recent years. The analysis of decision-making relates the processes of investment or disinvestment and hence innovation in new and existing facilities to the goals and the functioning of the industrial organization in question – be it a private or corporate firm, or a state-owned or state institutional organization – as also to the relationships between the organization and its environment. Empirical research into decision-making is mainly undertaken at the micro-scale, yet deductive research can relate its findings to organizations, to urban and regional systems and to communications, transport and contact networks at the macro-scale. Though a recent publication explores these issues in substantial depth through theoretical, conceptual and empirical evidence from Britain, Canada, Japan, Nigeria, the Soviet Union, the USA and Yugoslavia (Hamilton, 1974), important gaps remain.

Behaviour, though, is a broad term. It expresses the manner in which organizations – and the personnel managing them – or individuals conduct the making of decisions and the execution and results of actions. Behaviour is thus very complex and consists in the intricate interactions between: (1) organizational forms which shape the perception, mental image and actions of the decision-makers responsible for respective organizations; (2) the interpretation of the goals and functions of organizations by their respective individual or group managements; and (3) each organization, represented by its management, with the external environment which shapes the decisions made and the actions taken and which comprises other organizations, their policies, economic, legal, political and social conditions and trends therein at urban, local, regional, national and international levels.

Behavioural studies emerged as an expression of dissatisfaction with over-generalized, even erroneous, economic assumptions about the real world which provided the framework for classical and neo-classical theories (Hamilton, 1967, pp. 362–82). Yet the general methodology of Weberian and neo-Weberian schools, with its concern for cost relationships, is still relevant, even though technological changes and rising concern for environmental quality and social welfare have altered the parameters involved and *provided that it is cast within the behavioural framework of organizations, their goals and operation within general spatial societal systems.* Ample evidence of this is given in research into decision-making by individual firms (as by Rees and Stafford in Hamilton, 1974), into industrial linkage behaviour (as by Bater and Walker, 1970; Smith, 1970) and into optimizing the spatial allocation of functional units within an organization, a region, a nation or the world (as, for example, by Bandman, 1970–3). The notions of transport and cost minimization can be extended methodologically to the idea of the 'minimization of social effort' widely recognized as a means of maximizing social benefit in the planned socialist economies. Indeed, this has been a basic component of Soviet decisions in the quest for striking some planned balance between regional self-sufficiency and regional specialization through the application of the 'territorial production complex' concept. This concept was evolved from Lenin's idea of the *kombinat*, or production combine, 'processing raw materials in successive manufacturing stages even to the finished product'. Moreover, planners invoke the principles of locating industries, as appropriate, near their material or energy input sources or near their market in classic Weberian fashion – though these principles act rather as *directional paths* toward specific spatial, economic, social and political goals within the organizational framework of a planned economy. The writings of the late Professor Probst (1965, 1971) provide ample evidence of how costs of alternative locations are assessed in making these decisions.

The behavioural approach has placed the choice of location for a new (or closure of an old) unit within its proper context: as just one of several options which *may* be available to the management of any industrial organization in any investment (or disinvestment) decision process. No less spatial in their expression, these options include: the expansion (or contraction) of existing production or functions at existing sites; the acquisition (or nationalization) of (or by) another firm or organization; and the rationalization of existing facilities by 'reallocating' types and scales of functions among them. Indeed, given large and dynamic organizations, it is conceivable that several of these options will be combined simultaneously or through time as an almost continuous or at least cyclical process. Thus decisions concerning any single unit cannot be taken in isolation but must be related to the dynamics and to the functioning of the entire system of the organization and its socio-economic environment.

Thus behavioural study has not only led to a reappraisal of the 'initial' location decision, it has brought into proper focus the importance of the adaptive processes by which the organization adjusts both to changing internal situations and to a dynamic external environment. In geographic terms this demands the study of how adaptive processes express themselves in the pattern of individual (and aggregate) organizations – that is in the 'migration', 'diffusion' or locational inertia of their operations – and in the changing spatial relationships – that is the backward and forward linkages – of each and every unit and place in these organizations.

Research during the past decade has examined mostly the behaviour of individual, or of samples of similar or dissimilar organizations, or has presented general hypotheses about spatial behaviour (Hamilton, 1970, 1974; Pred, 1967). Increasingly, however, attempts are being made to translate the results of micro-level case studies into macro-scale patterns and processes. Indeed, the myriad of investment decisions being put into effect by the sum of many industrial organizations in any country interweave to produce urban, regional, national and international socio-economic (structural) and spatial change from the complex transmission of innovation via material, information, income and employment linkages between the functioning places (i.e., locations with extractive, processing, manufacturing, service, administrative, distributive or research functions) within and between each and every organization.

Regional and national spatial industrial structures can result from three sets of processes:

1. the exposure of potential industrial entrepreneurs – defined as individuals, families, groups or state organizations with investment resources – through contact with, or chance location in proximity to, environments which range from 'information-poor' to 'information-rich' and hence from 'low-innovation stimulating' to 'high innovation stimulating';
2. the perception by such entrepreneurs of actual or latent economic opportunities in the local or known environment and of their links with opportunities in other and in regional, national and international environments;
3. innovation by progressive entrepreneurs whose spatial distribution is random but whose power, vision, expertise and organizational ability enables them to dominate, spatially to monopolize and so to manipulate their socio-economic environment, building up advantages in it which either perpetuate their spatial monopoly or attract local and in-migrating entrepreneurs 'to follow or to serve the leader'.

The first two processes interact to generate tendencies towards a cumulative–causal spatial association between the scales, diversities and linkages of industrial activity on the one hand and the perception of economic opportunities by entrepreneurs in response to levels of innovation stimuli on the other. They establish the link between 'individual' and 'aggregate' behaviour in shaping, if unfettered, ranges of development from 'cores' of high-intensity economic activity, information-, innovation- and city-richness through to 'peripheries' of limited economic activity, information-, innovation- and city-poverty. The third process creates random industrial (and city) locations or distributions which introduce important 'eccentricities' into the spatial system.

Human perceptions of economic opportunities – motives (like sales and profits), conditioning factors or constraints (like resource or infrastructure availability, costs) and of space and place operate to yield macro-behavioural patterns of geographic relations between the scales, types, diversities and linkages of industries (and dependent functions) on the one hand, and the settlement and regional systems and intra-metropolitan zonation on the other. Originally generalized and synthesized by Hamilton (1967, pp. 361–2, 389–93, 403–10) from research by Alexandersson (1956), Bain (1954), Curry (1964), Florence (1948), Kolossovsky (1958) and Philbrick (1957), these relationships have been examined again by Norcliffe (1975).

Current spatial industrial structure results from long-term aggregate paths and cycles of organizational growth and change with their dependent locational and linkage adjustments. Empirical evidence to support hypotheses on the spatial growth and diffusion of individual or sample firms and other industrial organizations is still limited, despite recent studies (Chapman, 1974; Erickson, 1974; Hamilton, 1974; Steed, 1968). Great diversity in expansion paths is apparent nevertheless, and emanates from variety in the early historical experience among organizations and in the strategies for expansion open to them: growth in scale to penetrate existing markets more thoroughly; diversification into complementary products; backward and forward vertical integration, innovation of new technology in serving existing markets; penetration of new market with existing technology and products; diversification into unrelated products, technologies and new markets or into research and development. Each path can be followed either by innovation within the organization or by acquisition of – in a planned economy, cooperation with – other organizations. Knowledge of these processes for each and every significant organization, their variation in type, degree and timing as well as their spatial expression is essential: not only would this link micro- with macro-behavioural patterns, it would also facilitate prediction of future changes by types of technologies and products, of industries, and their impact upon the spatial structure of labour markets, infrastructure, resources and income-generation. Such information would aid government in designing longer-term policies to influence such processes for the betterment of mankind in general and of national and regional populations in particular.

For example, the following hypotheses can be presented. First, the variety of expansion paths open to the same organization are likely to produce different locational patterns of its facilities, so affecting towns, regions or nations differentially. Policy formation needs to be based on information which will guide the expansion paths of individual organizations so that aggregated organizational paths result in spatial changes which accord best with the national, regional, urban and socio-economic goals set by the policy-makers. Second, organizations diversifying into technological and product fields which are related or close to their initial product lines might have success rates which differ from organizations diversifying into unrelated fields. Case studies must establish how far such a correlation exists and under which conditions and which meaningful policy framework might be devised to guide organizations in the regional and national (and their own) interest. Third, the short-term advantages of the acquisition of 'available' organizations over expansion within the organization itself may be outweighed by longer-term disadvantages arising in the post-acquisition rationalization phase: again policy-makers must weigh this balance and act accordingly (Ch. 13).

Significant new interest has been aroused in the 1970s in the processes of locational adaptation and of linkage adjustment by organizations in response to their own internally-initiated, or environmentally-imposed, change. This interest is late recognition that investment decisions are not 'once-and-for-all' events to be forgotten after execution: unfortunately many governments (as in Britain) treat it so (see Warren in Hamilton, forthcoming; also Hamilton in Markowski, ed., forthcoming). Rather such decisions initiate new eras in which organizations must learn to adapt their operations and by altering the origins and destinations of linkages within the organization and between it and the environment.

This is a new guise for long recognized problems. Locational inertia could be explained in the 1950s as the successful adjustment of industrial production at certain (if not, indeed, many) places to changed economic environments by the substitution of inputs and their sources, of outputs and their destinations, of the scale of production and of technology or changed input:output ratios (Isard, 1956; Moses, 1958). The study of branch-plant characteristics became fashionable following the pioneering work of Luttrell (1962), who established that the types and intensities of linkages between parent and branch plants, and the production profiles of the branches, tended to alter as the distances separating parent and branch increased. Recent research has enriched our understanding of these processes within the behavioural framework. Linkages are examined (Chs 10–13) between facilities within organizations and between organizations and their environments. Types, intensities and distances of linkages vary significantly as between those that occur within an organization and those affected outside it.

The new focus has modified substantially the traditional study of linkages in several ways. First, the interpretation of linkage solely as a short-distance phenomenon and important in external economies of scale and agglomeration, following Florence (1948), has been broadened to include each and every kind of linkage *irrespective of distance*. Second, the spectrum of types of linkage has been widened from traditional manufacturing linkages (especially in intermediate production) to embrace all material, component, marketing, servicing, research, administrative and decision-making linkages made by organizations. Particularly new is the emphasis on service and sales linkages. Third, investigation has begun into how the spatial structure of linkages changes through time as organizations expand or contract, and alter their products in response to stress conditions. Watts (1975) examines the extension of market areas with corporate growth, while Moseley and Townroe (1973) and Lever (in Hamilton, 1974; in Collins and Walker, 1975) assess whether or not plant relocation leads to readjustments in linkage patterns. Fourth, viewing linkages in these ways has brought new insights into the processes of the transmission of growth and change through the spatial system, permitting modifications of classic diffusion theories postulated by Hägerstrand, and applied to industrial technology diffusion by Hamilton (1967, pp. 401–2) and recently elaborated by Feller (in Collins and Walker, 1975).

References

Alexandersson, G. (1956), *The Industrial Structure of American Cities*, Nebraska U. P., Lincoln, 134 pp.
Bain, J. S. (1954), 'Economies of scale, concentration and the conditions of entry in twenty manufacturing industries', *American Economic Review*, 44, pp. 15–39.
Bain, J. S. (1956), *Barriers to New Competition*, Harvard U.P., Cambridge, 304 pp.
Bandman, M. K., ed. (1970–3), *Ekonomiko-Geograficheskiye Problemy Formirovaniya Territorial'no-Proizvodstvennykh Kompleksov Sibiri.*, 5 vols., Novosibirsk (IE OPP SO AN SSSR).
Bannock, G. (1973), *The Juggernauts*, Pelican, London.
Bastié, J. (1975), 'Industrial activity in the Parisian agglomeration', in L. Collins and D. F. Walker, eds., *Locational Dynamics of Manufacturing Activity*, Wiley, London, pp. 279–94.
Bater, J. H. and Walker, D. F. (1970), 'Further comments on industrial location and linkage', *Area*, 4, pp. 59–63.
Beesley, M. (1955), 'The birth and death of industrial establishments: experience in the West Midlands Conurbation', *Journal of Industrial Economics*, 4 (1).
Bertin, G. M. (1973), 'La croissance des sociétés multinationales: bilan et perspectives', *Banque, Paris*, 323, pp. 983–90.
Chamberlain, E. (1933), *The Theory of Monopolistic Competition*, Harvard U.P., Cambridge, 213 pp.
Chapman, K. (1973), 'Agglomeration and linkage in the United Kingdom petrochemical industry', *Transactions Institute of British Geographers*, 60, pp. 33–68.
Chisholm, G. G. (1910), 'Geographical relation of the market to seats of industry', *Scottish Geographical Magazine*, 26, pp. 169–82.
Chisholm, G. G. (1914), 'The development of the industries of Edinburgh and the Edinburgh district', *Scottish Geographical Magazine*, 30, pp. 312–21.
Christman, H. M. (ed.) (1966), *Essential Works of Lenin*, Bantam Books, New York/London.
Collins, L. and Walker, D. F., eds. (1975), *Locational Dynamics of Manufacturing Activity*, Wiley, London, 402 pp.
Costa Santos, M. (1961), *Decentralizacao Industrial no Estado de São Paulo*, São Paulo, 74 pp.
Curry, L. (1964), 'The random spatial economy: an exploration in settlement theory', *Annals of the Association of American Geographers*, 54, pp. 138–46.
Dean, R. D., Leahy, W. H. and McKee, D. L. (1970), *Spatial Economic Theory*, Free Press, New York, 365 pp.
De Smit, M. (1966), 'Foreign industrial enterprises located in the Netherlands', *Tijdschrift voor Economische en Sociale Geografie*, 57, pp. 1–19.
Erickson, R. A. (1974), 'The regional impact of growth firms: the case of Boeing, 1963–68', *Land Economics*, 2, pp. 127–36.

18   The changing milieu of spatial industrial research

Feller, I. (1975), 'Invention, diffusion and industrial location', in L. Collins and D. F. Walker, eds., op. cit.
Fellner, W. (1949), *Competition Among the Few*, Knopf, New York, 328 pp.
Fetter, F. A. (1931), *The Masquerade of Monopoly*, Knopf, New York, 470 pp.
Florence, P. S. (1948), *Investment, Location & Size of Plant*, National Institute for Economic & Social Research, Cambridge, 211 pp.
Greenhut, M. (1952), 'Integrating leading theories of plant location', *Southern Economic Journal*, 18, pp. 526–38.
Greenhut, M. L. (1956), *Plant Location in Theory & Practice*, University of North Carolina Press, Chapel Hill, 338 pp.
Hall, J. M. (1976), *London: Metropolis and Region*, Oxford U.P., Oxford, 48 pp.
Hamilton, F. E. I. (1967), 'Models of industrial location', Chapter 10 in: R. J. Chorley and P. Haggett, eds., *Models in Geography*, Methuen, London, pp. 361–424.
Hamilton, F. E. I. (1970), 'Aspects of spatial behaviour in planned economies', *Papers of the Regional Science Association*, XXV, pp. 84–106.
Hamilton, F. E. I., ed. (1974), *Spatial Perspectives on Industrial Organization and Decision-Making*, Wiley, London, 533 pp.
Hamilton, F. E. I. (1976a), *The Moscow City Region*, Oxford U.P., Oxford, 48 pp.
Hamilton, F. E. I. (1976b), 'New directions in the spatial analysis of industrial activity', *Folia Geographica Series Geographia-Oeconomica*, Kraków, Poland, IX, pp. 7–18.
Hamilton, F. E. I. (1976c), 'Contemporary industrialization and the location of economic activities: IGU Working Group on Industrial Geography', *Geoforum*, 7 (3), pp. 237–41.
Hamilton, F. E. I., ed. (forthcoming 1978) *Industrial Change: International Experience and Public Policy*, Longman, London.
Hoover, E. M. (1937), *Location Theory and the Shoe and Leather Industries*, Harvard U.P., Cambridge, 323 pp.
Hoover, E. M. (1948), *The Location of Economic Activity*, McGraw Hill, New York, 310 pp.
Hotelling, H. (1929), 'Stability in competition', *Economic Journal*, 39, pp. 41–57.
Hyson, C. D. and Hyson, W. P. (1950), 'The economic law of market areas', *Quarterly Journal of Economics*, 64, pp. 319–24.
Isard, W. (1956), *Location and Space Economy*, M.I.T., New York, 350 pp.
Jansen, A. C. M. (1974), 'Elementen van een Vestigingsplaatsmodel voor Industriele "Multi-Plant" Ondernemingen', *Tijdschrift voor Economische en Sociale Geografie*, 65 (3), pp. 174–92.
Kaplan, A. D. H. (1954), *Big Enterprise in a Competitive System*, Free Press, New York, 250 pp.
Keuning, H. J. (1960), 'Approaching economic geography from the point of view of enterprise', *Tijdschrift voor Economische en Sociale Geografie*, 51, pp. 10–71.
Kolossovsky, N. N. (1958), 'Proizvodstvenno-territorial' nye sochetanye (kompleks) v Sovetskoi ekonomicheskoi geografii' in: *Osnovi Ekonomicheskogo Raionirovaniya*, Moscow, 200 pp.
Launhardt, W. (1882), 'Die Bestimmung des zweckmassigsten Standorts einer gewerblichen Anlage', *Zeitschrift des Vereins Deutscher Ingenieure*, pp. 106–15.
Lenin, V. I. (1916), 'Imperialism – the highest stage of capitalism', reprinted in Christman (1966), ed., op. cit.
Letwin, W. L. (1968), 'Monopolies', *Encyclopaedia Britannica*, Chicago, 15, p. 748.
Lever, W. F. (1975), 'Manufacturing decentralization and shifts in factor costs and external economies', in L. Collins and D. F. Walker, eds., *Locational Dynamics of Manufacturing Activity*, Wiley, London/New York, pp. 295–324.
Logan, M. I. (1966), 'Capital city manufacturing in Australia', *Economic Geography*, 42, pp. 139–51.
Loitard-Vogt, P. (1973), 'Ombres et lumières des entreprises multinationales', *Revue Economique Sociale*, 4, pp. 329–43.
Lonsdale, R. E. (1972), 'Manufacturing decentralization: the discouraging record of Australia', *Land Economics*, 4, pp. 321–9.
Losch, A. (1954), *The Economics of Location*, Yale U.P., New Haven, 520 pp.
Luttrell, W. (1962), *Factory Location and Industrial Movement*, Cambridge U.P., London, 2 vols.
Machlup, F. (1952), *The Political Economy of Monopoly*, Johns Hopkins Press, Baltimore, 544 pp.
Martin, J. E. (1966), *Greater London: An Industrial Geography*, Bell, London.
Marx, K. (1848), 'The Communist Manifesto', reprinted in Mendel, A. P., ed., (1961), *The Essential Works of Marxism*, Bantam Books, London/New York.
Massey, D. (1974), 'Towards a critique of industrial location theory', *Centre for Environmental Studies Research Paper*, London, 27 pp.
Mills, E. S. and Lav, M. R. (1964), 'A model of market areas with free entry', *Journal of Political*

Economy, 72, pp. 278–88.

Moseley, M. and Townroe, P. M. (1973), 'Linkage adjustment following industrial movement', *Tijdschrift voor Economische en Sociale Geografie*, 64 (3), pp. 137–44.

Moses, L. M. (1958), 'Location and the theory of production', *Quarterly Journal of Economics*, 72, pp. 259–72.

Muller, R. and Morgenstern, R. D. (1974), 'Multinational corporations and balance of payments impacts in less developed countries', *Kyklos*, Basel, 27 (2), pp. 304–21.

Norcliffe, G. B. (1975), 'A theory of manufacturing places', in: L. Collins and D. F. Walker, eds, op. cit., pp. 19–57.

Olsson, G. (1975), 'The dialectics of spatial analysis', *Antipode*, pp. 26–33.

Palander, T. (1935), *Beiträge zur Standortstheorie*, Uppsala, 419 pp.

Philbrick, A. K. (1957), 'Principles of areal functional organization in regional human geography', *Economic Geography*, 33, pp. 299–336.

Piotrowski, R. (1933), *Cartels and Trusts*, Kegan Paul, London, 376 pp.

Polli, R. and Cook, V. (1969), 'Validity of the product life cycle', *Journal of Business*, 42 (4), pp. 385–400.

Pred, A. (1967), *Behaviour and Location*, Gleerup, Lund.

Probst, A. E. (1965), *Lokalizacja Przemysłu Socjalystycznego: Szkice Teoretyczne*, P.W.N., Warsaw, 320 pp.

Probst, A. E. (1971), *Voprosy Razmeshcheniya Sotsialisticheskoi Promyshlennost*, Nauka, Moscow.

Pryor, F. L. (1972), 'Size of production establishments in manufacturing', *Economic Journal*, 326, pp. 547–66.

Richardson, G. B. (1972), 'The organization of industry', *Economic Journal*, 327, pp. 883–96.

Robinson, E. A. G. (1941), *Monopoly*, Nisket, London, 298 pp.

Robinson, J. (1933), *Economics of Imperfect Competition*, Macmillan, London, 352 pp.

Scherer, F. M. (1974), 'The determinants of multi-plant operations in six nations and twelve industries', *Kyklos*, 7 (1), pp. 124–39.

Singh, A. and Whittington, G. (1975), 'The size and growth of firms', *Review of Economic Studies*, Edinburgh, 129, pp. 15–26.

Smith, D. M. (1966), 'A theoretical framework for geographical studies in industrial location', *Economic Geography*, 42 (2), pp. 95–113.

Smith, D. M. (1970), 'On throwing out Weber with the bathwater: a note on industrial location and linkage', *Area*, 1, pp. 15–18.

Smithies, A. (1941), 'Optimum location in spatial competition', *Journal of Political Economy*, 49, pp. 423–9.

Steed, G. P. F. (1968), 'The changing milieu of a firm: a case study of the shipbuilding concern', *Annals of the Association of American Geographers*, pp. 506–25.

Steed, G. P. F. (1971*a*), 'Forms of corporate environmental adaptation', *Tijdschrift voor Economische en Sociale Geografie*, 62, pp. 90–4.

Steed, G. P. F. (1971*b*), 'Plant adaptation, firm environments and location analysis', *Professional Geographer*, 23, pp. 324–8.

Steed, G. P. F. (1976), 'Centrality and locational change: printing, publishing and clothing in Montreal and Toronto', *Economic Geography*, 52 (3), pp. 193–205.

Steed, G. P. F. (1976), 'Locational factors and dynamics of Montreal's large garment complex', *Tijdschrift voor Economische en Sociale Geografie*, 67 (3), pp. 151–68.

Stocking, G. W. and Watkins, M. (1948), *Cartels or Competition?*, Twentieth Century Fund, New York, 516 pp.

Stocking, G. W. and Watkins, M. (1951), *Monopoly and Free Enterprise*, Twentieth Century Fund, New York, 596 pp.

Thompson, I. (1973), *The Paris Region*, Oxford U.P., Oxford, 48 pp.

Vaupal, J. W. and Curhan, J. R. (1969), *The Making of Multinational Enterprise*, Harvard Business School, Cambridge, 505 pp.

Vernon, R. (1973), *Sovereignty at Bay*, Pelican, London.

Wadley, D. A. (1975), *Corporate Decision-Making during Recession*, unpublished Ph.D. thesis, Australian National University, Canberra, 316 pp.

Watts, H. D. (1975), 'The market area of a firm', in: L. Collins and D. F. Walker, eds., *Locational Dynamics of Manufacturing*, Wiley, London, pp. 357–84.

Weber, A. (1909), *Über den Standort der Industrien, I: Reine Theorie des Standorts*, otübingen, 246 pp.

Wood, P. A. (1969), 'Industrial location and linkage', *Area*, 2, pp. 32–39.

Chapter 2

Industrialization, location and regional development

Antoni R. Kuklinski

In 1967 the United Nations Economic Commission for Europe published a report, *Criteria for Location of Industrial Plants: Changes and Problems.* The preface provides the following substantive summary of the report:

The Study attempts to provide an overall picture of the experience of ECE countries in the application of various criteria for industrial location. Taking into account the institutional context of these countries, the study focuses more particularly on the growing importance assumed by macro-economic criteria and on the basic change affecting the mechanism of the decision-making process of industrial location. The effects on locational factors and criteria of the more significant developments in industrial technology, economic management, regional policies and economic integration on an international scale are examined in some detail. A special section of the study is devoted to evaluating the relevance of experience derived by industrialized countries to problems of industrial location faced by developing countries.

The basic conclusions of that study are still valid, indeed even reinforced by the events of the past decade, despite some criticism of the report's view that regional inequalities are less important in the early stages of industrialization in developing countries (Karpov, Sdasiuk and Utkin, 1973). Current attention, therefore, should be focused upon world-wide study of, and integration of socio-economic policies for, industrial location, industrialization and regional development.

In many countries, for quite a long time, industrial location, industrialization and regional development were recognized as phenomena belonging to different spheres of socio-economic activities and policies. The micro-economic and entrepreneurial approach dominated in the decisions in the field of industrialization policies and the criteria of social equality were, at least theoretically, recognized as the leading criteria in regional policies.

The promotion of national policies and plans to guide economic development and social change has created a new framework for an integrated approach to industrial location, industrialization and regional development. Within this framework there is a growing importance of macro-criteria in the field of industrial location. This shift from micro- to macro-criteria is building an important link between industrial location, industrialization and regional development. Thus the scope and structure of industrialization policies is also changing, becoming much more comprehensive. They incorporate not only classical technico-economic analysis but also regional, social and environmental analysis, making the interrelation between industrialization policies and regional policies quite evident.

Such changes in attitude and approaches are firmly rooted in changes in objective reality. The scale of investment decisions is growing. The decision to locate a small plant is not an issue of industrialization and regional development. The decision concerning the location of a large integrated plant is important enough to be recognized simultaneously as an issue of industrialization and regional development policies. The difference between the two situations is especially evident in regions and countries with low levels of industrialization where the new investment is not an incremental but a structural change.

The problem also has an institutional dimension. To what extent are the changes in objective trends, in attitudes and approaches reflected in the changing patterns of institutions responsible for decisions relating to industrial location, industrialization and regional development? The field of regional studies during the last decade has advanced many contributions which open new perspectives on the integration of different approaches. Two most important trends relevant in this context are the study of (a) growth pole theories and policies and (b) the integration of global, functional and areal planning. Sometimes the judgement is expressed that growth pole theory is the closest approximation to the general theory of regional development. It is not necessary to discuss this controversial issue here. There is no doubt, however, that the growth-pole hypothesis is stimulating new theoretical and methodological approaches which contribute to the integration of industrial location, industrialization and regional development. Recently this line of thinking was well advanced by Boisier (1975). This author is convinced that such study should be explored as an important guideline to work in industrial geography.

While concentrating attention on the technical substance of the growth-pole hypothesis, the controversial issue related to the ideological substance of this theory should not be forgotten. It is worthwhile to quote in this context a few lines from the challenging paper by Coraggio (1975):

Even the mildest review of the prescriptions for development through the establishment of growth poles leaves an uneasy feeling of unsatisfaction: a feeling that the essential components of the proposal are being subtracted from the analysis, i.e. the components concerned with the real functioning conditions of a system of regions operating within a framework of dependent capitalism.

The methodological validity of the analysis and its corresponding strategy are therefore questioned. Are they not an attempt to apply to our countries a theory elaborated on the basis of different factual situations, more specifically, those of the dominant countries? Is it not also true that only the mechanistic elements of this theory are selected, proceeding next to their superficial adaption to hazardous conditions, the essential content being left aside?

Finally, is this strategy of development poles not an ideological screen concealing the real process of increasing integration of our spaces to the dominant system?

In *socio-economic planning* different changes are occurring. One is the growing differentiation in that field: the continuous emergence of new types of planning which claim sometimes a semi-autonomous status. Such status is built up by partial interest and approaches. The role of the academic community is quite important in this situation, since it is developing new intellectual structures for new types of planning. At the same time, there is growing dissatisfaction with diversification: it could, under certain conditions, be equal to disintegration. Thus many national and international research organizations argue that the main problem is the integration of different planning activities. The issue of a general, integrative approach to global, functional and areal planning is discussed very vividly. To achieve progress along these lines not only new ideas on general integration are required but also new ideas and approaches on partial integration which are building new bridges to interlink the different planning sub-systems. From this point of view the most important studies concern the integration of sectoral and regional approaches to long-term planning. Especially relevant are models and approaches developed in Moscow (Baranov, 1974), Warsaw (Porwit, 1974) and Rotterdam (Waardenburg, 1974). These studies are creating a general framework for the integrative approaches to industrial location, industrialization and regional development.

Studies published during the last decade have chosen *grosso modo* the easy way of progress. This was the preference for conceptual and methodological studies where the research cycle is relatively short and the outputs really or seemingly significant in relation to inputs. Studies of this type can be implemented by individual efforts: only in exceptional cases the organization of large-scale teams, based on national and international cooperation, is necessary.

A quite different situation exists with empirical studies. Here the input–output relations are much less favourable. Sometimes a very large research project processing a vast amount of data yields few valid generalizations. The large-scale empirical studies are a domain of well-organized collective efforts working on a long-term basis. It is not an accident that this difficult way of progress has been chosen much less frequently, especially where empirical studies incorporate broad international comparisons. A deficiency of large-scale empirical research efforts is the fundamental weakness of the studies on industrial location, industrialization and regional development. The IGU Working Group on Industrial Geography (The Commission on Industrial Systems since 1976) can perform a good service for the international community of scholars and planners in promoting a large-scale empirical study on industrial location, industrialization and regional development. Naturally, some effort on the conceptual and methodical front is also necessary but the main task force should be concentrated on empirical studies.

The International Geographical Union can initiate an international research programme on industrial location, industrialization and regional development. This programme should integrate different national and international studies implemented in the last decade (especially within the United Nations framework) but the *main goal of this research is to create new empirical foundations for our thinking.* It is not an accident that a comprehensive title is proposed for this study. The problems of industrial location cannot be isolated from the broader framework of industrialization policies and regional development. The managerial assumptions of the proposed research programme should be based on the cooperation of about fifty scholars and planners representing a differentiated group of developed and developing countries. The proposed research programme can incorporate three main research projects.

1. The first project should investigate the decision-making process in the field of industrial location, industrialization and regional development. A set of studies could be designed and implemented analysing the structure and mechanism of the decision-making processes which are functioning in the multi-level policy

and planning systems developed in different countries in response to different social, political and economic conditions and institutional solutions. In this broad framework one could discuss again the criteria applied in the field. The new status achieved by social and environmental considerations could be tested in this context. Last but not least, one should review the controversial issue of conceptual and institutional integration and disintegration of different approaches to industrial location, industrialization and regional development.

2. Empirically-oriented research on industrial location, industrialization and regional development could concentrate on twenty national studies. The time-horizon of these proposed case studies could incorporate two perspectives: an historical perspective of the two decades 1950–70 and a futurological perspective of the year 2000. Naturally, the rigours in the comparative approaches in time and space should be limited to the historical perspective where standardization of analytical methods is already possible. The empirical content of the case studies should be as follows: each *industrial location* case study should discuss the five most important industrial location decisions of the years 1950–70. Each industrialization study should examine the economic, social and environmental problems of industrial development at the national and regional scales (Szczepanski, 1973). Changes in the patterns of industrialization in the years 1950–70 are tested via the application of the shift technique, supported by other methods (see papers on the UK, Italy and Poland in Hamilton, forthcoming). The distinction of the rate and volume of industrial growth could be applied in these studies. Each *regional development* study should critically evaluate the basic trends in regional development in the given country. Within such a framework one could answer the fundamental question: how important are the decisions in the field of industrial location and industrialization for regional development?

3. A theoretically-oriented research project on industrial location, industrialization and regional development should represent the second stage of the proposed programme. After the circulation of the preliminary results of the first and second research projects a start should be made on studying the issues involved in the following questions: in what direction the general theoretical framework of industrial location, industrialization and regional development should be changed to reflect the new situations which are generated by changes in objective reality and in the decision-making processes functioning in this reality?

Conclusions

The ideas and proposals expressed in this paper represent only a rudimentary scheme of academic and managerial thinking. This scheme should be revised and expanded. However, there is no doubt that the fundamental idea of this programme is valid and is designed as a logical continuation of efforts which were started successfully in the framework of the United Nations Economic Commission for Europe and the United Nations Research Institute for Social Development.

References

Baranov, E. F. (1974), 'A system of optional perspective planning', in: A. R. Kuklinski, ed., *Regional Disaggregation of National Policies and Plans*, Mouton, The Hague.

Boisier, S. (1975), 'Industrialization, urbanization, polarization – towards a unified approach', in: A. R. Kuklinski, ed., *Polarized Development in Regional Policy & Regional Planning*, Mouton, The Hague.

Coraggio, J. L. (1975), 'Towards a revision of growth pole theory', in: A. R. Kuklinski, ed., *Polarized Development in Regional Policy and Regional Planning*, Mouton, The Hague.

Hamilton, F. E. I. (forthcoming, 1978), *Industrial Change: International Experience and Public Policy*, Longman, London.

Karpov, L. N., Sdasiuk, G. V. and Utkin, G. N. (1973), 'Osobennosti i problemy regional'nykh ekonomicheskikh issledovanii v sisteme OON', in: Yu. M. Pavlov and E. B. Alaev, eds., *Regional'nie Issledovaniya za Rubezhom*, Nauka, Moscow, pp. 278–89.

Kuklinski, A. R. (1975), 'The spatial dimension in policy and planning', in: A. R. Kuklinski, ed., *Regional Development and Planning: International Perspectives*, Sijtoff, Leyden, pp. 433–44.

Porwit, K. (1974), 'Regional models and economic planning', in: A. R. Kuklinski, ed., *Regional Disaggregation of National Policies and Plans*, Mouton, The Hague.

Szczepanski, J. (1973), *Zmiany Społeczeństwa Polskiego w Procesie Uprzemysłowienia*, Instytut Wydawniczy CRZZ, Warsaw.

Waardenburg, G. (1974), 'Regional disaggregation of national development planning', in: A. R. Kuklinski, op. cit.

United Nations Economic Commission for Europe (1967), *Criteria for the Location of Industrial Plants: Changes and Problems*, UN, New York.

Chapter 3

Industrial location and the optimization of territorial systems

Mark K. Bandman

There have been substantial changes in the tasks, approaches and techniques of industrial geography in accordance with: (1) changes in social and territorial forms of division of labour and production organization; (2) the introduction of new technologies; (3) the widening of the range of raw materials being used and outputs produced; (4) the improvement of applied mathematics and computers. Most experts are right to maintain that the time has passed for research into the problems of locating single uni-product plants within isolated areas and of placing certain combinations of multi-product activities of one industry within territorial taxonomic divisions of various scales. It is the questions of the location of combinations of interrelated productive activities – intersectoral complexes and of the formulation of territorial-production systems within particular regions, countries and continents – that must be put on the agenda and require practical solution.

Such work has some peculiarities. It calls for new approaches and techniques of research. Its emergence and outlooks are caused, in our opinion, by a number of factors. First, the increase in specialization of productive activities has called forth an intensification of intra-sector and inter-sector linkages. This has resulted in a sharp increase in the role of optimization of the location and of the relationships of the units as a factor in raising productive efficiency.

Second, an increase in the concentration of production has put in new claims not only on the quantity of resources used directly but also on the qualitative characteristics of the environment. The natural factor has by no means lost its significance. On the contrary, its importance with respect to solving the problems of the location of productive activities has become greater.

Third, both specialization and concentration in production have essentially changed the conditions of manpower supply: the demand for the quantity and quality of manpower are higher than ever before. As a result, the dependence of the efficiency of alternative production locations on the size, composition and mobility of manpower, and on the established and future settlement systems has become tighter.

Fourth, the specialization and concentration of industrial units have not only intensified the cooperation and combining of productive activities within industry, the linkages of industry with natural and manpower resources, but they have also amplified the relationships of industry with the whole economic and social environment – productive and social infrastructure, population and management (administration). This all has caused the emergence of new forms of opening up and development of regional productive forces. The efficiency of productive activities is now to a considerable degree determined both by the rationality of the location and the linkages between the units and by the rationality of the schemes of developing and locating the entire spectrum of economic activities of a corresponding region.

The changes in the conditions for the forming and the functioning of productive activities has not only increased the number of factors but also turned some of them from those which have been taken into consideration in an indirect manner to those which are directly involved in the process of solving problems. This widens substantially the dimensions and complicates the structure of one of the most important types of industrial geographic problems – that of optimizing the location and migration of productive activities. However, structural complexity is caused not only, and perhaps even not so much, by the increase in the number of the factors being taken into consideration as much as by the intricacy and diversity of the forms of their influence, i.e. the existence of direct and indirect, direct and inverse relationships not only between the factors and production but between the factors as well.

Not only do the environment, infrastructure and manpower affect the location of productive activities but the development of productive activities affects the state of the natural environment, the formation of infrastructure and manpower. In addition, an increase in the number of infrastructural elements caused by the emergence of a new and development of an existing productive activity will call for an increase in the number of working people. This will require the expansion of infrastructure and, as a result, the increased population number and infrastructure will enhance the load on the natural environment. Conservation measures will in their turn call for more labour and development of particular infrastructure elements, and so forth. Thus, each direct relationship gives rise, as a rule, to an inverse one.

Both direct and inverse relationships may be direct and indirect, i.e. occur between a pair of the research subjects directly or by means of a third one indirectly. For example, the investments in social infrastructure contribute to an improvement of the living conditions for the population. As a consequence, the degree of the people's attachment to the area in question increases together with the opportunities to control the migration of the population. As a result, production is able to reduce expenditure in attracting and training labour force.

It is difficult to take account of particular interrelationships, because of the fact that their effect manifests itself usually with a certain lag both in space and time. So, for example, the 'return' from additional investments in purification installations for the oil industrial plants of the basin of the Middle Ob'-river will result in preservation of fish resources in the areas of the Lower Ob' and in the performance indices of fishing industry there. Or else the accumulation of the residues of annual 'permissible' waste may in a long time period exceed the standard limit and complicate considerably the conditions of water use and reproduction of some 'renewable' resources. Thus, without a proper examination of the whole interaction of locational factors it is impossible to determine the geography of a given productive activity. The above relationships manifest themselves differently in the solution of the problems of different scales and in the studies of the problems of locating productive activities in regions with different natural and socio-economic conditions. This predetermines not only the varied role of the above conditions but also the differentiating level at which each of them is examined. Both the role and the level are determined in each given case depending on the study objective, subject peculiarities, time-period duration, scale of the region under study and social-economic conditions. In our opinion, the most geographical dimension† characterises the problems of industrial location and migration within regions or small countries. At this level the regional factors and interrelationships calling for complex geographical studies assume the greatest importance.

At present it seems to be impossible to solve definitely the locational problem of individual productive activity separately, without taking account of other activities, without bringing the findings of these studies into accord with the results obtained by the representatives of other disciplines, without complex regional studies. It is just these reasons that seem to rouse interest in using modern techniques and computers in research into specialization, location, formation processes, internal and external linkages of inter-sectoral industrial complexes within limited areas. Very initial attempts of such studies have turned fruitful and enriched undoubtedly conventional research in industrial geography. However, some shortcomings of the new approach are evident. Most researchers affirm justly the new approach also does not guarantee that the inverse relationships and the impact of an industrial complex to be created upon the environment would be appropriately taken into consideration.

This convinces us once more that many conventional problems of industrial geography should be solved as a part of a more general task, that of optimizing the structure of the whole economy of an area under study and first of all territorial-production systems. In this case the resources are a prerequisite and the demand of the national economy for them determines the period and scale of their exploitation, whereas the exploitation method and production organization determine the character of industrial location, with the latter affecting the territorial distribution of the rest of the economy, population and the composition of the relationships. Thus, production is the basis for forming the units of the national spatial structure at all levels and it is impossible to optimize its territorial distribution without taking into consideration the optimization of the structure of the whole economy of an area in question.

One of the principal research directions of the Institute of Economics and Organization of Industrial Production, Siberian Branch of the Soviet Academy of Sciences (IEOPP SO AN SSSR) is the elaboration of the system of models for long-term territorial-production planning. Questions of industrial geography are dealt with at various levels of the system with regard to the aspects of both space or territory (the country as a whole, regions, territorial-production complexes and industrial centres) and sector (a sector as a whole, a sector within regions, particular plants) aspects. With that end in view a number of models of various classes have been proposed. These economic–mathematical models have been used in solving a series of practical tasks:

1. Emphasis is placed on taking account of the inter-sector linkages: instead of the locational tasks for the units of one industry, those for a complex of interrelated industries are solved, e.g. timber-logging–woodworking; oil and gas extracting–oil refining; aluminium–soda–cement–electricity, and so on.
2. Account is taken of direct and inverse relationships between industrial branches and particular infrastructure elements (construction sites, construction industry; energy, transport and power, etc.).
3. Account is taken of direct and inverse relationships of the production sector

---

† In the original version of this paper Bandman uses the new Russian term 'geografichnost' or, literally translated, 'geographicity' (Ed.).

with the rest of the economy of a region, with the population and environment, i.e. industry is represented as one of the elements in the formation of the units of the national territorial-production system or that of a region, territorial-production complex or industrial centre.

This last (third) way is realized within a framework using the technique of economic–mathematical modelling for optimizing the process of forming regional territorial-production systems. The goals of this work are:

(a) to identify the main taxonomic units of a territorial system;
(b) to analyse the prerequisites for developing productive forces;
(c) to optimize interrelationships of all economy elements, population and environment;
(d) to optimize the production and spatial structure of the economy, the settlement system and the schedule for protecting and renewing natural resources;
(e) to design a scheme for forming the main taxonomic units of a region under study, with all subjects in question being considered as interrelates elements of territorial-production complexes of an appropriate level (Fig. 3.1). Such a representation of production has two further advantages (in addition to those mentioned above) as compared with the 'purely' sectoral interpretation of industrial location and migration.

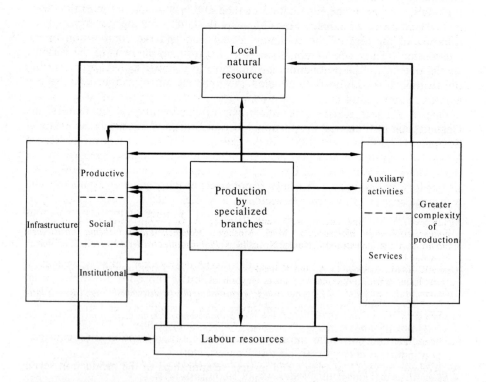

Fig. 3.1   Types of relationships in a territorial-production complex.

First, it is now possible not only to coordinate the location and development of industry with other elements of the economy of an area connected with it and with the supply of manpower over time but also to optimize this question with regard to the diversity of both direct and, which is of special importance, inverse relationships. Second, it becomes possible to analyse more thoroughly the probabilistic character of the research findings and increase their reliability. The effectiveness and 'life-expectancy' of the research findings depend largely on to what extent uncertainty of basic information is taken into account, on the variability of the economic environs, technological progress and other dynamic conditions. Uncertainty manifests itself in the optimization of the formation of the structural elements of territorial systems in different ways. A simultaneous consideration of industry with the other economic elements, manpower and natural resources makes it possible to analyse the uncertainty of forming not only separate units but also the entire aggregate of them. An opportunity occurs to devise the technique for studying adaptive properties not only of productive activities to economic, social and natural environments but also of the environment to a certain industrial location, development or migration alternative.

One of the IEOPP SO AN SSSR research outcomes is a version of the logical scheme and the tool for studying the role of industry in forming territorial-production systems and for optimizing the territorial distribution of industry as one of the elements of territorial-production complexes (TPC) of various levels. The logical scheme (the 'approach' of modelling the TPC formation) and the tool (the 'group of the models for forming TPCs') have been used in solving a number of practical problems in pre-planning studies of Siberia. To our mind, one of the lines of development of international research in the years to come could be represented by a study of conditions for forming and functioning of industry within local territorial-production combinations in various regions and countries. These studies could be both theoretical (research into the laws of location, relationships and place of industry) and applied (the solution of practical optimization problems). They should contribute to the improvement of research, to mastering the new technique and to intensifying the linkages with other scientific disciplines.

References

Aganbegyan, A. G., Bagrinovski, K. A. and Granberg, A. G. (1972), *Sistema modelei narodnokhoziaistvennogo planirovania*, Mysl, Moscow; *Metodicheskie polozhenia otraslevogo planirovania v promyshlennosti*, Nauka, Novosibirsk; *Planirovanie otraslevykh sistem*. Ekonomika, Moscow, 1974.

Alekseev, A. M., Kozlov, L. A. and Kriuchkov, V. N. (1974), *Setevye modeli v perspektivnom planirovanii razvitia proizvodstva*, Nauka, Novosibirsk.

Bandman, M. K., ed. (1969–75), *Formirovanie Territorial'no-proizvodstvennykh Kompleksov Sibiri*, IEOPP SO AN SSSR, Novosibirsk, Vols. I–VI.

Bandman, M. K. *et al.* (1971), *Modelirovanie Formirovania Territorial'no-proizvodstvennykh Kompleksov*, IEOPP SO AN SSSR, Novosibirsk, and Nauka 1975.

Bandman, M. K., ed. (1975), *Formirovanie Territorial'no-proizvodstvennykh Tompleksov Angaro-Yeniseiskogo Regiona*, Nauka, Novosibirsk.

Bandman, M. K. *et al.* (1975), *Metodocheskie Polozhenia Optimizatsii Prostranstvennoi Struktury Ekonomicheskogo Raiona*, IEOPP SO AN SSSR, Novosibirsk, 1975.

Chapter 4

The metropolitanization of industry

Gerald J. Karaska

Industrial geography has seen a number of paradigms spanning the last three decades. One early phase in industrial geography emphasized the case study, wherein the geographer was concerned with elaborating and measuring the numerous factors which were responsible for the location of an industry or firm. While there were many facets to this approach, it was distinctly empirical, calling upon real world facts and relationships. The 1950s saw the work of regional economists and a few geographers begin to expand upon the pioneering work of Weber, Lösch and others. Industrial location theory became the predominant wave of thinking and research. These developments have been followed by yet another paradigm, a wave of collective thinking which parallels developments in other subfields of geography, and which evolves as a combination of the two previous paradigms. The earliest themes and research were devoid of theory, while studies of location theory were too abstract and neglected fundamental properties of the real world. The new paradigm combines reality with a sincere respect for theory, while consciously considering social and 'human' issues. It has roots in general systems theory, is closely related to questions of economic development and is derived from the geographer's social conscience that his work become more relevant and useful. Such changing themes of industrial geography may be expressed in the context of general systems. The early case studies focused upon the elements of the system. To the location theorists, the important emphasis was the relationships between the elements. In modern industrial geography, the concern is with the total system.

Dimensions of the recent paradigm

The research which is on the frontier of the most recent paradigm in industrial geography has a distinctive focus. Its emphasis lies in an *interdependence* framework. That is, the firm or industry is seen as only one element in the total system or milieu, and the industry is viewed as related to all other elements in the system. Any change in the firm is seen as not only affecting everything else, but the impacts 'feedback' to create yet another change in the original firm. While interdependence is the distinguishing feature, there are other dimensions or manifestations of the research effort: behavioural aspects, impact statements, dynamic properties, sub-system properties and a perspective of relative space.

The behavioural dimension

The manufacturing-regional system is viewed as focusing upon *man* and his personal, subjective behaviour. While this view certainly adds a 'human' quality to the system, it also endeavours to point to a very critical factor in the system, namely decision-making. Geography has long recognized that the location of industry is influenced by a decision of the owner-manager. Yet, only recently has research probed the character and reasons behind any particular decision. The earlier paradigms had acknowledged the subjective and personal influences upon decisions, but more recent research has emphasized the decision-maker as a product of complicated cultural and historical forces which influence his values. These values are profoundly affected by policy and goals attributable to political economy. Examination of psychological influences upon the character of the decision-maker is still in embryo.

Impact statements

Impact and multiplier analyses are familiar. Especially popular are the economic base and input/output frameworks. Inherent in these analyses is another view of the new paradigm. Industry is linked and connected not only to other industry by other businesses and institutions. In fact, any single firm can be shown to be connected to *all* other elements in the system. Thus, the answer to the question of the location of a firm or industry lies in articulating the complex set of linkages in the system. The patterns of wholesaling and retailing, for example, bear a critical relationship upon the pattern of industry. So, too, do journeys to work and consumption habits influence industrial location. Thus to understand location one must comprehend all the processes at work in the system, including the influences of the natural environment and political institutions.

The manufacturing sub-system

Within that total milieu the complexities of the firm, that is, corporate structure and organization, must be recognized. The modern industrial firm is not a simple, one-man management system. It is a highly complex business organization comprising many men and a myriad of decisions. In addition, the firm is frequently interlocked with the corporate structures of other firms and even with other national systems. It is only very recently that we have begun to probe inter-industry relationships: highly complex linkages as products move through many stages of fabrication to final consumption. Most industries sell to other industries. We have yet to clearly articulate these patterns, let alone explain or model them. Recent work has revealed that *wholesaling* is an extremely critical and vital element in these inter-industry relationships. A huge volume of industrial sales filters through 'middlemen'. It is essential to analyse what this fact must mean for the location of industries and the establishment of industrial complexes. This dimension of the manufacturing system also included other management attributes of the firm. One operation of corporate structure which has been sorely neglected is the financial-investment phase. Financial linkages with banks, investors, interlocking corporate arrangements, and even foreign institutions are factors which critically influence the location and level of production.

The perception of space

Geographers have begun to acknowledge that space and maps may be portrayed in relative rather than absolute metrics. The distance between two places need not be measured in miles or costs per mile, but may in fact be measured in psychological and social costs. To *modern* industry it is not the transportation charges and costs which are considered, rather it is the speed, efficiency and dependability of supply, and the sets of mental maps which ultimately determine the buying–selling relationship. Further, the procurement and sales relationship is often determined by personal face-to-face contracts. Here we include such considerations as embraced by recent studies on mental maps, spatial perceptions and social spaces.

Dynamics properties

The interdependent flavour of the recent paradigm in industrial geography may also be considered dynamic in the sense that each stage or level of the system evolves to yet another stage. Thus, not only are all elements of the system interconnected so that impacts or changes are transmitted throughout the region, but the total system can be seen to develop in predictable patterns. In a very real sense, then, a theory of industrial location is inextricably bound to a theory of regional economic development.

While linkage or impact statements focus upon change and, in one sense, the dynamic properties of the system, there is a kind of overriding 'stage' of the system. Manufacturing processes, management and locational patterns have meaning only in this general or 'totality' context, which implies change and evolution through time. The stage of development critically affects the process, behaviour and patterns of the industrial systems. The temporal, economic development sequence that nations have undergone is well documented. Here attention focuses on the American scene to postulate that it represents one leading, advanced stage. Other scenes (nations) are hypothesized as eventually evolving toward the American pattern.

Some evidence on a theme

Views of the new paradigm in industrial geography are guided by some observations on the behaviour and the patterns of industry in the USA. These observations appear as contradictions to traditional locational concepts and themes. They suggest the basis for not only the re-formulation of industrial location theory, but the creation of a new theory. These critical facts are:

1. There exists a 'friction free' flow of products from industry to industry. The procurement patterns of American industry reveal a random spatial pattern.
2. Industry location is dominated by a concentration in metropolitan areas and regional complexes.
3. The industrial composition or structure of the metropolitan areas is remarkably similar to each other: 'industry is everywhere the same'.

Random flows

Our literature describes the location of industry under such headings as market-orientated, material-orientated and footloose, etc. These terms were derived from our traditional preoccupations with profit maximization, cost minimization and transport-distance costs. They were reflections of our naivety and rather narrow perspective of the contributing factors or forces. One cannot be too critical, for, indeed, in the early stages of economic growth and industrialization, the locations of raw materials, the restrictions of physical space and the simplicity of production were real. These terms, and this naive perspective, however, lose sight of the facts of modern industrial life. The modern firm is a sophisticated and complex enterprise which critically depends upon communication and active participation. In addition, contemporary manufacturing processes are highly complicated and technically advanced, comprising a myriad of products of almost infinite variety. And, most important, it is a standardized process: anyone can make products of comparable quality.

The manufacturing process is a long chain of fabrication, wherein the product of one firm becomes a component to another firm, which moves to another factory for assembly into another product, and so on. For example, the 1958 input/output table of the US economy reported that most industrial output was

Table 4.1 The number of manufacturing sectors selling directly to final demand (US input/output table 1958)

Per cent	Number	Cumulative per cent
90–100	0	100
80–89	1	100
70–79	9	98
60–69	5	81
50–59	7	71
40–49	4	58
30–39	4	50
20–29	2	42
10–19	6	38
0–9	14	27
Total	52	

destined for other industries (Table 4.1). At the same time, this chain of component assembly is not linear. It is a multiple chain or stream. That is, each firm specializes in the production of a standardized (even specialized-standardized) piece which can be sold to many different production streams.

Finally, the cost of these material inputs to a firm comprises only a small proportion of the total costs. The 1958 input/output table reveals that for most industries these material costs are less than half the cost of the final product (Table 4.2). Therefore, it is *not* the costs of delivery of materials and products which are critical to the enterprise, and which determine industrial location. Nor are the location factors dominated by the linkages or proximity to other industries. Transport costs and agglomeration economics are not the critical factors, rather the critical metrics of geographic space are 'metropolitan externalities' which are measured in terms of speed, efficiency, dependability and reliability of goods, services and information.

Metropolitan concentration

The most favourable location for a producing unit, then, is where there exists a localized concentration of other producers, businesses, people and institutions. This factor of concentration should not be confused with the industrial complex notion or the agglomeration factor, for it is not necessarily efficient nor critical that the firms in the complex feed on each other. Rather, their existence depends upon the presence of economic, social and institutional externalities which determine economic, social and political spatial efficiency.

A significant proportion of manufacturing costs are attributable to non-material

Table 4.2   Input coefficients from primary and secondary industries by industry class (1958 input/output table)

Industry class	Coefficient	Industry class	Coefficient
Food	0.056818	Heat-plumbing and structural	
Tobacco	0.43507	metals	0.50850
Broad textiles	0.61939	Stamp-screws and bolts	0.54625
Miscellaneous textiles	0.51471	Fabricated metals	0.45578
Apparel	0.52038	Engines and turbines	0.48676
Miscellaneous fibre		Farm machinery	0.57882
textiles	0.67168	Construction goods	0.45789
Lumber and wood	0.47662	Materials handling	0.50981
Wood cuts	0.48740	Metal working	0.37615
House furniture	0.44547	Special industries	0.43148
Other furniture and		Industrial machinery	0.44483
fixtures	0.42960	Machine shops	0.34959
Paper and allied	0.42735	Office computer and	
Chemicals (selected)	0.44022	accounting machinery	0.28735
Plastics and synthetics	0.49107	Service industries	0.53189
Pharmaceuticals	0.34443	Electrical industries	0.39144
Paints	0.49689	Household appliances	0.44988
Petroleum	0.64983	Electric light	0.40014
Rubber and miscellaneous	0.38252	Radio-TV	0.44026
Leather	0.55932	Electric components	0.41421
Footwear	0.45195	Miscellaneous electrical	
Glass	0.27010	machinery	0.45751
Stone and clay	0.32841	Motor vehicles	0.58567
Primary iron and steel	0.44053	Aircraft and parts	0.46704
Primary non-ferrous		Other transport	0.49720
metals	0.52522	Scientific and control	0.40286
Metal containers	0.56584	Optical-opthalmic	0.28829
		Miscellaneous manufacturing	0.39014

(input) costs, namely: wages, sales-advertising expenses, capital availability, wholesaling and even taxes (municipal services). Further, industrial organization is controlled by a very broad (horizontal) system of financial–legal corporate linkages. Industry is replete with branch offices, corporate headquarters, distribution sites and sales offices, not to mention an elaborate set of management controls and multinational organizational precepts. For example, it is becoming increasingly difficult for enumerators to distinguish between manufacturing employment and service employment. One could, thus, speak of the 'tertiarization of secondary employment'. The theme of a dominant locational pull by the metropolitan areas upon industry location serves to emphasize that our theory be directed toward interdependence and total systems notions.

Compositional similarity

Observation shows that the industrial composition of American metropolitan areas is remarkably similar. One should not describe industrial location in terms of textiles in the South, or electronics in New England. The existing regional specializations, while real, are negligible and misleading descriptions of the true state. The logic behind this theme derives from the preceding argument or discussion, but to this must be added some additional insights. First, the US economy not only produces sophisticated components and products, but its *consumption* is voluminous, beyond comparison. Thus, not only is the pattern of the flows complex and random, but the volume of these flows or streams is great. The only logical solution to explain or control these flows is to say that the production units are evenly distributed among all the sub-areas, so that each sub-area has a similar composition. The 'underdevelopment' of certain parts of the USA is only a relative term: regional personal incomes have been equalizing at an extremely rapid rate.

This logic still does not imply a distribution which is determined by consumption. Rather, it says that because of the spatial efficiency of agglomerations or complexes, particularly reflecting their externalities and infrastructures, each complex must develop and advance in response to its total production–service requisites. Second, the production–service complexes are arranged in a nested, hierarchical pattern similar to central place theory: an incidence matrix for the number of manufacturing firms, arranged by size of metropolitan area for a portion of the Midwest, shows a symmetry comparable with that found in the classical central place matrix.

A scenario

The intended meaning of the preceding discussion can be best conveyed by presenting a scenario of industrial location in the USA. American manufacturing was established on the basis of settlement patterns, innovative behaviour (inventions, etc.), the location of critical raw materials and the overall economic, cultural and political developments in the history of the USA. One might point to some significant date, say 1940, and state that the primary concentrations of industry were well established. Since that time, very few major new concentrations have appeared, major trends being toward a decentralization which was two-fold: first, away from the centre of our cities toward the peripheries (i.e. suburbanization) and second, a movement toward the more under-developed parts of the USA.

By 1970 all parts of the country have felt the economic effects of industry. Most important, extremely rapid growth in transport and urban systems has yielded the net effect of including everyone in our urban society. Even the rural farmer in Kentucky has exposure to, and participation in, all the amenities, goods and services of our modern society. Instead of distinguishing our population into urban *vs.* rural components, today all are urban and arranged by metropolitan areas. Berry's maps of commuting patterns to metropolitan areas beautifully describe the 'filling up' of our space by metropolitan zones of dominance.

At the same time, in 1970 the manufacturing processes are well standardized. Inventions are not only very small in number, but they can be adopted by anyone to produce a comparable component. For example, the inventions in electronics which founded the Boston–New England complexes have become so standardized that they have been adopted everywhere, and one finds most new electronics factories (even corporations) being born in 'medium-sized towns' in Texas. What, then, is the trend in the migration (birth, death, transfer) of new plants? The evolving pattern is metropolitan–hierarchical. Many migrations are *intra*-metropolitan and reflect industry's response to everyday, or short-run, changes in their financial or cost structures. These movements still maintain the critical ties of participation in a metropolitan economy. There are a set of *inter*-metropolitan moves which reflect the same responses to everyday cyclical changes. Industry moves to another metropolitan area to gain some short-run benefits (also inducing some added short-run costs); these firms are still dependent upon metropolitan externalities.

The preceding moves represent kinds of 'random' movements. That is, they are responses to a multitude of forces, the explanation of which are singularly un-predictable, but in aggregate are predictable. For some industries their migration can be explained by some elements from the random process, but another part of the explanation rests in the opening up of new growth areas. Smaller metropolitan areas are conducive to the growth of new industries which act as service com-ponents to the total system-region. Each smaller metropolitan area will strive to develop its food, printing, plastics, paving materials, cement, foundries, forgings, fabrications and machinery industries. Some higher order metropolises will add another set of industries which interact with a larger region or set of metropolitan areas. The total system, then, looks like a hierarchical nest similar to central place theory.

It is conceivable that the future development of the scenario has the US par-titioned into equalized, nested sets of industrial composites. The metropolitan areas at each rung of the hierarchy would have similar industrial compositions. Specialization of industry, then, would apply to higher order metropolitan areas. Of course, there would exist anomalies or distinctive specialization, describing those industries which are still tied to sources of raw materials or unusual cost advantages.

Chapter 5

The limits of regional agglomeration and social cost

Kiyoji Murata

Traditional location theory

The gap between the theoretical explanation of industrial agglomeration and reality is so wide that it is of limited use in understanding the size of existing industrial regions. The possibility of excess-agglomeration was not adequately considered. Weber (1909, pp. 126–8) divided the concept of agglomeration into two categories, namely, 'enlargement of plant' at a low stage and 'social agglomeration' at a high stage where multiple plants are located close to each other. He thought that the forces encouraging social agglomeration were the same as those creating large-scale plant. Therefore, the terms 'low stage' and 'high stage' were not devised to consider the expansion in the size of a single plant, the concentration of multiple plants in the development phase, or to question the relevance between the two. No remarkable significance can be seen in the classification itself. Moreover 'social agglomeration' does not involve analysis of the social factors promoting agglomeration but simply questions the technical possibility of the parallel existence of multiple plants close to each other in the same area: it is thus nothing but 'regional agglomeration'.

Production activities can save costs by enjoying 'agglomeration advantages' and can expand their market areas correspondingly. Industrial production creates industrial areas by increasing plant size and by attracting many production units, although this process differs according to the types of industries, amount of capital and the resources of the area: Weber neglected these factors. A small number of large industrial areas tend to dominate wide market areas while other places tend to specialize in products with short distance range or to function as a link at some point in the chain of production of large enterprises. But enlargement of agglomeration cannot continue without limit as long as agglomeration results from the behaviour of enterprises in pursuing economic rationality, i.e. when 'pure agglomeration' is assumed.

Production costs, market areas and agglomeration

Weber (1909, pp. 128–31) cites examples of advantages which commonly generate scale and regional agglomeration, but argued that when agglomeration reaches a certain stage, 'opposing tendencies' resulting from the size of the agglomeration begin to operate. Weber attributed such counter tendencies to the rise in land values. *Ceteris paribus*, land values rise proportionately with increased demand for land resulting from growth of the agglomeration, so promoting a rise in warehousing costs of materials and products and in labour costs, so beginning to play a deglomerative role. Weber knew, therefore, that the growth of agglomeration itself would, in time, decrease the agglomeration advantages and that, accordingly, there was a certain limit to its growth.

Ohlin (1935, Ch. 10) thought that 'agglomeration and deglomeration tendencies balance': longer distance movement of raw materials and products would mean higher transport costs and higher prices for natural resources as demand rose through growth of an agglomeration. Isard (1956) added increases in the rental charge for land and in the costs of municipal services resulting from the concentrated land use, growth in population density and increased costs of food supply due to distance from rural areas (Hamilton, 1967, pp. 393–5).

Weber, Ohlin and Isard all concluded, theoretically, that the agglomeration process tends to accentuate the operation of deglomerative factors towards an equilibrium at a certain stage. However, they were mostly concerned with production costs and neglected relations between agglomeration and the expansion of the market. Yet Ohlin shows that, *ceteris paribus*, the volume of sales decreases proportionately with extension of the market area as shipping costs of the product rise proportionately with distance. Lösch (1954, p. 108) agrees: 'every economic commodity has its own maximum shipping distance, beyond which it cannot be sold', the limit to aggregate sales being the limit to the growth of agglomeration.

We may now examine this issue in terms of market competition between two areas. According to Hoover (1937, pp. 95–8), at location A production costs are lower than at B as a result of agglomeration advantages there. As the market distance of A spreads towards B, market price rises as shipping costs increase, but A enjoys greater agglomerative advantage from the economies of larger-scale production, so the superiority of the agglomeration A offsets increased shipping costs and permits extension of its market to B which thus cannot compete with A and cannot develop industries. To a lesser extent the same would be true where A and B have equal local agglomeration conditions but A derives advantages of superior transport which lowers shipping costs from A so that area A can supply a greater market distance than B. Then intersection of the margin lines of A and B becomes the boundary between the markets of A and of B. Any further agglomeration in either A or B cannot be realized unless it is accompanied by a loss in sales in the competing market, i.e. through a drastic reduction in price. Naturally such analysis assumes an equal density of demand in each market area; however, even if the extent of the market is the same, a higher density of demand in one area will facilitate greater agglomeration in that area as a result of a higher market threshold and greater opportunities for realizing internal and external economies of scale.

The limits to regional agglomeration

Thus agglomeration and deglomeration are often assumed to maintain an equilibrium with no possibility for any 'excess-agglomeration' beyond a certain limit. In reality, such equilibrium is not maintained. Does this arise solely because of a rift between theory and reality? Since Von Thünen and Weber, location theory has traditionally been static: issues are treated as the product of contemporary interdependencies without including a time element. Although Hoover (1948, Part Two) describes change in location and agglomeration, no dynamic theoretical analysis has been made concerning the growth process whereby the population, capital and technology change simultaneously. Weber felt the elaboration of such problems as 'dispersion after agglomeration has reached a certain limit' were outside the theory. Accordingly, the deglomeration factors mentioned by Weber were concerned only with how much they weakened agglomeration tendencies, or with whether or not pure agglomeration was formed.

To begin to fill the gaps in analysis, brief reference must be made to the following factors:

Immobilities

However stressed that immobility of capital equipment is not a sufficient factor to prevent, but does restrict relocation. Mises (1949, p. 506) and Ezawa (1954, pp. 89–90) emphasized the peculiar indivisibility of capital. Agglomeration is limited by the substitution relationships between given labour and capital in individual industries, but the indivisibility of capital has a tendency to promote agglomeration. When capital is invested, it forms the units of a fixed indivisible scale and tends to be fixed spatially because of its restricted 'convertibility', so restricting relocation in the physical sense, but not hindering spatial change so much (Chs 1, 13). A similar problem arises from the relative immobility of labour of an area. Nevertheless, in reality relocation in the search for cheap or adequate labour is a very active process.

Decreased transport costs

The basis of Weber's location theory was transport costs, so that agglomeration was portrayed as a deviation from the place of minimum transport costs. Ohlin argues that such costs are basic on limiting agglomeration: the higher transport costs are, the more equalized or dispersed is industrial location. Since transport is the means of overcoming distance in space it was reasonable for Von Thünen in the 1820s to assume that transport costs by wagon, and for Weber in 1900 to assume that railway costs, were proportionate to distance.

But Hoover emphasized the influence of 'long haul economies' on the selection of location and agglomeration and, by partially amending the conclusion of Weber, related the function of agglomeration to its growth.

Kuklinski (United Nations Economic Commission for Europe 1967, pp. 2–5) stresses how the locational importance of transport costs has decreased drastically. For example, while the transport distance of iron ore imported to Japan has trebled since 1945, the proportion of transport costs in total ore delivery costs to Japanese steelworks has decreased from 33 to 45 per cent to 19–44 per cent depending on source. Chisholm (1966, pp. 162–4) further indicates that such a decrease has tended to promote agglomeration. Karaska emphasizes 'location free from the friction of distance' (Ch. 4). So improved transport has raised the limits to regional industrial agglomeration, largely through the reduction of both time and costs of transporting goods, services and people. While, however, differences in transport costs among locations and regions are now far less than formerly and hence less strict in defining the limits of agglomeration, this has given greater play to other factors of an agglomerative or deglomerative character in the location of industry.

Pure regional agglomeration

Theories describe agglomeration as 'pure'. Weber argues that even if a material resource or a market creates an agglomeration in fact, this is simply 'fortuitous agglomeration' which lies outside the compass of agglomeration theory. Discussion here relates then to the limits of pure agglomeration. If we suppose that pure regional agglomeration generates dynamic growth, the theoretical limit of regional agglomeration is the point at which the marginal agglomeration advantages approach zero. These advantages relate to the existing industrial region as a whole and alter according to the last production unit intended to be newly located or to the latest expansion of a production unit which already exists in the region. Hirschman (1958) indicates that when social overhead capital is not increased, total productivity in aggregate direct production activities also does not increase.

Compound regional agglomeration

This can be understood by the following example. Suppose an industrial region has reached a stage in development where it has realized pure agglomeration and every enterprise is enjoying agglomerative advantages. Then if a firm is newly located or an existing firm expands there, production costs will rise as a result of the increase in land values, and efficiency will be measurably reduced by traffic congestion resulting from the increased volume of transported goods. Thus, *ceteris paribus*, if production units continue to increase in numbers or enlarge the agglomerative advantages of the region will be reduced and will eventually reach zero. This point will be the limit of regional agglomeration, as further expansion must result in negative agglomerative advantages,

Thus marginal agglomeration advantages relate to the whole region, and not solely to individual enterprises. Since the location theory originally evolved as a theory of capitalist economy, agglomeration theory has been seen as a question of advantages enjoyable by, and thus analysed only from the viewpoint of, individual firms. However, the influence of agglomerated industrial regions extends spatially beyond individual firms, and supports regional economies as limbs of, and often systems within, the national economy. It is thus a defect of agglomeration theory that it deals with the problems of regional economies only at the level of individual enterprises.

However conceivable the limit of regional agglomeration is in theory it cannot be identified in practice. Regional agglomeration in reality is only partly pure agglomeration since it also includes fortuitous agglomeration, and hence better termed 'compound'. Agglomerative advantages actually identified by enterprises are not as great as commonly supposed: a large existing industrial region plays the roles of market and supplier of intermediate production units. Such a region is also a zone of minimal transport cost. This means that agglomerative processes are accelerated by non-agglomerative advantages, which during the process of expansion become bigger whilst agglomerative advantages become smaller. This actual state can be best explained by Gunnar Myrdal's 'principle of circular and cumulative causation' rather than by existing agglomeration theory: according to Myrdal (1957), concentration of economic activities in a certain region generates 'backwash effects' which leave other regions in a depressed state, so increasing imbalance among regions. Even when agglomerative advantages cease to exist, many factors still accelerate the cumulative expansion in a region formed by compound agglomeration, whilst other regions must continue to endure backwash effects.

Other problems exist in the real world. Weber observed the agglomeration of manufacturing industry in general but noted that the response to the limits of regional agglomeration varies according to the type of industry. Some types of industry are forced to disperse as land prices rise, while others can tolerate the rise of land prices rise, while others can tolerate the rise of land prices by making more intensive use of it. The same phenomenon arises as a result of industrial water shortages. Moreover, if such bottlenecks can be eliminated by public investment, then the limits to regional agglomeration will be raised. The whole question of agglomeration may be summarized as in Fig. 5.1.

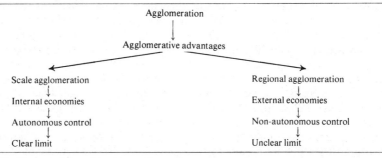

Fig. 5.1. The Characteristics of Agglomeration

Agglomeration which is accelerated by agglomerative advantages can be divided into two types, scale agglomeration and regional agglomeration. The former is mainly supported by internal economies, while the latter mainly depends on external economies. Given a fixed level of technology the expansion of scale agglomeration eventually reduces marginal profit towards zero, this point being the limit of scale agglomeration. Over time, technological developments tends to override the falling trend of marginal profits, and the limits of scale agglomeration are expanded, but there is no changing the fact the new limits appear autonomously under new technological conditions. By contrast, since regional agglomeration is compound agglomeration, which has complicated combined effects on both the regional and the individual enterprise, it is mainly supported by external economies, and autonomous control cannot operate. As a result, a limit to regional agglomeration cannot exist.

Excess agglomeration and 'unpaid costs'

Social costs and economics

Agglomeration theory can explain the rationality of industrial enterprises, but not the rationality of a regional economy or agglomeration. Although individual enterprises may be rational in their production, they may generate many negative effects which reduce regional efficiency and worsen the community's living environment. The simultaneous existence of rationality in individuals and irrationality in aggregate is no more than the manifestation of 'excess-agglomeration'. An agglomeration theory which can explain excess agglomeration is clearly important for location policy. To do this the concept of 'social costs' must be introduced. Generally, social costs are the negative consequences which the community sustains as a result of production processes, and for which private entrepreneurs or individual organizations are not held accountable (Kapp, 1950). Social costs also include certain social opportunity costs which take the form of avoidable wastes and various social inefficiencies.

The concept of social costs is not new. Adam Smith recognized them as the 'obligation of a sovereign'. Alfred Marshall divided the production economies into external and internal economies. Often external economies bring greater advantages to the enterprises than internal economies so that industrial location is almost always decided upon the extent to which the external economies can be tapped. 'External diseconomies', however, yield negative effects to enterprises and originate in the expansion of industrial agglomeration. The external economies and diseconomies classified by Marshall were considered within the limits of their influences on the structure of costs and the consequent profits of enterprises. The fact that economic effects appear outside the enterprises means the existence of a difference in interests between the areas as a whole, where the enterprises are located and the individual enterprises comprising it. This equals the gap between private (or individual) marginal net product and social marginal net product dealt with by Pigou (1952, pp. 134–5, 184). Social marginal net product is greater than private net product where, for example, afforestation of privately-owned land contributes to improved underground water supplies or serves as a windbreak. But when industries pollute or damage the natural or built environments, the social marginal pure product becomes less than the private (or individual) marginal pure product since the damages caused are not compensated by the private sector.

While Marshall made the enterprise the object of analysis, Pigou considered the whole of society. But it is possible to extend Marshall's concept to Pigou's, and external economies may be considered a plus difference between the investment and social pure products, the external diseconomies its minus difference. According to Pigou, differences should be removed by the appropriate encouraging or restricting policies of government. (For a recent analysis see Cumberland in Hamilton, forthcoming, 1978.)

Thus it is untrue that in the past no account was taken of social costs. Yet it was never dealt with as an integral part of value or price theory, but rather treated exceptionally in a separate system of welfare economics. Kapp (1950) suggests the reasons: that in keeping with scientific thought in their day the nineteenth-century economists doubted the existence of 'natural order' in economic affairs which would maximize welfare. Thus classical economists explored that order in terms of the images conveyed by their philosophical prejudices. When 'political economy' became 'economics', theoretical analysis – particularly value theory – was limited to the study of market phenomena; economics examined only matters which could be measured by their value in exchange. The social ends or means which could not be expressed in market prices came to be regarded increasingly as 'non-economics' and, as such, outside the scope of economic analysis. The neo-classical school applied the rationality of human behaviour to economic analysis and tried to prove a social justice based on the mechanism of private interests, i.e. it assumed that costs and returns of enterprises equate with the total costs and total returns to society. Traditional economics thus deemed the 'unpaid' as a natural result and accepted the pretended 'equilibrium' as the result of 'rational' activities.

Social costs and regional agglomeration

No agreement has yet been reached on social costs in economics. For instance, Michalski (1964) limited the issues to theoretical consistency and operational scope in existing economics. Mishan (1969) extended the discussion further to cover the comparison of 'goods' with 'bads', the latter being negative effects of economic and social processes. Kapp was first to analyse costs systematically, such costs comprising the impairment of human factors of production; social losses by pollution; diminution of animal resources; losses due to soil erosion, decreased fertility and excessive deforestation; losses from disorderly location and agglomeration. Private productive activities give rise to various social costs which were not reflected in enterprises' expenditures. Measures for preventing and recovering such social losses are taken by State policies.

In reality, under market conditions, firms do not pay all production costs. They retain their managerial rationale by internalizing the external economies and externalizing the internal diseconomies generated by the production process. Such externalization yields big social costs in environmental pollution, traffic congestion and shortage of transport facilities. Improving these conditions is principally a public responsibility. Yet amelioration of the evils of a region of excess agglomeration is nothing but stop-go treatment and is a waste of public funds. Enterprises not only take advantage of such investment, but further expansion of the agglomeration is accelerated by corresponding improvement of the production base: the vicious circle of cumulative causation continues.

To raise national efficiency and to achieve balance in national land use, it is essential to plan industrial decentralization, even if realization may be difficult. If regional policy, therefore, is to achieve the necessary industrial migration, the internalization of social costs is fundamental. At present there are no specific standards for clearly calculating social costs. But this much is certain: the cost of preventing environmental pollution, and the costs of removing the disbenefits of excess agglomeration of industries, can be regarded as social costs, and should be internalized by the enterprises concerned. The proposal to internalize social costs within the firm is new and is not easily assimilated by agglomeration theory. Yet this innovative idea will give a better insight into the actual state of regional agglomeration and into the effectiveness of location policy.

Some experts fear that the internalization of social costs will inevitably limit output, increase costs and raise risks of recession. This hypothesis can be countered by two arguments. First, shifting social costs from regional communities to enterprises should decrease aggregate costs by restricting the root causes of such costs. Second, societal standards can, do and must change to rationalize scarce resources use and to create a worthwhile environment for man: today labour costs are the largest factor in production yet no one would wish to bring back slavery, prohibit unionization or neglect industrial safety in an effort to reduce such costs. Moreover, in Japan, the government obliges enterprises to internalize social costs of pollution: and though this has now reached 15–25 per cent of investment in equipment by heavy and chemical industries, no bankruptcies have resulted.

Finally, many experts maintain that the costs of redevelopment and expansion in existing industrial regions are less than the costs of industrial dispersal to new regions. The following example is an appropriate answer to this point. Average

44   *The limits of regional agglomeration and social cost*

railway construction costs per metre in Japan in 1970, were: Surface railway (in Tohoku Region) £220 per metre; overhead railway (outer ring of Tokyo) £1400 per metre; and underground railway (in inner Tokyo) £11 500 per metre. The differences among the three construction costs represent social opportunity costs in the ratio 1:6.3:52.5 and such unit outlays are replicated in varying degrees in other infrastructures. Big expenditures per unit in large cities accelerate new congestion and invite only greater negative effects. Thus investment in highly agglomeration regions is wasteful, even from simple comparisons of *accountable* costs. The formation of a proper scale of regional agglomeration in developing countries, and the decentralization of industries and related activities connected with a new proper scale of regional agglomeration in developed countries, are important problems for spatial analysis and regional policy.

References

Chisholm, M. (1966), *Geography and Economics*, Bell, London, pp. 162–4.
Ezawa, J. (1954), *Economic Location Theory*, Tokyo (in Japanese).
Hamilton, F. E. I. (1967), 'Models of industrial location', Ch. 10 in R. J. Chorley and P. Haggett, *Models in Geography*, Methuen, London.
Hamilton, F. E. I., ed. (forthcoming 1978), *Industrial Change: International Experience and Public Policy*, Longman, London.
Hirschman, A. O. (1958), *The Strategy of Economic Development*, Yale U.P., New Haven, pp. 89–90.
Hoover, E. M. (1937), *Location Theory and the Shoe and Leather Industries*, Harvard U.P., Cambridge, pp. 95–98.
Hoover, E. M. (1948), *The Location of Economic Activity*, McGraw-Hill, New York.
Isard, W. (1956), *Location and Space Economy*, M.I.T., New York.
Kapp, K. W. (1950), *The Social Costs of Private Enterprises*, Asia Publishing House, London.
Lösch, A. (1954), *The Economics of Location*, Yale U.P., New Haven.
Marshall, A. (1961), *Principles of Economics*, Macmillan, London, 9th edition.
Michalski, W. (1964), *Grundlegung Eines Operationalen Konzept der 'Social Costs'*, Hamburg.
Mises, L. von (1949), *Human Action: A Treatise on Economics*, Hodge, London.
Mishan, E. J. (1969), *Growth: The Price We Pay*, Nelson, London.
Myrdal, G. (1957), *Economic Theory and Underdeveloped Regions*, Duckworth, London.
Chlin, B. (1935), *Interregional and International Trade*, Harvard U.P., Cambridge.
Pigou, A. C. (1952), *The Economics of Welfare*, Macmillan, London.
United Nations Economic Commission for Europe (1967), *Criteria for Location of Industrial Plants*, Geneva.
Weber, A. (1909), *Über den Standort der Industrien*, Tübingen.

Chapter 6

New technology and organization patterns: their impact on planning industrial areas

Karl H. Hottes

A major element in modern planning lies in the *space* requirements of industries (used in the West German sense of mining and manufacturing units with a minimum of ten employees). The broad distribution of land among uses in most countries shows clearly, however, that the proportion of area actually used for industrial production is comparatively small: in the German Federal Republic it does not exceed 1 per cent of the nation's territory. On this basis, therefore, further expansion of the area for industry would seem to be without risk. Nevertheless important constraints are to be clearly observed.

First, industrialization generates remarkable indirect demand for land in that large areas have to be reserved for non-industrial purposes which serve, or are consequent upon, mining and manufacturing (Hottes and Kersting, 1976; Podolsky, 1975). Such areas include the following: *Residential areas* are required since any form of industrialization results in agglomeration of population in urban areas which must then absorb both the migration and natural increase of population. In contrast to urban zones, where residential areas may have to expand substantially, such areas in the countryside may change relatively little and may actually decrease. *Transport and traffic areas* are needed in greater amounts to cope with the increased freight and passenger traffic generated by industrialization (Mikus, 1974). In addition to the changing requirements of active and passive forms of surface transport (roads, canals, ports, railways, airports), certain zones are limited in their free use of, or access to, other means of transport such as pipelines or electricity lines which 'neutralize' the utility of land lying respectively above or below them. *Other infrastructure areas* are required by the functions directly or indirectly serving industrialization such as banking, commerce, chambers of commerce and law, industrial training facilities and warehouses and may not occupy land adjacent, or even near, the industries themselves. *Agricultural and forest areas* are sometimes changed in the pattern of their use by industrialization and in such a way that certain crops are extended or introduced to provide a sufficient input of raw material for the respective industry – like sugar-beet, vegetables for canning, pinewood for mines or as raw-material for cellulose-mills.

Second, however, most attention here is paid to the direct consequences of industrialization. These manifest themselves in: (*a*) the demand for land for production purposes – which depends upon structure and type of industries, size of unit, required storage area, the technology applied and organization pattern; (*b*) the demand for areas for related non-production purposes in and adjacent to the production areas such as offices, social areas, internal traffic and transport; (*c*) the reserve land requirements in the immediate neighbourhood resulting from the

45

specific methods of industrial production, including a maximum economic use of existing installations and sites and to meet possible expansion of the production area; (*d*) the 'consumption' of land by opencast coal and ore-mining sector, gravel and clay pits, which leave large areas devastated and produce extensive waste heaps and waterlogged depressions or by other industries which emit polluted water and gaseous products.

Reasonable environmental protection of the population may require specific distances be left between industrial sites and other forms of land use: regulations established by the provincial government of Nordrhein-Westfalen are strict in this respect. Now it is necessary to approach the problem of the extent to which the *direct* demand for industrial land is influenced by new technologies and organization patterns. Geographers should discuss both the individual unit in the system of an industrial location complex (Hottes, 1976) and the *types* of industrial location complexes, i.e. the 'ensemble des firmes'. This leads to the consideration of the following main points: development trends in technologies and organization in modern industries; the spatial effects of trends; and industrial area demands by different systems (such as in the spatial system, in the contrasting systems of developing countries and industrialized countries and in different economic and political systems).

Development trends in modern industrial technology and organization

Since the early days of 'manufacture', industrial production has been progressing on a path from mechanization to partial automation and eventually complete automation. The process includes both production and transport. Evolution is from the simple foot-driven drill to transmission-driven lathes, from there to self-powered lathes and turret-lathes, and finally to fully automatic lathes shaping the complete part. There is also a progression from manual pulling to hand-driven pulleys, cranes and finally electronically-operated cranes as well as from manual transport to carts and conveyor belt systems. Organizational changes also occurred from production from a single machine through production from groups of machines to assembly lines and complete automation. Branches that cannot make use of assembly lines will use modern fork-lift trucks for internal transport. Some industries, such as chemicals or beverages, use mostly pipes.

The trends are different in respective units depending on capital investment and the readiness to invest, and in various types of industries as determined by production requirements. Cakes can be produced fully automatically, cars only partially so! Those industries which produce single units or small 'runs' (as in steel-construction and rolling) will be limited to an optimum level of mechanization in their production and transport activities. Although there is a great variety, some general statements are relevant:

1. The changeover from handicrafts to mechanized production led to concentration of linear processes because of the power sources (steam engine or water power): a number of buildings with specialized functions have to be erected within an industrial unit instead of one former all-purpose building.
2. Introduction of carts and trucks (*Flurfördermittel*) in Germany since 1950 requires wider transport alleys inside the units. The greater spread of transport vehicles leads to the spatial separation of storage and production areas because products can be moved further. Since such vehicles are very sensitive to steep

slopes, production units and most other installations have to be placed on the same level, generating a greatly increased demand for production and surface storage space and sometimes the disappearance of multi-storeyed factories.

3. Introduction of the assembly line (car-manufacturing) or mechanized production leads to a reverse concentration movement of production processes: substantial investments, mass production and continuity are essential for making profits so that all necessary ancillary units and depots will be placed immediately on, above and under the production line. The first process, described above, is reversed, i.e. 'spatial retreat' by concentration by using, for example, multi-storeyed shelves. The intensity of capital investments reduces land costs to a minimum. But such manufacturers have to separate certain units from the production line, such as research laboratories or the production of prototypes, on another site perhaps in another place, often to make use of certain contacts with neighbouring universities or computer centres. Application of computers and advanced electronics not only reduces labour on the production process, but leads also to a greater intensity of production per unit area and more rational internal control of both the technical and the administration activities. Such concentration in space leads to relatively reduced area demands. The absolute rate of investments enforces the concentration of diverse functions of different units into one central head office, and sometimes the construction of the head-office in a new location. This process may be called 'autonomization' (see below).

4. Introduction of completely new production processes and industries like plastics-manufacturing make new demands.

5. The adaptation both in site, area and investment to modern transport facilities. The trend towards new bulk-carrier ships calls not only for new port and storage installations, but also for enlarged production units because of the larger quantities to be shipped. A prototype for such trends is Dunkerque with its new port and heavy industries complex. Another aspect is the more rational use of the infrastructure provided by third parties, i.e. the concentration of new production units near to motorway-interchanges or junctions or power stations. In such cases it is not the single unit which saves space, but the common use of infrastructure, as on industrial estates (Hottes, 1976).

6. The 'autonomization' (not to be confused with 'automation') is a modern organization technique used by large concerns, by which identical production processes are concentrated in one location to make best use of modern technology while other functions may be concentrated in separate sites or locations elsewhere. This is often preceded by acquisitions of competitors (Ch. 13). Sometimes internalization is enforced by new environmental standards, because in certain places dangerous production processes may be prohibited. Sometimes 'autonomization' leads to increased area demands, but generally less space will be required.

Spatial relevance

Thus different technologies and organization patterns in industries create varied area requirements. Assuming equal output, the trend to mechanize production processes and especially transport operations increases the demand for industrial space. Assembly lines and automation, however, lead to contraction and thus to reduced area demand. Areas left free in such a process may be eventually left idle. This may be observed, for example, in the steel industry as a result of the introduction of modern high-speed rolling mills: it is well recorded in aerial photographs before and after the introduction of such mills at the Krupp Plant in Bochum (Dodt and Mayr, 1976). With generally increasing market demand for products, however, most units will expand production and make use of such areas by installing more machines (as happens in the paper industry) or by using the empty space for storage purposes.

Where only intermediate technology is introduced, i.e. a mechanization of transport operations, site requirements increase, but of more importance is the *quality* of the site in that it is of extensive size and flat. Thus attention turns to areas which were previously used for agricultural purposes. Crowded sites left idle by old industries, especially those depending on water power in narrow valleys, are more or less lost since they can hardly be re-used by industry. Such sites in cities, however, may be required for large-scale re-use in combination with other functions.

Organizational innovations have resulted from the introduction of computers for business control, auditing, technical operations or necessary internalization after the takeover of competitors can create additional demands which are met both in rural areas and in central city business districts on former residential or other uses of land. Previous forms of intensive land-use disappear. In situations where environmental damage may occur, industry is steered to vacant land or low quality heaths, forests or coastal and estuarine marshlands.

Industrial site demand

On the *micro-level* of spatial patterns a reduction in site-area because of technological changes is seldom accompanied by structural changes. When units specialize, the division and separation of production processes appears more clearly. The same applies to cases where, without technological changes, higher production or increased storage requirements (e.g. of military raw materials) lead to bigger site area-demand. Only if in the course of expansion some units have gained a dominant position might the pattern itself change. Obviously, however, completely new units do change the existing pattern, especially when new 'autonomized' units are set up, such as experimental and research laboratories or computer centres. Similarly existing patterns will change substantially as a result of new infrastructure such as new ports to handle very large ships. Demand for sites for very noisy or environmentally-dangerous industries is mostly met on less valuable ground sometimes distant from populated areas. Examples are the non-ferrous-metal works and nuclear power-stations in the Dutch and Belgian Campine or formerly the dynamite and ammunition factories on sandy land to the east of Cologne.

On the *macro-level* aspects vary according to the general geographical structure. If the Ruhr is regarded as a major zone for heavy industries, then society can be grateful for the saving effects of modern technologies, as when a larger number of small and medium-sized steelworks is replaced by better-equipped and more efficient large units. Environmental control is easier, former industrial areas may serve as sites for new industries so that desirable structural change is made possible (Hottes, 1967a, 1971; Jarecki, 1967). Large-scale regional development plans may also be introduced more easily for the region. This phenomenon may be seen in the Pittsburgh–Youngstown area, the Ruhr, the British coalfield regions and Upper Silesia (Schlenger, 1955; Buchhofer, 1975).

Industrial regions with a predominance of lighter industries widely dispersed over a region of mixed industrial and agricultural functions – such as in Northern Italy – will have to encroach on valuable rural areas. There a balance must be struck between (1) a possible dominance of industries, as for instance in the textile region to the north-west of Milan or the FIAT region near Turin, (2) an adequate infrastructure for commuters living in villages and (3) an efficient and profitable farm production base.

If one approaches the problem in the context of regional planning models – like that of development (or 'growth') poles and axes – then our modern industries may be considered as *industries motrice* in the sense used by Perroux, irrespective of whether they are newly-established or still occupying their old locations. Industries in that case are active components both in development poles and development axes. At a pole their role may be that of a central tertiary function, although originally based on production, as in the case that the activities concerned are administration and research. The production units, however, are a welcome factor strengthening development axes. When production is moved from a development pole, desirable urban clearance effects may be observed from the point of view of town planning, while the pole is also relieved of goods and commuter transport (Hottes and Dewey, 1976). Industrial and regional planning can thus create important opportunities for cooperation and coordination.

The context of developing regions

The change to new patterns of organization and technologies is extremely rapid in developing countries. Site demand can generally be met with ease but, with the exception of open-pit mining, the demand resulting from housing and infrastructure is very much higher than from industry. Analysis is required of the extent to which the establishment of consumer industries and the relocation of handicrafts and repair-shops from old bazaars to new industrial estates leaves room for town-planning measures in the old quarters. That it is substantial is an impression gained at least in Baghdad, Teheran and many medium-sized towns in Turkey. In many cases new industrial models are used such as industrial estates which not only provide room for new medium-sized industries but also for many handicraft units which are changing over to mechanized small-scale industrial production (Aufderlandwehr, 1969; Hottes, 1976). Most Third World countries have the advantage that the planning or relocation of industrial areas is subject to national, regional or local planning. Therefore these new locations should offer better conditions for future industrial production than equivalent locations in industrialized nations which have often developed 'wild' in the early capitalist period without respect to regional planning. Frequently, however, such hopes are shattered by the actual (and disappointing) trends in the young nations, where town planning control of real sprawl is seldom achieved ('gece-condu' settlements in Turkey, i.e. 'wild' slums). There is also a tendency to locate workers' colonies in the immediate neighbourhood of new industries because of traffic problems, so re-creating the mixed industrial–residential zones of the capitalist period. Moreover, there is a tendency to disregard basic environmental requirements so that already in the near future industries recently innovated will have to be reshaped as new technologies become available.

There is, however, another important aspect. The adaptation of new technologies and the level of university teaching in many developing areas have reached the point, where in connection with 'autonomization' certain production units are moved not only from developed to underdeveloped regions of Europe (for example, to the Mezzogiorno), but also from developed to developing countries. This includes not only units for the mass production of low-value goods or for the supply of medium-value investment goods to overseas markets, but also the installation of high-precision optical goods or complete research units. The 'migration' of a pharmaceutical research laboratory managed by Hoechst from Frankfurt-am-Main in the German Federal Republic to Bombay in India may serve as just one example.

The context of different economic systems

The supply of additional sites and the planned re-use of former industrial areas is arranged more easily in planned socialist economies than in capitalist market economies. In the former the declaration of industrial areas depends only on the setting-up of a 'plan'. Where compensation of private parties or rural cooperatives is necessary the amounts are also fixed by the State administration, and there are no objections. There is also the advantage that in many States large reserves of unused space exist so that no decision has to be made concerning competing land uses: Siberia is an example. The concentration of industries into large combines, the stress on more applied research (as compared with Western countries) in universities and academies of science in socialist countries and also the centralization of trade through respective boards have always encouraged the process of autonomization, so that relocation is more rare.

In capitalist market economies, however, the supply of industrial sites and the re-use of former areas meets with considerable difficulties. The fact that in many such countries the free use of property is guaranteed by law is a serious restriction on the provision of larger units as required for modern planning. Although the government may expropriate areas for infrastructure against proper compensation in the public interest, industrial areas that do not fall under this rule have to be obtained with difficult legal procedures, large financial outlays or by exchange of equally valuable locations. More and more, therefore, models are required, under which the provision of large-scale industrial sites and their necessary infrastructure will become easier without unduly restricting basic constitutional rights. One way is the so-called 'master-plan' – similar to a German 'Flächennutzungsplan' – which declares certain areas for industrial use after proper democratic decisions: until needed for industrial use, the proprietor who owns plots in those areas is free to continue the existing use of the site. Another method is the sale of land parcels by public order within a given time limit at *market* prices to an organization set up by public bodies. The organization then sells leases or rents out the plots to future entrepreneurs after having developed the area for industrial purposes. Therefore the respective organization will have to be equipped with considerable financial resources; normally it is only the central government which provides and guarantees such funds. Another model aims at common ownership of individual private plots in the form of an 'owners' society' which, on a cooperative basis, sells or leases the land. This last suggestion is in some way similar to socialist rural cooperatives – only without production targets – but carries substantial disadvantages regarding the sale or transfer at will of the shares.

Conclusion

Site requirements change as a result of the introduction of new products, the continuous expansion in output, of existing industrial products based on ever-increasing consumption and also changes in technologies and organization patterns inherent to industry. Such changes as result are, on the one hand, *quantitative* in the expansion or reduction in the size of industrial sites and, on the other hand, *qualitative* in the type of use. The impact of modern technologies and organization patterns in industry do not only express themselves in production itself, but also in the spheres of administration, social services, storage, transport needs, waste-disposal and environmental safety. Within both the regional and the international contexts the trend towards 'autonomization' can be observed, i.e. the segregation of production and related processes into spatially-separated units. Although industrial sites have only a minor share of the total land area, the industrial geographer has to watch the trends with respect to an overall supply of the cultivated areas in the world to ensure a maximum restriction of industrial sites, devastated areas and industry-related infrastructural zones in favour of farm areas, recreation zones and suitable settlement areas. That is why the industrial geographer must think not only in economic and social terms, but also in technical terms in order to extend the research introduced by Kruger (1942) under the title of 'Engineering Geography' (Ingenieurgeographie) and Gerling (1949 and 1969) under the title of the 'Geography of Technology' (Technikgeographie).

References

Aufderlandwehr, E. (1969), 'Die moderne Industrialiserung in Hyderabad/Indien als Beispiel für eine Industrieansiedlung in tropischen Ländern', *Ruhr-University* (Bochum) *Geographisches Institut*, mimeographed.

Buchhofer, E. (1975), 'Die gewerbliche Wirtschaft Oberschlesiens seit 1945', in: R. Brever, ed., *Oberschlesien nach dem Zweite Weltkrieg*, Marburg.

Dodt, J. and Mayr, A. eds. (1976), 'Bochem im Luftbild', *Bochumer Geographische Arbeiten*, Sonderreihe 8, Paderborn.

Fels, E. (1967), 'Der wirtschaftende Mensch als Gestalter der Erde', *Erde und Weltwirtschaft* (2), Stuttgart.

Gerling, W. (1949), *Technik und Erdbild, Die Erscheinungsformer der modernen Technik in der Landwirtschaft – Aufbau und System der Plantagen*, Würzburg.

Gerling, W. (1969), *Wirtschaft – Technik – Landschaft. Probleme der Wirschaftsgeographie und Raumforschung*, Würzburg.

Hottes, K. (1967*a*), 'Das Ruhrgebiet im Strukturwandel. Eine Wirtschaftsgeographische Zwischembilanz', *Berichte zur Dt. Landeskunde*, **38**(2), pp. 251–74.

Hottes, K. (1967*b*), 'Die Naturwerksteinindustrie und ihre standortprägenden Auswirkungen – eine vergleigende Untersuchung, dargestellet an ausgewählten europaischen Beispielen', *Giessener Geographische Schriften*, **12**.

Hottes, K. (1971), 'Wie läst sich der von Waibel für die Landwirtschaftsgeographie entwickelte Formationsbegriff für die Industriegeographie verwenden?', *Heidelberger Geographische Schriften*, **36**, pp. 35–41.

Hottes, K., ed. (1976). 'Industrial estate, Industrie und Gewerbepark – Typ einer neuen Standortgemeinschaft', in: K. Hottes, ed., *Industriegeographie*, Darmstadt (Wege der Forschung).

Hottes, K., Buchholz, H. J. and Hieret, M. (1971), 'Bochum-Gerthe, Analyse und Vorschlage zur Entwicklung', *Materialien zur Raumordnung aus dem Geographische, Institut der Ruhr-Universität Bochum, Forschungsabteilung für Raumordnung*, p. X.

Hottes, K. and Dewey, W. J. (1976), *Das punktaxiale System zwischen Rhein-Ruhr und Antwerpen-Calais. Schriftenreihe Landes- und Stadtentwicklungsforschung*, Dortmund (Inst. f. Landes- und Stadtentwicklungsforschung des Landes NW).

Hottes, K. and Kersting, H. (1976), 'Der industrielle Flächenbedarf – Grundlagen und Mebzahlen für seine Entwicklung', in: *Neue Konzeptionen der Industrieansiedlungen. Sonderveröffentlichung des Siedlungsverbandes Ruhrkohlenbezirk,* Essen.

Jarecki, C. (1967), 'Der neuzeitliche Strukturwandel an der Ruhr', *Marburger Geographischen Schriften,* **29.**

Kruger, K. (1942), 'Die Ingenieurgeographie in den Wirtschaftswissenschaften', *Die deutsche Volkswirtschaft*, pp. 431–3 (Berlin).

Mikus, W. (1974), 'Verkehrszellen, Beiträge zur verkahrsräumlichen Gliederung am Beispiel des Güterverkehrs am Boder Grossindustrie ausgewählter EG-Länder', *Bochumer Geographische, Arbeiten*, Sonderreihe Bd. 4.

Minister fur Arbeit (Gesundheit und Soziales des Landes Nord-Rhein Westfalen (NW) (1975), 'Abstände zwischen Industrie – bzw. Gewerbegebieten und Wohngebieten im Rahmen der Bauleitplanung', *Runderlab* (1).

Muller-Wille, W. (1963), 'Die Ackerfluren im Landesteil Birkenfeld und ihre, seit dem 17. Jahrhundert', *Beiträge zur Landeskunde der Rheinlande N.F.,* 5.

Perroux, F. (1964), 'La firme motrice dans le région motrice', *L'économie du XXe siècle,* 2.

Podolsky, J. P. (1975), *Methodik der Ermittlung und Anwendung von Flächenkennzahlen bei der Grobplanung bon Fabrikanlagen,* Dissertation TU Hanover.

Schlenger, H. (1955). 'Der Ausbau des Oberschlesisch-Mährischen Industrieraumes zum 'Westkombinat der Ostblockstaaten', *Deutscher Geographentag Essen 1953.* Tagungsberichte und Wiss, Abhandlungen (Wiesbaden), pp. 48–66.

Chapter 7

Introducing the environmental effect into normative location planning models

Anette Reenberg

The main emphasis in 'western' research in industrial geography has been on elucidating the essential characteristics, interdependencies and trends of development. Greater attention has been focussed on developing normal models in other parts of the world. There seems to be a tendency to avoid normative and planning-oriented approaches in favour of static descriptions of past, present or future structures. If the industrial geographer wishes to provide practically applicable research results, it is necessary to work with normative models for planning industrial location, though current empirical research must continue to provide the fundamental knowledge of actual relationships.

Basic models and problems in model-building

Several types of quantitative models are relevant for industrial geographers, but those based upon input–output tables and location–allocation are among the most important. Input–output models are essential because they describe the relationships (flows) between different sectors of the economy and are of vital importance to the industrial complex concept. The term 'location–allocation' models refers to mathematical models which are established to find the solution of a problem with the following structure:

The best location is sought for producers (sources) which are to satisfy the demand of consumers in geographical space. The following are known: the location of the consumers, the demand of the consumers, the producers' capacity, the cost of delivery from producer to consumer (transport costs) and production costs. We wish to find out the number of producers, the location of producers, the allocation of consumers to producers and the quantity transported and the amount produced at the site of production. In most cases, the location–allocation problem cannot be solved exactly but acceptable approximate solutions can be derived either by exact methods such as linear-programming, integer-programming, mixed integer-programming or dynamic programming, total enumeration, efficient search procedures (for instance branch-and-bound) or by heuristics. Location–allocation models are well suited to the study of many spatial-industrial problems: they can be used in the search for the best location for the producer when the spatial distribution of demand is known, or for the best location when the available inputs (raw materials or semi-finished products) to industry are known, or they can be guidelines for choosing which present industries or plants to close in a rationalization process.

Characteristically, many elements are relevant to the locational process and thus deserve attention in a model built to describe a locational system and its behaviour. *Economics of scale* are one of the most important phenomena causing non-linearity. This is highly inconvenient, as linear models are much easier to handle than non-linear models. *Restrictions* on the spatial configuration of a locational problem will also complicate model construction (i.e. non-feasible localities, non-feasible interaction patterns and thresholds for the delivery-distance). Industries which are, or embody, obnoxious facilities have a *negative environmental effect*, here used in the sense of a detrimental effect on the physical environment: these, too, produce complications in model-building.

Models incorporating environmental effects

The treatment of environmental effects in models may be difficult because of the special economic characteristics of most waste products: the cost (or damages) caused by the environment-disturbing industry are, in most cases, very difficult to price. This matter has been discussed at length by Herfindarl and Kneese (1974). For example, where an industry uses lake-water for cooling, some long-term ecological changes may occur in the lake as a result of the heating of the water. How can this be expressed in monetary terms?

Even when it is possible to price environmental effects, another difficulty may confront an economic evaluation. The fact that, in most cases, costs incurred by an environment-polluting industry is paid for by society implies that the optimal production level is most likely not the same for the industry as for the society as a whole. Thus normative models which include environmental effects are of relevance only for communities (1) which have overcome the problem of integrating all economic decisions, or (2) where the law prescribes certain restrictions on the environmental effects (such as maximum acceptable pollution) and (3) where no economic trade-off between production and decline in environmental quality is accepted. With these limitations in mind let us now return to the two types of models previously mentioned.

Input–output models are often used for impact-analysis, i.e. to establish the total production necessary to cover a certain specified final demand on industrial sectors and possibly on regions. Originally, the input–output table was only a registration framework for the monetary flow equivalent to the flow of goods and service for intermediate and final demand. Recently, however, various attempts made to incorporate ecological variables in the model yield possibilities for studying environmental effects as they are related to different levels of production. Leontief (1970) presents an essential example, interpreting environmental pollution into a standard type input–output model. The main structure of the input–output balance is shown in Fig. 7.1 (the flow is measured in physical units). Evidently the detailed structure of the table depends on whether industries as well as households are generating pollution and on the manner the pollution abatement is financed. The structure shown provides an opportunity to determine the direct and indirect effects on the production pattern and on the pollution pattern resulting from changes in final demand. The approach is best suited to solving problems where the location of the environmental effect matters neither for natural nor for policy reasons. This is the case for instance if the model is used to analyse the influence of different patterns of final demand on CO_2-discharge, because globally such discharge will be more or less diluted.

Examples of similar models may be quoted. Cumberland (1966) uses a treatment of environmental relationships which is closer to cost–benefit analysis since he considers only aggregated cost and omits linear input–output coefficients in the environmental sector. Isard (1969) and Daly (1968) present more comprehensive models which take into account the interaction both between and within the economic and environmental sectors, while Victor (1971) has elaborated a model which represents a compromise between the Isard and Leontief models. Commonly these models determine the environmental effects for a given production level.

The input–output framework can also provide the core of a simple normative model which finds the optimal production level, given certain restrictions concerning the environment. This kind of model requires information about the value of

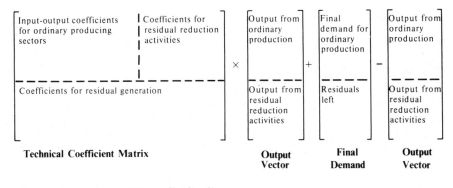

In normal input-output rotation: A X + Y = X

Fig. 7.1 The main structure of an input–output balance.

the different outputs in addition to the coefficients stating the technical relationships in the production and pollution processes. The structure of the model is best explained by a simple example: Consider an economy with two producing sectors only, 1 and 2. The interdependence between these is given by the technical coefficient matrix:

$$a = \begin{Bmatrix} 0.1 & 0.6 \\ 0.5 & 0.2 \end{Bmatrix}$$

In the production process there are three scarce resources: capital $1(R_1)$, capital $2(R_2)$, and labour (L) (say, $R_1 = 13$, $R_2 = 8$ and $L = 14$ units). The amounts used per unit output in the two sectors are:

in sector 1: 0.2 units R_1, 0 units R_2 and 0.1 units L

and in sector 2: 0 units R_1, 0.1 units R_2 and 0.1 units L.

If the values of the sectorial outputs (X_1 and X_2) are 0.45 per unit in sector 1 and 0.12 in sector 2 the best production-mix will be the combination of X_1 and X_2 which maximizes the objective function

$Z = 0.45X_1 + 0.12X_2$

and at the same time satisfies the restrictions caused by scarce resources (Table 7.1).

Environmental and spatial aspects relevant to a geographer can be considered in a way similar to capital and labour. Table 7.2 shows for example additional equations expressing (1) demand for space per unit production in sector 1 and 2 equal to a_1 and a a_2 – maximum space available is A, and (2) pollution from sector

Table 7.1 Linear programming model: constraints and objective function

	Production activities		Production final demand		Production unused resources			Production maximum value
Level of activity	X_1	X_2	X_1^d	X_2^d	R_1	R_2^d	L^d	
Industry 1	−0.9	0.6	1	0	0	0	0	0
Industry 2	0.5	−0.8	0	1	0	0	0	0
Capital to Ind. 1	0.2	0	0	0	1	0	0	13
Capital to Ind. 2	0	0.1	0	0	0	1	0	8
Labour	0.1	0.1	0	0	0	0	1	14
Objective function	0.45	0.12	0	0	0	0	0	

Reading instructions, as an example line 1:
$-0.9X_1 + 0.6X_2 + X_1^d = 0$

Table 7.2 Additional constraints for space and pollution

	X_1	X_2	X_1^d	X_2^d	R_1^d	R_2^d	L^d	A^d	F^d	Maximum value
Space	a_1	a_2	0	0	0	0	0	1	0	A
Pollution	f_1	f_2	0	0	0	0	0	0	1	F

1 and 2 equal to f_1 and f_2 per unit produced – maximum tolerable total pollution is F. In the same manner other environmental considerations may be expressed in the model.

When considering the environmental effects in *location–allocation models* one may distinguish roughly between two types of approaches:

1. Assume that a certain level of environmental effects can be accepted if it implies a sufficient level of economic benefit for an industry. To find the optimal solution it is necessary to use a model in which the economic advantage for the industry is traded-off against the diseconomies resulting from the environmental effects. This approach, termed the 'facility-package' approach, is represented by the work of Austin, Schmith and Wolpert (1970), Hinman (1974), Morris (1972) and Anderson (1971).
2. A slightly different type of model is necessary if trade-off between diseconomies for the society and benefits for the industry is not acceptable. The alternative the most frequently used is that a maximum acceptable environmental effect is defined. This second approach is adopted by Marks and Jirka (1971), Nijkamp and Paelinck (1972).

The basic idea of *'the facility-package' approach* is that when a noxious facility is located in an area, it may cause opposition from people in the neighbourhood. This may result in interruptions, delays, changes in design and thus an increase in the cost of the project. In some cases the adjustments necessary are known, and it is possible to evaluate the expected additional costs of introducing auxiliary facilities to compensate for the negative environmental effect so that the costs caused by the opposition may be decreased. If so, it is suggested that one should consider the location of 'facility-packages' instead of a single facility, i.e. the location of possible combinations of the main facility (industry) with different auxiliary facilities. As stressed by Wolpert (Mumphrey, Seley and Wolpert, 1971), the approach does have the drawback, however, that it does not ensure that the negative environmental effects are reduced to a minimum level, because powerful political groupings in society ensure that their interests are given a high priority (vis-à-vis less powerful groups).

One model formulation of the facility-package approach is suggested by Austin, Schmith and Wolpert (1970). This finds the optimal location for one main facility together with auxiliary facilities which minimizes total costs for the establishment, for maintenance of the facilities plus the cost caused by the opposition. The opposition variables are expressed in an objective function. Variables in the model are:

F_{OL} = main facility in location L
F_{jL} = auxiliary facility in location L
$E(C_{OL})$ = expected costs by F_{OL}
$E(C_{jL})$ = expected costs by F_{jL}
F_L = 'facility-package' consisting of F_{OL} and some (or all) auxiliary facilities F_{jL}
$P_i(F_L)$ = the probability of opposition against F_L in population group i
$E_i(F_L)$ = expected costs caused by the opposition against F_L in population group i

If only the main facility is considered the objective function will be:

MIN. $E(F_{OL}) = E(C_{OL}) + \Sigma_i E_i(F_{OL})P(F_{OL})$

Introducing auxiliary facilities changes the function to:

MIN. $E(F_L) = E(C_{OL}) + \sum_{j=1}^{k} E(C_{\propto j,L}) + \Sigma_i E_i(F_L) P_i(F_L)$

where $\propto_j$ stands for a given combination of auxiliary facilities. The inequality:

$\Sigma_j E(C_{\propto jL}) + E(C_{OL}) \leqslant B$

ensures that the optimal solution satisfies the budget restrictions.

The main difficulties arise in attempting to estimate the cost caused by the opposition. The method suggested is based on a weighting of some 'attributes' (i.e. positive or negative effects of the industry). Stated generally, in my opinion it is doubtful if the approach is significantly different from cost–benefit analysis, which is asserted to be the alternative, because the subjective mutual weighting of environmental effects criticized is only moved to another place in the model.

Alperovich (1972) presents a model based on the same idea as Austin's but different in formal structure. It is expressed as a linear programming problem with the objective function:

$$\text{MAX } Z = \Sigma_i \Sigma_j b_{ij} x_{ij}$$

where:

b_{ij} = the value per unit service delivered from j to i
x_{ij} = the amount of units shipped from j to i

The opposition is now expressed in one of the constraints. Two inequalities are of interest in this connection:

$$\Sigma_j \alpha_{ij} \cdot S_j - \Sigma_j b_{ij} \cdot x_{ij} - \Sigma_s \Sigma_j Y_j^{sj} \cdot \beta_{ij}^{sj} \cdot C_j \leqslant \overline{\overline{\alpha}}_i$$

where:

$\overline{\overline{\alpha}}_i$ = maximum acceptable net loss (i.e. no opposition below this limit)
β_{ij}^{sj} = the increase in land value at location i resulting from one unit of invest-
      ment to decrease the negative effects from the industry (size S, location j)
C_j = money spent to decrease negative effects from an industry located in j
S_j = industry located at location j
α_{ij} = decrease in land value at location j per 'unit' industry located in j
Y_j^{sj} = 1, if there is an industry located at j
      0, if there is not an industry located at j

The inequality ensures that the decrease in land value caused by the industry and the increase because of investment in abatement facilities are in balance, i.e. the net loss is less than $\overline{\overline{\alpha}}_i$. A second inequality ensures that costs of establishing and maintaining the main facility (industry) plus investment in the abatement facilities are less than the total budget:

$$\Sigma_j P_{s_j} \cdot S_j + \Sigma_j C_j \leqslant B$$

Contrary to Austin, Alperovich uses one index, land value, to express the opposition. In this way he avoids weighting difficulties, but when using the land value to express the actual effects of a noxious facility he has to accept the hypothesis that the market system works perfectly.

Hinman (1974) suggests another model using decreases in land value to measure negative environmental effects. The model determines the optimal location for an industry defined as the one causing the least net decrease in land value.

One assumes knowledge about a function, $f(d_{ij})$, expressing the decrease in land value in i due to locating an industry in j, and to V_i, the land value in i.

If the fixed cost for the industry is the same everywhere in the planning region, a mathematical model locating at least m industries will be:

$$\text{MIN } Z = \Sigma_j \Sigma_i X_j \cdot V_i \cdot f(d_{ij})$$

$$\Sigma_j X_j \geqslant m$$

$$X_j = \begin{cases} 0 \\ 1 \end{cases}, vj$$

Morris (1972) suggests a model for locating one facility. The basic idea is the willingness to accept a cost higher than the absolute minimum in favour to trade-off some environmental effects. The objective function is:

$$\min_i A_i = R_i + S_i$$

where R_i are the working and construction costs in location i and S_i are social costs. The evaluation of S_i is based on a weighted average (E_i) of environmental qualities (recreation, aesthetic values, etc.) multiplied by a percentage expressing the expected decrease in quality. To make S_i commensurable with R_i it is calculated as

$$S_i = \beta \cdot \frac{E_{max} - E_i}{E_{max} - E_{min}}$$

where β is the acceptable higher cost mentioned before. An iso-cost line map (A_i) is constructed to find the optimal location. For criticism of this approach see Markan (1974).

Finally, Anderson (1971) should be mentioned since his work provides another model based on mutual weighting of environmental characteristics.

The following two models serve to illustrate two different approaches explicitly incorporating a *specific limit to the environmental effects that are tolerable*. Marks and Jirka (1971) design a model which seeks the optimal location for nuclear power plant in a situation where the running and distribution expenses are known. The model involves a general location–allocation algorithm of mixed-integer type, finding the location and size for several facilities in a discrete space. There is also an additional algorithm which calculates the cost of bringing the cooling-water temperature back to normal (as prescribed by the law) in all potential localities. This evaluation is based on physical expressions for temperature diffusion in different environments, i.e. in rivers, lakes or sea. All costs are summed and the location allocation problem is solved as a minimization problem. The formal structure of the model is shown in the appendix.

Nijkamp and Paelinck (1972) present a somewhat different method of considering environmental effects. Instead of calculating the costs of reducing the environmental effects they insert a physical upper limit for the distortion which is expressed as inequalities in a minimization model:

$$\sum_{r'=1}^{R} h_k^{r'r} \sum_{j=1}^{J} b_{kj}^{r'} \cdot q_j^{r'} \leqslant d_k^{or}$$

where:

r' = the region where industry ji located
q_j^{r} = the production level of industry j in region r
b_{kj}^{r} = the amount of pollutant k per unit
$h_k^{r'r}$ = the part of k originated in r and transmitted to region r
d_k^{or} = maximum acceptable amount of pollutant k in region r

The inequalities $(r \times k)$ ensure that the total pollution of type k in a region does not exceed the levels acceptable.

The advantage of this approach is that it avoids the problems of economic evaluation of the environmental effects. However, it does not ensure a feasible solution to the model for small values of d.

Conclusion

The approaches analysed may clearly result in models which differ markedly according to the details incorporated. Although little research shows whether or not highly detailed models provide a significantly better result than simpler models, the few analyses investigated tend to indicate that this is not so (Markan, 1974). Thus, when using mathematical models in industrial location analysis and planning, attempts should be made to elaborate models which embody the main structure of the described system rather than incorporate too many details which would make a solution difficult or impossible. Another essential point to remember is that model results can never be more than a guideline for the final evaluation prior to decision-making. However, modelling is a necessary prerequisite for making any system evaluation and description consistent and thus an essential part of research in industrial geography.

References

Alperovich, G. (1972), 'Welfare criteria and models for locating public facilities', in: *Research on Conflict in Locational Decisions,* University of Pennsylvania Regional Science Department Discussion Paper, 19.

Anderson, M. G. (1971), 'A computer-based model for nuclear power site selection', *Area,* 2, pp. 35–41.

Austin, M., Schmith, T. E. and Wolpert, J. (1970), 'The implementation of controversial facility complex programs', *Geographical Analysis,* 2, pp. 315–29.

Cooper, T. (1963), *Location-Allocation Problems,* Operations Research II.

Cumberland, J. H. (1966), 'A regional inter-industry model for analysis of development objectives', *Papers and Proceedings, Regional Science Association,* 17, in Hamilton (1978).

Daly, H. E. (1968), 'On economics as a life science', *Journal of Political Economy,* 76.

Hamilton, F. E. I., ed. (1974), *Spatial Perspectives on Industrial Organisation and Decision-Making,* Wiley, London/New York.

Hamilton, F. E. I., ed. (1978), *Industrial Change: International Experience and Public Policy,* Longman, London.

Herfindahl, O. C. and Kneese, A. V. (1974), *Economic Theory of Natural Resources.*

Hinman, I. (1974), 'A location model for public-facilities with neighbourhood effects', *Research on Conflict in Locational Decisions,* Discussion Paper, 13.

Isard, W. (1969), 'Some notes on the linkage of the ecological and economic systems', *Papers and Proceedings Regional Science Association,* 22, pp. 85–96.

Leontief, W. (1970), 'Environmental repercussions and the economic structure: an input–output approach', *Review of Economics and Statistics,* 52, pp. 17–26.

Markan, Anette (Reenberg) (1974), 'Location-allocation models and their application in public facility planning', *Kulturgeografiske Skrifter,* 9 (in Danish).

Marks, D. H. and Jirka, G. H. (1971), 'An environmental screening model for the location of power generating facilities', Unpublished Paper, *Operation Research Society of America Meeting,* Dallas.

Morris, D. (1972), 'Inclusion of social values in facility location planning', *American Society of Civil Engineers, Journal of the Urban Planning and Development Division,* 98, pp. 7–32.

Mumphrey, A. J., Seley, J. E. and Wolpert, J. (1971), 'A decision model for locating controversial facilities', *American Institute of Planners' Journal,* November, pp. 397–402.

Nijkamp, P. and Paelinck, J. H. P. (1972), 'An interregional model of environmental choice, an application of geometric programming', *Foundations of Empirical Economic Research,* Netherlands Economic Institute, 6.

Optimale Zweig und Standort Planung (1969): translations of papers from Russian.

Richardson, H. W. (1972), *Input–Output and Regional Economics.* Penguin, Hardmonsworth.

Victor, P. A. (1971), *Input–Output Analysis and the Study of Economic and Environmental Interaction,* Ph.D. Thesis, University of British Columbia.

Appendix

The mathematical formulation of the model by Marks and Jirka.

Objective function: $\text{MIN } Z = \sum\limits_{i=1}^{m} F_i \cdot Y_i + \sum\limits_{i=1}^{m} \sum\limits_{j=1}^{m+P} (V_i + c_{ij}) x_{ij} +$

$$\sum\limits_{k=1}^{P} \sum\limits_{j=1}^{P+m} t_{kj}^* \cdot x_{kj}^*$$

Constraints:

$$\sum\limits_{j=1}^{P+m} x_{ij} \leqslant c_i y_i \qquad\qquad , i = 1,2,\ldots,m \qquad\qquad (1)$$

$$\sum\limits_{i=1}^{m} x_{ik} + \sum\limits_{h=1}^{P} x_{hk}^* = \sum\limits_{j=1}^{P+m} x_{hk}^*, k = 1,2,\ldots,p \qquad\qquad (2)$$

$$\sum\limits_{i=1}^{m} x_{ih} + \sum\limits_{k=1}^{P} x_{kh}^* \geqslant D_h \quad , h = 1,2,\ldots,n \qquad\qquad (3)$$

$$\sum\limits_{i \in sr} Y_i \leqslant 1 \qquad\qquad\qquad\qquad (4)$$

$$y_i = \begin{cases} 0 \\ 1 \end{cases} \qquad\qquad \forall_i$$

x_{ij} og x_{ij}^* are positive integers

where:

$y_i \quad = \begin{cases} 1, \text{ if facility } i \text{ has been constructed} \\ 0, \text{ if not} \end{cases}$

$x_{ij} \quad = $ flow from facility i to point j

$x_{ij}^* \quad = $ flow from intermediate point i to point j

$c_{ij} \quad = $ per unit transport cost of flow from facility i to point j

$t_{ij}^* \quad = $ per unit transport cost of flow from intermediate point i to j

$F_i \quad = $ fixed cost for facility i

$\forall_i \quad = $ variable per unit cost for facility i

$C_i \quad = $ capacity of facility i

$D_h \quad = $ demand in point h

$S_r \quad = $ subset of mutual exclusive facilities

$m \quad = $ number of alternative facilities

$p \quad = $ number of intermediate network-points

$n \quad = $ number of demand areas

Chapter 8

The location of non-manufacturing activities within manufacturing industries

John B. Goddard

Closer linkage is required between research on the behaviour of organizations viewed spatially and aggregated studies of urban systems. The spatial structure of corporate organizations, when defined in the location of non-manufacturing functions and their information flow networks, underlies and steers a number of aggregate urban and regional development processes – like the spatial diffusion of technical innovation, multiplier leakages, polarized development and regional external economies. This paper reviews theoretical and empirical studies under three headings: (1) changes in the aggregate distribution of employment in various non-manufacturing activities; (2) changes in the spatial structure of corporate organizations, particularly the division of functions between locations; (3) studies of intra- and inter-organizational information flows. Under each heading particular emphasis is placed upon research that has aimed at building bridges between different aggregation levels. Management of contact networks through investment in advanced telecommunications, 'communication audits' and the designation of growth centres based on functions for exchanging information can become an important policy instrument for both organizations and public sector agencies concerned with regional development.

The basic features of regional inequalities in economic and social development within economically-advanced countries are relatively well documented. The emergence of the 'post-industrial society' with its associated relative or absolute decline of employment in purely manufacturing activities and increase of employment in 'non-productive' administrative research and technical functions has resulted in an increase rather than in an amelioration of regional inequalities. Regional concentration occurs especially in office-type jobs in which individuals are principally involved in the processing of information within organizations and its exchange between organizations using personal contact. This has important social implications for social mobility and migration and significant economic implications for development and change which are steered by the diffusion of new information.

Though the growth and changing location of information activities is recognized few attempts have been made to modify traditional location theory. Several writers refer to the inappropriateness of theory developed in the time of the single-product, single-plant firm to a situation where the multi-location, multi-product corporate organization dominates (Hamilton, 1974). Yet a comprehensive body of theory which can satisfactorily explain the location of various corporate functions, particularly those not directly concerned with physical production, has yet to be developed. Much recent behavioural research on organizations has focussed on location-decision processes rather than on factors which affect the performance of various organizational functions located in different places.

Attempts to apply traditional location theory, with its emphasis on regional variations in operating costs, to the location of non-manufacturing functions have substituted flows of information for flows of goods as a key variable in the cost equation (Törnqvist, 1970). Though sources of information, like materials, are not ubiquitous, it is doubtful whether concepts or methods of analysis applied to commodity flows (or even movements) are appropriate for examining the effect of location on different organizational functions. This is because there are greater possibilities for adapting communication behaviour to different locational situations than there are of changing sources or market outlets for manufactured products. That substantial adjustments can occur in the spatial structure and behaviour of organizations — the divisions of various functions between locations and the contact patterns of these functions — with few physical manifestations like new buildings, also creates difficulties for planning control. Corporate mergers and reorganization often lead to more significant changes in the geographical distribution of employment in non-manufacturing functions than of employment in physical production. Such changes seldom enter the realm of public policy: indeed, public-sector agencies often make these changes themselves with little consideration of their regional implications.

The lack of an adequate theory for the location of non-manufacturing corporate functions compounds the problem of policy intervention. Research is developing on office location but this has mainly been concerned with head office location or the location of independent service firms in the 'quaternary sector'. Few attempts to set head office location within the context of the spatial structure of corporate organizations though a recent study is an exception (Hamilton, 1974).

An obvious source for basic concepts is thus modern organization theory. This stresses the need for a holistic or 'systems' view of organizations (Emery, 1969; Haire, 1959; March and Simon, 1958). However, few organization theorists have explicitly considered the effect of location of the operations of organizations. Yet location is obviously important. The so-called social–technical systems theorists emphasize the open nature of organizational systems and the importance of interaction between an organization and its social and technical environment (Emery and Trist, 1965). To a regional analyst the term 'environment' also has a particular spatial connotation. The location of various non-production functions within a multi-unit organization influences its pattern of access to an environment which is composed of other parts of the organization located elsewhere and other organizations. Such patterns of access are reflected in information flows which can be mapped into geographical space. It is these information flows rather than the formal structure of the organization that ultimately define how the firm operates, particularly how it will be able to adapt to changes in the environment by developing new products, selecting new supplies and so on.

Aggregation problems

One most pressing issue facing research into the management of urban systems is the aggregation problem: the need to build at least a conceptual bridge between individual organizations and the whole urban system. The critical questions seem to be: what is the relationship between the spatial structure of organizations and growth and change in these organizations? How do these differences feed through into the aggregate performance of different cities and regions? The need to relate the behaviour of individual organizations to the overall pattern of urban change suggests the importance of a contextual framework for future research where the behaviour of various corporate units is examined in different regional and organizational environments.

The relationships between different levels of analysis are suggested by Fig. 8.1. Discriminating or contextual variables enter at each level. Sometimes these are

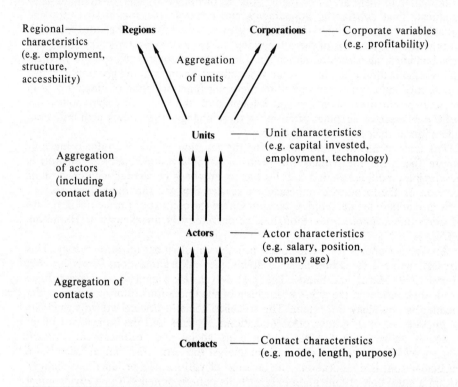

Fig. 8.1   Aggregation levels: contacts, business units, organizations and regions.

more than the sum of behaviour at lower levels. The geographical distribution of contacts of different types at the lowest level relates the organization to its external and internal environment. The actors having these contacts may therefore be differentiated according to the amount and type of their contact as well as other non-contact or contextual variables such as salary, company age or length of time in a particular job at a particular place. Establishments are composed of collections of actors classified by contacts: they are also characterized by a number of other variables which indicate the position of the establishment within the company (e.g. office space as a percentage of the total), its performance (e.g. R. and D. input, turnover, value added, changes in product line) and most important material flows with various segments of the environment (inputs and outputs from its own region as a percentage of the total). Firms in turn may comprise collections of establishments and have aggregate characteristics like profitability which cannot be readily attributable to individual parts. At the same level, regions comprise collections of establishments characterized by aggregation of all of the preceding variables plus regional factors such as industrial investment, industrial and occupational mixes and accessibility (particularly contact potentials).

The spatial structure of corporate organizations

Regional development processes: theory

Recently the structure – that is the division of functions between spatially separate units of the organizations – of corporate organizations have been related to the spatial structure of national urban systems (EFTA, 1973; Goddard, 1973*b*). Connection with the national system of cities is stressed because many functions are administrative activities predominantly concentrated in urban regions. The simplest example is that provided by Wärneryd, who has mapped three hypothetical organizations with a rigidly hierarchical bureaucratic structure into geographical space (Wärneryd, 1968). Various levels in the organization (group head office, divisional head office, plant management) are located in cities all at different positions in the urban hierarchy (national capital, regional centre, local centre). A complex set of linkages of interdependencies exists within and between the units of these organizations at different levels of the urban hierarchy. Internal linkages take the form of lines of administrative responsibility and ownership ties, while external linkage exist between different organizations with service firms in particular urban centres.

Pred has further explored the relationship between corporate structure and regional development processes (Pred, in Hamilton, 1974) adding to Wärneryd's original models an additional link across the hierarchy ('big city interdependence' or links between divisional headquarters). He suggests that the regional development process basically consists of three sub-processes: (1) the generation of non-local multiplier effects; (2) the diffusion of growth-inducing innovations; and (3) the accumulation of organizational operational decisions at particular levels in the hierarchy. All three processes tend to reinforce the existing urban system, particularly the dominance of the largest cities. Thus, the spatial structure of linkages within the organization tends to steer the spread of non-local multiplier effects. Expansion of activities at a branch plant may lead to additional administrative employment at a divisional or group head office rather than locally. If that expansion is an existing product field simply involving more inputs of the same type as previously then decisions about purchase sources are predefined and may be made at the local level. But if new or specialized inputs are required this decision is likely to be made at a higher level and possibly not involve local sources. For example, specialist consultancy services may be purchased by the head office from its own local environment. The possibility of using such services is one of the chief external economies offered by urban areas to manufacturing organizations.

Thorngren (1967) has distinguished between two types of external economy, the controllable and the uncontrollable (Fig. 8.2). Significant direct financial savings can be gained by contracting out business services like legal advice: the link between the administrative part of the organizations consists of information

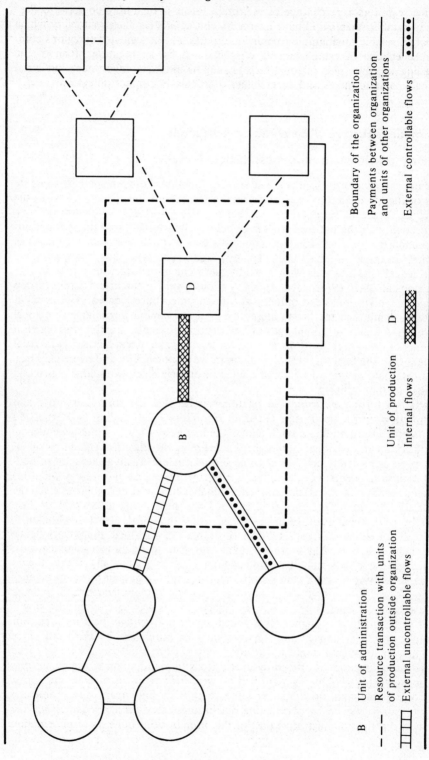

B   Unit of administration

---   Resource transaction with units
       of production outside organization

▥▥▥   External uncontrollable flows

———   Boundary of the organization

———   Payments between organization
       and units of other organizations

●●●●   External controllable flows

       Unit of production   D

▩▩▩   Internal flows

Fig. 8.2   Flows of information and external economies.

flows and parallel monetary flows. Such pecuniary economies are equivalent to those gained by contracting out part of the production process from the production unit: in this case material flows are paralleled by monetary flows. Uncontrollable external economies arise from information flows in which no monetary transactions are directly involved: for example, information about new markets, suppliers or production processes on which the long-run survival of the organization might depend. This information, while vital to the third process – the spread of growth inducing innovations – may (though not necessarily) flow along the established network of interdependencies within and between organizations. Substantial advantages accrue from location in an agglomeration where complexes of interlinked functions are found. Because of the steep distance decay effect on flows of specialist information, the industrial complex or growth pole has more meaning as a spatial concept in terms of this type of interaction than material flows (Hermansen, 1971).

The increasing concentration of manufacturing production into a limited number of large corporate organizations makes these generalizations particularly relevant to regional development (Parsons, 1972; Watts, 1972). The development of organizations from small single-function firms through national organizations engaged in several activities in many regions to multi-divisional and finally multi-national corporations have been discussed by Westaway (1974b) drawing upon the work of business economists like Ansoff, Chandler and Redlich (Ansoff, 1965; Chandler and Redlich, 1961). The emergence of the national corporation has involved both a horizontal division of management into specialist departments (finance, personnel, purchasing or sales) and a vertical system of control devised to connect and coordinate departments. The head office's responsibility has been to coordinate, appraise and plan for the survival and growth of the corporation as a whole. The expansion of such corporations through mergers and take-overs tends to lead to greater concentration of administrative employment through elimination of functions formerly duplicated in the separate organizations prior to amalgamation. External services which smaller organizations had to contract out are internalized: they can now be economically provided for the larger group. In the multi-divisional corporation, each division is concerned with one product line and is supervised by its own divisional head office while a group head office plans for the enterprise as a whole. Services for which there is substantial demand may be contracted out to companies which are wholly or partly owned by the corporation. The service firm meets the needs of the parent company at commercial rates, and competes in the open market for other work. In this way the linkages in the urban system become more complex and connections across the hierarchy (big city interdependencies) take on greater significance.

To see how the development of the corporate hierarchy relates to the spatial concentration of control, Westaway highlights a scheme, devised by Chandler and Redlich (1961) of three levels of business administration, three time horizons, three levels of tasks and three levels of decision making within an organization which have a bearing on location. In the early stages of corporate development – the small single-function, single-unit firm of classic location theory – all three levels are embodied in one entrepreneur. As the company expands into a national corporation, level three, which is concerned with the day-to-day management of production, is separated both functionally and geographically from the higher levels. Level two, concerned with the medium-term coordination of a number of production plants, operates from a head office located in an accessible large city.

Level one comprises top management whose function is to determine long-term goals and plan company strategy, thereby setting a framework within which all other levels operate. In the multi-divisional corporation this highest level may be separated from level two in the form of a group head office located in a capital city – principally because of the need for close connections with the money market, the media and government.

Empirical evidence: the location of non-manufacturing functions and employment

Empirical support for these contentions concerning the spatial structure of corporate organizations and the urban system comes from studies both of the changing location of administrative functions and of non-manufacturing employment. The territorial extent of large corporations is readily apparent when the location of various units are mapped out (Rees, in Hamilton, 1974). Seen alongside the distribution of urban centres in Britain or the USA the duality of the corporate and organizational system is readily apparent. Nevertheless, such maps tell little about the roles and interrelationships of units with an organization. Such information can only be obtained by sample surveys of the type reported by Parsons of 224 manufacturing operations in the UK (Parsons, 1972). This showed that although the South-East region accounted for only 28 per cent (507) of all operating units of these corporations, it contained 74 per cent (51) of group head offices; 48 per cent (15) of central service units (i.e. those functions concerned with administering the corporation at geographically distinct locations from the head office); 69 per cent (66) of corporate control units (i.e. group head office plus central services): 42 per cent (36) of divisional head offices; and 48 per cent (41) of research and development units. Comprehensive figures collated by Buswell and Lewis (1970) emphasize the importance of the South-East region outside London for research and development in the public and private sector: the region contained 49 per cent of all such establishments in the UK (Buswell and Lewis, 1970).

Most attention has been paid to the location of head offices: Westaway (1973a) indicates that the head offices of the 1000 largest companies in the UK are highly concentrated in London, with an almost perfect correlation between firm size and propensity to locate in the capital: 86 of the 100 largest firms have their head office in London compared with 32 of 100 smallest. Concentration appears to be increasing over time: between 1969 and 1972 the number of head offices located in London increased by 30 while all other large cities recorded losses. Firms with head offices outside London tend to be those that operate in fairly narrowly-defined sectors of the economy. Similar patterns of concentration have been documented in the United States (Goodwin, 1965; Armstrong and Pushkarev, 1973) and Sweden (Pred, 1973b). The 21 largest S.M.S.A.s in the USA contained 348 head offices of the 500 leading industrial corporations in 1968 and 163 of these were located in New York City. Similarly of the 148 leading companies in Sweden, 57 had their head office in Stockholm. The studies suggest that three broad types of spatial structure could be relevant: (1) multi-unit corporate organizations with head offices in the national capital; (2) multi-unit corporations with head offices outside the national capital, and (3) small independent firms outside the corporate hierarchy.

Studies of the changing location of non-manufacturing employment have proved more difficult principally because product-orientated industrial classifications have failed to isolate the non-manufacturing function within organizations. The paucity of official data on the occupations of employees by place of work is remarkable in view of the growth of such employment in all advanced economies. The 1966 census was the first time such data were published in the UK. Prior to that only residence-based occupational data were available and was generally meaningful only at the regional level. Analysis at this level shows the concentration of *all* office occupations in the prosperous regions (Burrows, 1973; Rhodes and Kan, 1972). No analysis of those employed in non-manual occupations in manufacturing industry which is available by region has been published. Residence-based occupational data are only meaningful when related to relatively closed labour market areas. Westaway (1974*a*) analyses the changing distribution of professional, managerial, clerical and manual occupation groups between 1961 and 1966 for Metropolitan Economic Labour Areas and shows an increasing concentration of managerial and professional occupations in Labour Markets in the South East, though there is some regional distribution and local decentralization of clerical occupations. Occupation-by-industry data has been equally difficult to obtain in the USA. 'Central Administrative Office and Auxiliary' employment is reported by the US Census but only for selected industry groups. Armstrong and Pushkarev (1973) analyse such data by S.M.S.As and indicate that 'manufacturing administrative jobs are either decentralizing gently to smaller metropolitan areas, in the wake of production plants, or if they have to be centralized, prefer to locate in or near New York'. Growth rates for manufacturing office employment appear to be inversely related to the size of metropolitan area. With the exception of New York, there is a close correspondence between the industrial composition of all manufacturing jobs in a region and the industrial composition of office employment, but this often results from one or two large employers for as in Britain, sectors that are highly concentrated in particular regions tend to have their office in that region (e.g. vehicle producers in Michigan with head offices in Detroit).

Relations between regional and organizational structure: behavioural research

Few studies have been directly concerned with relating the distribution of non-manufacturing activities and employment to regional development processes. Most research concerns relationships between organizational structure and geographical distribution of service purchases. This involves examination of the extent to which particular services (e.g. banking and finance or legal services) are provided within or outside the organizations. Britton (Ch. 10) has studied service supply in contrasting regions of Canada for single-plant firms and multi-plant corporations, concluding that there are pronounced differences in the willingness of managements of single-plant firms and those of branch plants to undertake certain tasks within the unit (i.e. to internalize).

His findings are corroborated in Norway by Stenstadvold and in Sweden by Byström. Both examine service use from the viewpoint of demand by manufacturing plants and supply of service firms. In less accessible regions of Norway Stenstadvold observes that management tends to use low-order service functions to provide high-level services: a bank manager is asked to give advice on long-range financial planning. Even though services may be available locally, branches' plants tend to be steered to Oslo while single plant firms are often unaware of the existence of possible service suppliers in nearby towns. Byström relates expenditure on external services to size of firm: expenditure on lower-order services like accounting decline with size of firm while that on high-order services like advertising increase with size of firm. Routine services required frequently or at short notice tend to be supplied locally while infrequent services are supplied from more distant sources.

Such studies of service provision relate principally to Pred's sub-process of 'the spread of non-local multiplier effects', although they impinge to a certain extent on his 'accumulation of operational decisions' (i.e. the level at which purchase decisions are made). Few studies, apart from Pred's own historical investigations (e.g. Pred, 1973c), have related the spread of innovations to the spatial structure of corporate organizations: most refer principally to non-industrial innovations (Berry, 1972). Yet there is much literature in organization theory on the innovation process, particularly the relationship between corporate structure and adaptation to environmental change. Socio-technical systems theorists place great emphasis on the environment when explaining innovation. Their main questions concern the kinds of formal organizational structure that can most effectively relate environment, technology and organizational members together. While a classical hierarchical structure may be appropriate in a stable environment more flexible arrangements are required in fields of activity subject to continual change (Burns and Staulker, 1961; Emery and Trist, 1965; Jefferson, 1973). Insofar as 'corporate structure' and the 'environment' can be defined in geographical space, the spatial structure of organizations can have an important bearing on the innovation process.

One study explicitly attempts to relate organizational and environmental characteristics in a spatial context. Back, Dahlborg and Otterbeck (1970) selected five regions in Sweden with varying population size, density and growth characteristics and the six largest manufacturing firms with head offices in each region. Data were collected for all units of these firms in the country as a whole. The final sample consisted of 22 firms with 80 units in 55 regions. Data on the changing organizational characteristics of units were then related to the characteristics of the regions within which the units were located. This contextual analysis thus links the two highest levels in the hierarchy of investigations outlined in Fig. 8.1. Organizational variables relate the unit to the organization as a whole (e.g. level of administration) and to the aspatial technical and social environment (e.g. variability in the scope of activity), while the characteristics of the spatial environment were defined in population size, growth and density of the immediate region. Linking the three sets of data through correlation and cluster analysis suggested that dense growing regions contained units that were heavily involved in administrative activities (high percentage of salaried employees), research and development (R. and D. employees a high percentage of total), which had experienced a high degree of variability in their level of activity (average fluctuation in number of employees over a five-year period) and scope of activity (technology, production mix and markets). In contrast, units with more stable activities tended to be found in the less dense and slower growing regions.

These findings indicate the importance of the immediate environment for industrial establishments. The process by which the local environment influences management decisions (and vice versa) is clearly reflected in the pattern of information flows between the unit and its internal and external environment.

Information flows and regional and organizational development processes

Theory

Information flows are a key process by which corporations monitor, manipulate and respond to their environment. Understanding of the manner whereby (organizations) adapt to changing conditions requires (1) indices of the range of their information inputs and their processes of decision making, i.e. the way in which information from the outside environment is channelled through the organization to the places where appropriate action can be taken, and (2) discovering how organizations scan their environment and their modes of scanning,

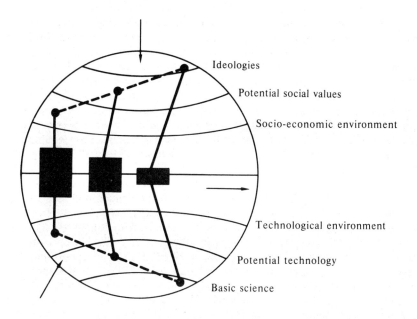

Fig. 8.3 Sources of information in the development space.

particularly which mode is associated with what information needs, how mode assignments are made and what procedures operate to alter their rules of scanning (Aquilar, 1967; Dill, 1962; Steed, 1971).

Thorngren (1970) suggests three principal modes by which organizations scan their environment. The environment or 'development space' (Jantsch, 1967) can be divided into two halves – a knowledge and a values environment (Fig. 8.3). Each part of the environment is divided into a series of distinct time horizons. The first type of interaction between the organization and its environment referred to as 'orientation' processes by Thorngren link the furthest segments of knowledge and values environment (basic sciences and ideology). This type of relation concerns the very long run future of the organization. With a motor manufacturer, this might involve considerations of developments in basic science that could provide an alternative to the car and possible changes in societal values with respect to personal mobility. The second type of relation or 'planning' process link potential social values and technology and involve the development of specific products identified by earlier orientation relations. As Fig. 8.3 suggests, planning relations involve a less random scanning of the environment than orientation processes. In the case of the car manufacturer these processes may involve the development of say a battery-operated vehicle. Finally, the bulk of an organization's external relations operate within established technological and social environments and are concerned with the control of existing resources. These 'programmed' relations are structured according to a pattern laid down by earlier orientation and planning relations. In the case of car manufacturers such relations might be concerned with producing next year's models.

The important point for regional and organizational development is that these three processes tend to involve different contact networks or 'modes of scanning' with some types of spatial environment being more appropriate for one type of contact than another. Thorngren suggests that orientation relations tend to occur in large pre-planned meetings involving wide-ranging discussions between people often coming into contact for the first time. It is the widening or divergent character of the contact network that distinguishes orientation processes. Only the largest metropolises offer the wide range of potential contacts with government, researchers, financial institutions and other business organizations, contacts which are essential for the conduct of orientation processes (Meir, 1962).

Planning processes by contrast tend to involve limited sets of familiar individuals with more clearly-defined objectives and information search tasks. Unlike orientation, planning activities are less dependent on random contact: indeed the great variety of information generated in the large metropolis may conflict with the development of a specific project and lead to communications overload (Ramström, 1967). Being familiar with one another, individuals involved in planning contacts can use telecommunications provided there are opportunities for regular (e.g. monthly) personal meetings (Goddard, 1971). The location of research and development activities in relative remote locations in the outer South East of England is remarkably consistent with this theory.

Finally, the great majority of external relations are concerned with routine matters. They involve specific discussions between familiar participants who are in frequent contact usually about matters directly related to buying or selling. Theoretically there is no reason why such activities could not be conducted in relatively remote locations using telecommunications. However, the sheer volume of contact may prevent this. Because of their routine nature these types of contacts are likely to have a relatively steep distance decay function and be confined to the local environment.

Regarding development processes, organizations without scanning units in information-rich environments could be slow to adapt to changing circumstances. Yet if all units are located in such an information-rich environment, conflicts could arise between the long- and short-term objectives associated with different processes. Relocation of activities to appropriate environments may therefore bring considerable benefits. For example, decentralization of routine activities from a city centre head office could release time for more essential orientation processes. However, relocating orientation functions to an environment dominated by programmed activities inevitably means that the orientation function diminishes because the function of a particular unit is an expression of its interaction with the external environment: by relocating a unit the pattern of access to the environment changes.

Empirical research

Best known of the studies of flows of information within and between organizations are Törnqvist's case studies of the gross amount of external contacts of manufacturing organizations with head offices in different locations in

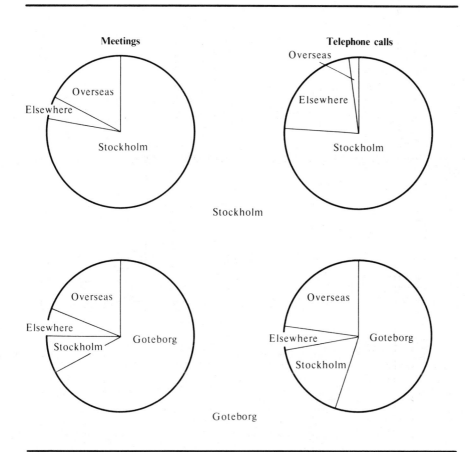

Fig. 8.4 Geographical distribution of external contacts of firms located in four Swedish towns.

Sweden. Most striking is the importance of the local environment regardless of the location. With the exception of Stockholm, between 40 per cent and 50 per cent of all contact time is spent at the home location. After that the other major urban centres account for the bulk of external contact time. Not surprisingly the firms in Stockholm can meet 71 per cent of their external contact needs in Stockholm itself. Thus the urban system is composed of discrete and remarkably self-contained centres. The importance of the near environment is also demonstrated by other studies. In a communications survey of 100 units located in four different urban regions of Sweden (Stockholm, Gothenburg, Sundsvall and Umeå) 76 per

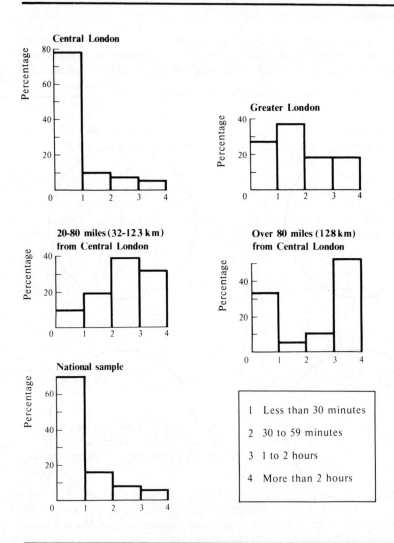

Fig. 8.5 Length of journey for business contacts.

cent of all contacts involving travel were with places less than 30 minutes away (Fig. 8.4).

Despite substantial differences in density, a remarkably similar figure (78 per cent) was recorded in a survey of 72 commercial offices located in central London (Goddard, 1973*a*). Another communication survey for the Post Office of 115 establishments throughout the UK has indicated that 70 per cent of meetings involving persons from other establishments gave rise to journeys of less than 30 minutes (Connell, 1974). An exception to this generalization is provided by 22 offices that have decentralized from London and attempt to maintain contact with the capital, involving themselves in long business journeys (Goddard and Morris, 1974). Nevertheless, decentralized offices in locations beyond London's shadow (over 60 miles) do have more local contacts and shorter journeys than those moving to locations in South East England (Fig. 8.5).

The importance of the local environment thus depends on urban spatial structure and on how far the sectoral composition of its local economy can meet the contact needs of the activity in question. This may be represented in the form of one row of an inter-sectoral inter-regional contact matrix (Fig. 8.6) showing the external telephone contacts of the head office of a wholesale and retail newsagent which has decentralized to Swindon, just over 60 miles from London. Contacts with the local environment are dominated by low-order ubiquitous services like transport and distribution. London is relatively unimportant except for contacts with the publishing sector which is nationally concentrated in the capital. Since manufacturing activity is dispersed throughout the country, the head offices of manufacturing firms in central London have a more widespread contact network than financial or service activities – although professional service firms have more of a national and regional role than business service firms (Table 8.1).

Table 8.1 Geographical distribution of contacts of central London offices by sector (from Goddard, 1973a)

	Manufacturing	Finance	Business services	Prof. services
Telephone				
Central London	47	74	71	37
Greater London	22	12	17	20
S.E.	11	4	4	11
Rest of UK	16	7	7	27
Overseas	4	3	1	5
Total (100%)	2096	1797	764	
Meetings				
Central London	53	76	83	37
Greater London	20	8	9	20
S.E.	7	3	2	11
Rest of UK	10	6	5	27
Overseas	10	7	0	5
	1045	855	366	

Törnqvist has revealed a close connection between occupational status and contact intensity. Variations in contact intensity also occur between functions and locations: individuals in decentralized offices have fewer contacts than their central London counterparts (Table 8.2) partly because the extent to which individuals of different status and in different types of departments play an internal or an external role within organizations. Middle management has a more internal role as do accounts departments especially in decentralized locations. Thus, regardless of the labels attached to them, ostensibly similar departments function in a different way in different locations.

Differences between telephone contacts and personal meetings moreover suggest that contacts using the two media perform different roles within the organization. This becomes more apparent when the various characteristics of the two communication channels are considered. The telephone is used principally for short, unarranged contacts which are concerned with one specific subject (Table 8.3). Most interesting is the way in which the same channel is used in different locations; in decentralized offices both meetings and telephone calls occur far less

Sectoral and regional distribution
of external telephone contacts

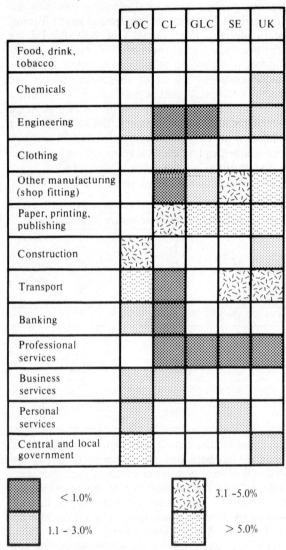

Fig. 8.6 Sectoral and geographical distribution of external contacts of a decentralized office.

frequently, meetings last longer, are arranged further in advance, involve more participants and wider ranging discussions. Location has quite a fundamental influence on communication behaviour. The effect of location on different contact networks can best be summarized if contacts are assigned to orientation, planning and programmed classes. Thorngren has pioneered the use of latent profile analysis to achieve this classification. Orientation contacts are assumed to take place in meetings where a large number of people come together for the first time for wide ranging discussions. Planning contacts also involve much feedback but occur more frequently and involve both the use of the telephone and face-to-face meetings. Programmed contacts are short, usually unarranged, regular contacts involving specific discussions (Classes I, III and II respectively in Fig. 8.7).

Table 8.2 Contact intensity: central London and decentralized offices (from Goddard and Morris, 1974)

	No. of external meetings per respondent (3 days)		No. of external calls per respondent (3 days)	
	Central London	Decentralized	Central London	Decentralized
Managing director, Chairman, Senior Partner	3.2	0.3	10.3	9.0
Director, Company Secretary, Junior Partner	2.3	0.6	7.0	8.4
Manager, Section Head	2.6	0.8	7.9	3.5
Assistant Manager, Professional	1.9	0.4	6.7	3.0
Executive	1.3	0.6	8.5	3.6
Clerk	0.4	0.2	5.1	2.6

Though all three contact types can be identified in most organizations in most locations, the relative importance of each does vary. Table 8.4 shows that orientation contacts are less important in decentralized locations than in central London, reflecting the fact that fewer contacts are with the information-rich environment of the city centre. The division of contacts into those that are internal and external to the organization shows that the planning function is essentially an internal one. The characteristic of contact networks have an important bearing on location decisions: firms that have rejected decentralization from central London (the non-movers) have significantly more external orientation contact than firms about to decentralize (24.1 per cent compared with 14.8 per cent) and also significantly more internal planning contacts (32.2 per cent compared with 17.7 per cent). These differences can again be largely attributed to the geographical distributions of contacts with non-movers having significantly more contacts with other firms in the city centre than the non-movers (63 per cent compared with 42 per cent) for telephone contacts and 79 per cent compared with 50 per cent for meeting contacts). Movers also record a lower intensity of contacts (an average per week of 6.2 calls and 1.3 meetings compared with 19.2 calls and 3.0 meetings for the non-movers).

The limited opportunities for orientation contacts with the local environment probably account for the lower intensity of this type of relation in decentralized offices. Thorngren noted that orientation contacts are predominantly with Stockholm, while local orientation contacts are better developed in Umeå (which has a university) than Sundsvall (which is dominated by heavy industry). Yet there are few connections between the two centres even though they are relatively near to one another. Thus the characteristics of the local environment and its accessibility to the national economy have an important bearing on processes of information exchange.

The developmental significance of regional variations in opportunities for contacts of different types is difficult to assess. One attempt by Collins (1973) uses stepwise multiple regression to link Thorngren's contact data to the characteristics

Table 8.3   External contact characteristics: decentralized locations and central London (from Goddard and Morris, 1974)

	Telephone		Meeting	
	DEC (%)	C.L. (%)	DEC (%)	C.L. (%)
Length				
2–10 mins	90	87	7	19
11–30 mins	10	12	27	29
31–60 mins	0	1	19	19
1–2 hours	0	0	25	18
Over 2 hours	0	0	22	—
Arrangement				
Not arranged	85	83	15	17
Same day	9	9	5	13
Day before	4	4	13	12
2–7 days	3	2	32	31
More than 1 week	1	2	35	27
Initiation				
Myself, own office	54	52	52	49
Other	46	48	48	51
Frequency				
Daily	8	18	0	14
Once a week	20	23	6	10
Once a month	16	14	18	13
Occasionally	40	34	42	38
First contact	16	11	33	25
Main purpose				
Give order	16	13	9	7
Recieve order	3	3	0	1
Give information	21	11	8	7
Receive information	26	26	14	9
Give advice	2	5	1	6
Receive advice	1	9	4	5
Exchange information	17	20	26	28
Negotiation*	8	3	13	8
General discussion	4	7	15	13
Other	2	5	4	16
Range of subject matter				
One specific subject	86	84	47	57
Several subjects	13	15	38	35
Wide range of subjects	1	1	15	8
Number of people at meeting				
One other			45	61
2–4			36	26
5–10 people			11	8
More than 10 people			7	5
Total number of contacts	1160	5266	193	1554

* Not strictly comparable with Central London.

of the seventy respective establishments at one point in time as well as changes in these characteristics during the previous year. This analysis corresponds to levels one and three of Fig. 8.1. No attempt has yet been made to link such analysis with the higher level regional and organizational variables that were considered by Back, Dalborg and Otterbeck. In one such model with the total number of con-

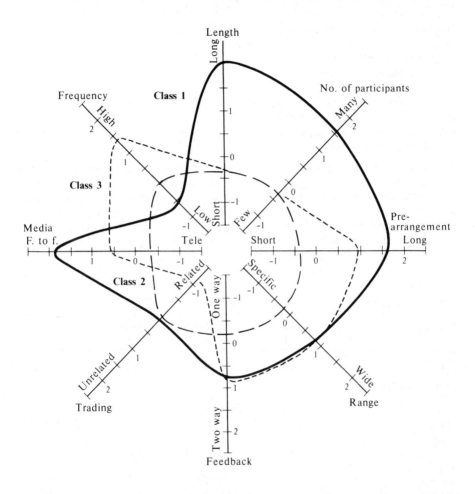

Fig. 8.7 Multivariate classification of the external contacts of central London offices.

tacts per head as the dependent variable, there were significant (99.9 per cent level of confidence) positive contributions from the following variables:

salaried employees as % of total;
office space as % of total;
turnover (in Kroner);
total number of product lines;

median salary level (in Kroner);
growth proportion of office space;
growth in value added due to new products;
growth in proportion of value added accounted for by smallest product line;
growth in salary of highest quartile; and
growth in salary of lowest quartile.

There were also highly significant negative contributions from:

proportion of organizations' total employees in the unit;
proportion of all input from Sweden outside unit's own region;
proportion of output to unit's own region;
salary of highest quartile;
salary of lowest quartile;
service nature of product (1 = manuf.; 1 = service);
growth in proportion of all employees in unit;
growth in proportion of input from own region; and
growth in median salary

The proportion of variance explained by this model is 64 per cent. The results suggest that units with a large and growing office component, especially those on rising salaries rather than those in the middle levels, tend to generate a large amount of external contact. The nature of the product and geographical environment also seems to have a bearing on contacts. Change and diversity in product structure leads to more contact activity while dependence upon the local region for inputs and outputs leads to less contact activity. The position of the unit within the corporate environment is important, with small units in large organizations having the greatest amount of contact.

Table 8.4   Classification of contacts (from Goddard and Morris, 1974)

Location	Orientation (%)	Planning (%)	Programmed (%)
Central London			
External	14.5	4.2	81.2
Decentralized locations			
Internal	7.3	17.7	74.9
External	10.3	1.1	88.6
Movers			
Internal	6.5	17.7	75.8
External	14.8	3.5	81.7
Non-movers			
Internal	6.9	32.2	60.9
External	24.1	8.5	67.4

Conclusions

Many interesting findings have originated in Sweden, yet isolated studies suggest that they are also applicable in the different British geographical context, with its relatively easy access between cities, a more continuously industrialized area and 'overlarge' conurbations with decaying physical and industrial infrastructure. Yet the importance of the local environment for organizational development and connections between corporate structure and the urban system could stem principally from the unique spatial structure of the Swedish economy: a hierarchically-ordered system of discrete cities separated by relatively 'empty' areas. Nevertheless, forces are at work in the growth of corporate organizations which, when related to the development of national (and increasingly international) systems of cities, appear to transcend obvious geographical differences. There is a pressing need to bring together researchers and policy-makers concerned with understanding and managing both organizational and urban systems at the international level. And if the importance of inter- and intra-organizational information flows as a factor shaping corporate and urban system development is accepted, then this dialogue should include workers from the telecommunications field to identify how current advances in technology can be used to steer future development in desired directions. The following outlines possible elements in an international research programme.

The most obvious task is to establish some inventory of the present and likely future changes in the distribution of various corporate functions, i.e. the spatial structure of organizations, within and between national urban systems. Much information can be obtained from directory resources, company reports and the management press, but a strategic view of corporate organizations and answers to difficult questions like the affect of recent mergers on the distribution of different functions, interviews with top management are necessary.

To assess the aggregate significance of changes in corporate structure for the development of the urban system it is essential to study the changing geographical distribution of employment in non-manufacturing activities. The advantage of a labour market definition of urban areas is that residence-based occupation data can be related to relevant employment centres. But the problem still remains that most census classifications of occupation inadequately describe the functions of non-production workers.

Empirical studies of contact patterns of actual *information flows within and between geographically separate units of large organizations* can provide valuable behavioural insights into mechanisms underlying a wide range of processes: management of organizations and the urban system through public involvement in the decisions of organizations, in investment in advanced telecommunications and designation of growth centres based on information functions; early warning of future changes, since flows of information are a necessary precursor of future changes in suppliers which will ultimately be reflected in new patterns of goods and money flows with consequent impacts on employment levels for contractors in different regions.

Because of fundamental time–geographic considerations, changes in the location of administrative functions have a profound impact on the way individuals communicate, ultimately on the patterns of interdependence in an urban system. Relocation can be used as a positive tool in management: to bring together departments that need to communicate more with each other and perhaps less with other firms; to improve linkages with other firms that are located elsewhere, perhaps in newly emerging spheres of interest for the organization; to encourage the devolution of some functions to lower levels in the organization thereby creating space and time in a head office for decision-making activities.

The success or otherwise of the relocation will need to be maintained by regular communication surveys or 'audits'. These data may suggest additional changes in the formal organizational structure or new telecommunication devices that are needed to derive the maximum benefits from the new locations. In such contact surveys limited attention need be paid to the direct costs of communications. Because of the uncertainty and the speed with which changes can occur in environmental conditions, a process of monitoring a selected strategy, coupled with appropriate adjustments in that strategy, is probably more appropriate than 'one shot' cost–benefit analysis. Relocation of administrative functions should thus be seen not solely as a short-run economic decision with respect to such factors as rents, labour costs and telephone bills, but as part of a process by which organizations can adapt to changing environmental conditions.

Public policies are concentrated decentralization of activities from capital cities are needed as a means of reducing regional inequalities in economic and social development (EFTA, 1973). Already dispersal of routine administrative functions from metropolitan cities is occurring, though mostly this comprises short-distance moves to relatively minor centres. Studies of intra- and inter-organizational communications can identify opportunities for converting some moves into more significant transfers to distant centres high in the urban hierarchy. Such moves do not necessarily disadvantage individual organizations as short distance relation, which predominates at present, discourages the establishment of the new local linkages that might be an essential component of an administrative decentralization strategy. It is thus necessary to distinguish between *dispersal* of administrative functions (which is purely a geographical concept) and *decentralization* (which is also a functional concept) which geographical separation may encourage.

Widespread dispersal of information-processing activities is both undesirable and unrealistic. Yet existing investment in physical infra-structure in sub-national urban centres, whose level of functional significance in the corporate hierarchy may well be below their rank size in population terms, implies considerable underuse of scarce resources which can only be remedied by major decentralization programmes. Within such centres relatively inexpensive 'narrow band' telecommunications (e.g. document transmissions and group audio) can be used for intra-urban contacts while public studios can be used for intercity 'broad band' video telecommunications. Greatest potentialities exist for the use of 'narrow band' systems in low level contacts which are characteristically intra-urban rather than inter-urban. Telecommunications are most effective where the participants are also in regular personal contact, which again is only possible in large urban centres.

Other benefits may be gained by decentralizing decision-making functions to larger urban centres in development areas: opportunities for establishing complexes of interrelated information exchanging activities as a stimulus for growth and change in the surrounding region. Although growth-centres based on propulsive industry may be unrealistic in material linkages, such centres could have very real meaning in locating administrative functions and their associated information flows, so making provincial centres the terminal points for intra-regional linkages rather than simply staging posts for connections with the capital.

Concentrated decentralization of administrative functions within private sector organizations clearly requires new policy instruments to bring about the detailed steering of economic activities that this strategy implies. Traditional systems of blanket controls on physical development applied over wide areas of a country are very blunt tools. The subtle ways in which firms can adopt to environmental changes through administrative reorganization which may include alterations in the divisions of functions between locations suggests that the location process for non-productive functions is even more difficult to control than the location manufacturing plants. Contact patterns are the very key in the process of change *and* control. Organizations frequently make sub-optimal decisions because of a failure to appreciate fully the information constraints imposed by their own limited contact networks. Communications audits administered by a public agency could be a very powerful tool in urban and regional policy by highlighting for firms opportunities for alternative locational/organizational arrangements, especially the advantages to be gained through locating different but complementary functions in the same city. While governments frequently become involved in the field of industrial reorganization, mergers and the like, attention is seldom paid to the spatial implications of the interventions. Communications surveys can reveal for example the possibility of linking up complementary functions in nearby cities; a public agency could thus become a 'contact wholesaler' without becoming directly involved in the financial affairs of private organizations.

The emergence of the post-industrial society emphasizes that without national urban policy that takes account of the influence of contact possibilities on regional development, existing spatial inequalities are likely to remain. Indeed, investment in communications infrastructure such as conference video facilities and advanced passenger trains that are uncoordinated with location policy are only likely to increase regional differentials in contact opportunities and ultimately in economic and social development. Impact studies of the dispersal of government agencies from Stockholm and London conclude that relocation leads to an increase in travel unless groups of inter-connected agencies are concentrated into large centres. This represents a closed systems view of organizations with little consideration of the possibility of new patterns of communication developing in the new locations. Open systems modelling of these processes is clearly a major priority for future research.

References

Ansoff, H. I. (1965), *Corporate Strategy*, McGraw-Hill, New York.

Aquilar, F. J. (1967), *Scanning the Business Environment*, Macmillan, New York.

Armstrong, R. A. and Pushkarev, B. (1973), *The Office Industry: Patterns of Growth and Location*, MIT Press, Cambridge, Mass.

Back, R., Dahlborg, H. and Otterbeck, I. (1970), *Location and the Economic Structure of Organizations*, EFI, Stockholm School of Economics (English summary).

Berry, B. J. L. (1972), 'Hierarchical diffusion: the basis of developmental filtering and spread in a system of growth centre', in: Hansen, N. M., ed., *Growth Centres in Regional Economic Development*, Free Press, New York.

Britton, J. (1974), 'Environmental adaptation of industrial plants: service linkages, locational environment and organization', in: Hamilton, F. E. I., ed., *Spatial Perspectives on Industrial Organization and Decision Making*, Wiley, London.

Burns, T. and Staulker, G. M. (1961), *The Management of Innovation*, Tavistock Press, London.

Burrows, M. (1973), 'Office employment and the regional problem', *Regional Studies* (7), pp. 17–31.

Business International (1974), 'Quantifying external relations: a useful mode-', November, **22**, pp. 374–75, New York.

Buswell, R. J. and Lewis, E. W. (1970), 'The geographical distribution of industrial research activity in the U.K.', *Regional Studies* (4), pp. 297–306.

Chandler, A. D. and Redlich, F. (1961), 'Recent developments in American business administration and their conceptualization', *Business History Review*.

Collins, H. (1973), *Analysis of Face to Face and Telephone Contact Generation in the Private Sector*, Communications Studies Group, London (P/73200/CL).

84   The location of non-manufacturing activities

Connell, S. (1974), *The 1973 Office Communications Survey*, Communications Studies Group, London (P/74067/CN).

Dill, W. R. (1962), 'The impact of environment on organizational development', in: Mailick, S. and Van Ness, E. H., eds., *Concepts and Issues in Administrative Behaviour*, Prentice Hall, Englewood Cliffs.

EFTA (1973), *National Settlement Strategies: a Framework for Regional Development*, Geneva.

Emery, F. E. and Trist, E. L. (1965), 'The causal texture of organizational environments', in: Emery, F. E. (1969), *Systems Thinking*, London, Penguin Books.

Emery, F. E., ed. (1969), *Systems Thinking*, London, Penguin Books.

Engström, M. G. and Sahlberg, B. W. (1973), *Travel Demand, Transport Systems and Regional Development*, Lund Studies in Geography (b), No. 39.

Goddard, J. B. (1971), 'Office communications and office location: a review of current research', *Regional Studies*.

Goddard, J. B. (1973*a*), *Office Linkages and Location*, Progress in Planning (1), Pergamon Press, Oxford.

Goddard, J. B. (1973*b*), 'Information flows and the urban system: theoretical consideration and policy implications', *Proceedings of the Third Urban Economics Conference*, Centre for Environmental Studies, London.

Goddard, J. B. (1973*c*), 'Office employment, urban development and regional policy', in: Bannon, M., ed., *Office Location and Regional Development*, An Foras Forbartha, Dublin.

Goddard, J. B. (1973*d*), 'Civil service for the regions', *Town and Country Planning*.

Goddard, J. B. and Morris, D. M. (1974), *Office Communications in Decentralized Locations*, Location of Offices Bureau, London (mimeo).

Goodwin, W. (1965), 'The management centre in the U.S.', *Geographical Review* (5), pp. 1–16.

Haire, M., ed. (1959), *Modern Organization Theory*, Wiley, New York.

Hamilton, F. F. I., ed. (1974), *Spatial Perspectives on Industrial Location and Decision Making*, Wiley, London/New York.

Hermansen, T. (1971), 'Development roles and related theories: a synoptic view', in: Hansen, N. M., ed. (1972), *Growth Centres in Regional Economic Development*, Free Press, New York.

Jantsch, E. (1967), *Technological Forecasting in Perspective*, OECD, Paris.

Jefferson, R. (1973), *Planning and the Innovation Process*, Progress in Planning (1), Pergamon Press, Oxford.

March, J. G. and Simon, H. A. (1958), *Organizations*, Wiley, New York.

Meir, R. L. (1962), *A Communications Theory of Urban Growth*, MIT Press, Cambridge, Mass.

Parsons, G. (1972), 'The giant manufacturing corporations and balanced regional growth in Britain', *Area* (4), pp. 99–103.

Pred, A. (1973*a*), 'The growth and development of cities in advanced economies', in: Pred, A. and Tornqvist, G., *Systems of Cities and Information Flows*, Lund Studies in Geography (B), No. 38.

Pred, A. (1973*b*), 'Urbanization, domestic planning problems and Swedish geographic research', *Progress in Geography*, (5), pp. 1–76.

Pred, A. (1973*c*), *Urban Growth and the Circulation of Information: The U.S. System of Cities 1790–1840*, Harvard U.P., Cambridge, Mass.

Ramström, D. (1967), *The Efficiency of Control Strategies*, Stockholm.

Rhodes, J. and Kan, A. (1972), *Office Dispersal and Regional Policy*, Department of Applied Economics, Cambridge.

Steed, G. P. F. (1971), 'Changing processes of corporate environment relations', *Area* (3), pp. 207–11.

Thorngren, B. (1967), 'Regional economic interaction and flows of information', in: *Proceedings of the Second Poland-Norden Regional Science Seminar*, Committee for Space Economy and Regional Planning of the Polish Academy of Sciences, PWN, Warsaw.

Thorngren, B. (1970), 'How do contact systems affect regional development?', *Environment and Planning* (2), pp. 409–27.

Thorngren, B. (1973), 'Swedish office dispersal', in Bannon, M., ed., *Office Location and Regional Development*, An Foras Forbartha, Dublin.

Törnqvist, G. (1973), 'Contact requirements and travel facilities: contact models of Sweden and regional development alternatives in the future', in: Pred, A. and Törnqvist, G., *Systems of Cities and Information Flows*, Lund Studies in Geography (B), No. 38.

Törnqvist, B. (1973), 'Contact requirements and travel facilities: contact models of Sweden and regional development alternatives in the future', in: Pred, A. and Tornqvist, G., ???.

Wärneryd, O. (1968), *Interdependence in Urban Systems*, Gothenburg.

Watts, H. D. (1972), 'Giant manufacturing corporations: further observations on regional growth and large corporations', *Area* (4).

Westaway, E. J. (1974*a*), 'Contact potentials and the occupational structure of the British urban system', *Regional Studies* (8), pp. 57–73.

Westaway, E. J. (1974*b*), 'The spatial hierarchy of business organizations and its implications for the British urban system', *Regional Studies*, (8), pp. 145–55.

Chapter 9

Swedish industry as a spatial system

Gunnar Törnqvist

The purpose of this chapter is to study the Swedish production or 'activity' system spatially (Fig. 9.1). In this hypothetical production system workplaces or establishments are distributed among several regions. Establishments are interdependent, being linked together by the transport of physical goods, persons, information and paralleled by flows of payments. The production system also comprises ownership and power relationships. Establishments in region A form a comparatively closed sub-system: they depend very little on units in other regions. In regions B, C, D and E, however, many workplaces are linked with units in other regions. Regional borders 'cut up' the system to make useful comparisons based on aggregate data difficult between regions. In a modern society, the operations of different workplaces are often highly specialized, yielding marked division of labour within a national production system. Production results that can be measured in one region (like region E in Fig. 9.1) are achieved by cooperation between units, some of which are nearby within the observed region, but most of which are far away in other regions. Changes identifiable in one region may thus be the result of events and circumstances in other regions. Interdependencies in a system of the kind illustrated in Fig. 9.1 are complicated, and very difficult to *quantify* as our knowledge of the processes operating in spatial systems is extremely limited.

Research organization

Figure 9.2 shows that research is divided into three consecutive stages: (1) survey, (2) analysis and (3) experiment. A second dimension is included, called the aggregation level: at the lowest level the objects are individual employees and workplaces while the highest level comprises entire urban regions within and outside Sweden.

1. A strong motive force in urbanization and the attendant concentrations of some activities in large urban regions is the need for contacts in the exchange of information between increasingly specialized job functions in society (Fig. 9.3). To test this assumption the survey stage studied both direct personal and telephone contacts between employees in various firms and other organizations and the spatial organization of employment in Sweden using the same functional classification. Thus far, research constitutes *observations of actual behaviour* in a national activity system.
2. Interest in the next stage shifts to the *limitations on and possibilities for* the functioning of different kinds of activities in varying locations. Analysis of the

86

possibilities of maintaining direct personal and telephone contacts and of transporting goods demands study of the transport system. The time-distances and costs characterizing the transport system have been used to determine the accessibility of different localities and regions relative to each other. *In micro-studies* the observation units to be located are employees, job functions,

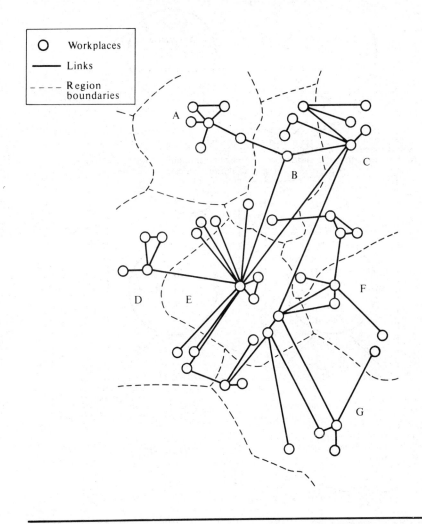

Fig. 9.1 A hypothetical production of system in a geographical perspective.

workplaces or entire organizations. Measurements in time and costs are made of the effects of hypothetical relocations on contact activity and transportation of these units. Assumptions about the scale and orientation of transport in various locations are based upon observations of actual contact-pattern and transport behaviour in a real transport system. *The macro-studies* are represented in Fig. 9.2 by analysis of 'contact landscapes' using aggregated data. Contact requirements in various urban regions are calculated by imposing data of contact requirements of different work functions on aggregate

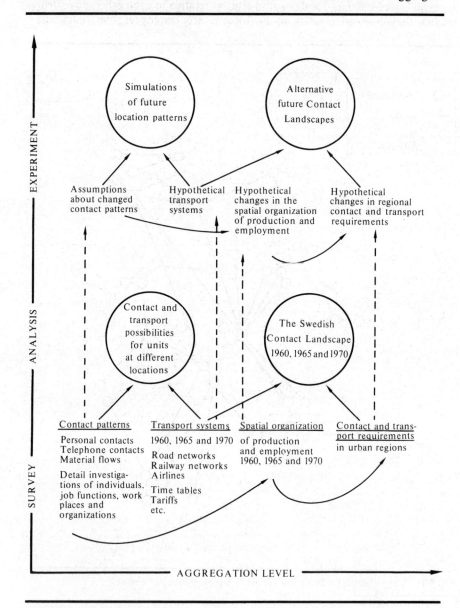

Fig. 9.2   Organization of work.

functions in each region. The contact landscape then shows the regional balance or imbalance between these contact requirements and the travel supply available in the existing transport system. These studies complement each other by revealing the advantages and disadvantages of each method. Macro-studies show the interplay and interdependence between the location of economic activity and public administration on the one hand and configuration

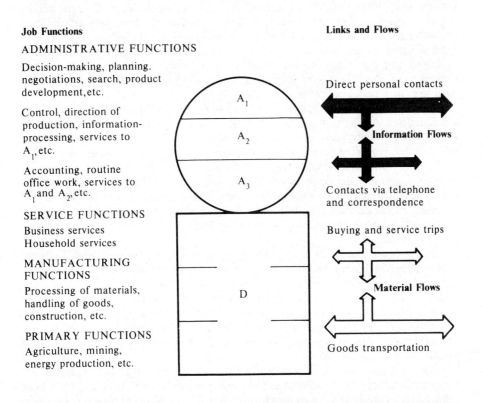

Fig. 9.3   Diagrammatic representation of an activity system consisting of job functions connected by links and flows.

of the transport system on the other, but the results are very difficult to inter-pret. The micro-studies comprise only a few case studies, yet yield deeper un-derstanding of links existing in a complex activity system.

3. By experimenting with operational models one can identify constraints upon policy opportunities for shaping the future spatial organization of society. These experiments are based on purely hypothetical distributions of workplaces and settlements and transport system, but use both micro- and macro-studies.

Links in a national production system

The nature of links between workplaces in Fig. 9.1 depends upon the types of ac-tivities located at different workplaces. Figure 9.3 shows four groups of job functions likely to be found in the units of production (activity) system studied. Several functions occur simultaneously in many establishments within a production system: for example, functions relating to physical production and handling of goods usually predominate in production units. But within each unit there are also service and administrative functions of varying significance though official statistics classify them as manufacturing jobs. Service functions particularly characterize commerce, transport, communications, education, health and medical services, social welfare, business and recreational services. Administrative functions are probably present in all types of modern activity, though their presence can vary from very slight (e.g. on a farm) to overwhelmingly predominant (e.g. in a public administrative agency).

Figure 9.2 also shows the types and flows of contacts that characterize various job functions. As each establishment included in the production system (Fig. 9.1) may simultaneously accommodate several job functions, the units are also linked together by several different kinds of contacts. Information is transmitted via direct personal contacts requiring journeys of one or more of those involved, via telephone contacts and correspondence. Services also require the transport of people, whereas the manufacturing functions and primary functions are linked together by goods transportation. The flows binding together the objects in the system are often paralleled by corresponding flows of payments moving in the opposite direction.

All types and flows of contacts shown in Fig. 9.3 have been identified, analysed and compared with one another. *Micro-studies* are based on descriptions of direct personal and telephone contacts, the buying and selling (flows) of services and goods for individual companies and other organizations. *Macro-studies* are based on aggregated data of direct personal and telephone contacts, buying and selling (flows) of services and goods within and between entire urban regions in Sweden. Direct personal contacts of organizations and urban regions have been analysed already (Törnqvist, 1970).

Figure 9.4 gives results of a micro-study: it shows the outgoing telephone calls from a manufacturing firm in Malmö in one week in May 1973. Calls have been allocated to a mesh of squares measuring 20 × 20 km. Squares receiving less than 0.5 per cent of calls are shaded grey. This investigation used an *automatic traffic reader* which registers calls going through the exchange of the firm studies. The calls are located using the dialling code, and the first figures in each telephone number show which automatic telephone station connects each outgoing and incoming call: in 1973 Sweden had 6687 such stations. Since they are assigned coordinates, the computer can map the registered telephone call data. Such telephone-call networks are registered for many companies, other organizations, private households and entire urban regions throughout Sweden.

Figure 9.5, an example of a macro-study, shows geographical distribution of sales of goods by manufacturing companies in 1970. All the companies included are located in Malmö and its environs, Sweden's southernmost urban region. Deliveries, like the telephone calls, have been plotted over squares measuring 20 × 20 km. Figure 9.6 gives a corresponding view of the manufacturing companies purchasing of goods during one year. Similar maps exist for various Swedish urban regions.

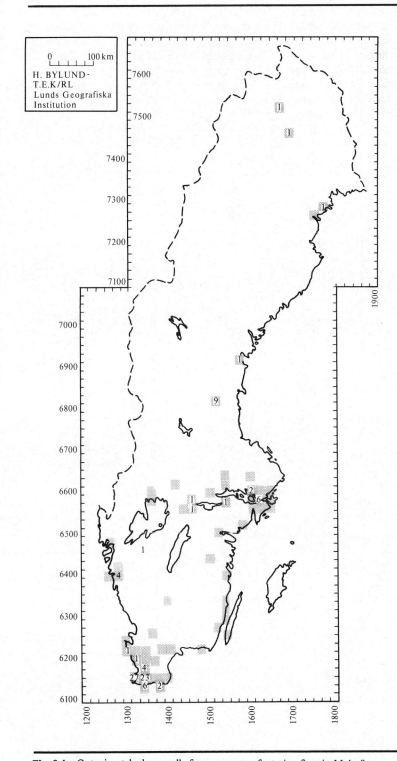

Fig. 9.4 Outgoing telephone calls from one manufacturing firm in Malmö.

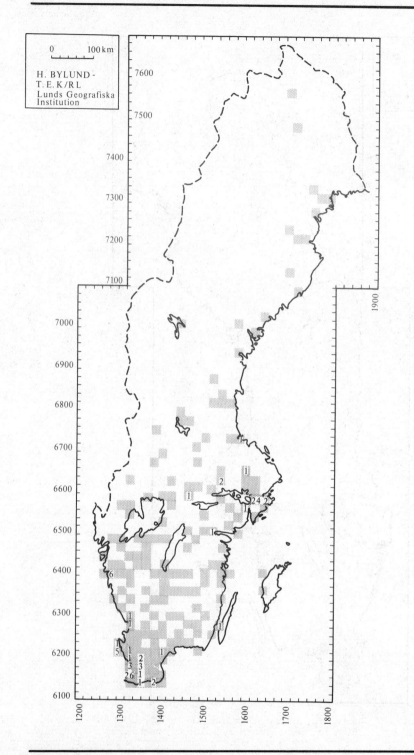

Fig. 9.5   Sales of goods. All manufacturing firms in Malmö.

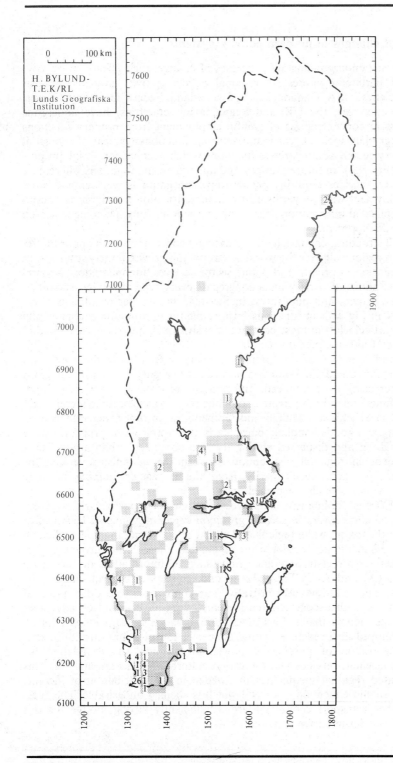

Fig. 9.6 Purchasing of goods. All manufacturing firms in Malmö.

Employment changes in modern activity systems

Activity systems undergo constant processes of change: their effects on employment are of particular interest to regional policy. Activity systems in post-industrial societies (USA, Canada, Japan, Switzerland, Federal Germany, France, the Benelux countries, the UK and Scandinavian countries) have undergone marked shifts in concentrations of gainful employment from primary functions (typical of agrarian society), via manufacturing functions (typical of industrial society) to service and administrative functions which account for a high proportion of jobs (Fig. 9.3). In future primary and manufacturing functions will require less manpower, services requiring person-to-person contacts will demand more labour. Employment will rise very sharply in administration functions, as a result of more complicated information processing, decision-making, planning, research and product development.

So far such structural changes have increasingly concentrated job opportunities in large urban regions all over the world. Metropolitan growth largely results from dynamic expansion in private and public sector services administration. Around these agglomerations of control units congregate every type of service, radio and television, newspapers and publishers. In Sweden, the number of administrative employees (A in Fig. 9.3) in functions responsible for information exchange and processing, particularly the most contract-intensive (A_1), has risen very rapidly: from 150 000 (1960) to 250 000 (1970).

Regional redistribution of occupational activity in Sweden in the 1960s has been *selective*, functional differentiation between the seventy major urban regions becoming increasingly pronounced. Information processing, control and administrative functions in both private and public sectors have become increasingly concentrated in Stockholm, Malmö and Gothenburg, in that order. Meanwhile, manufacturing and goods handling, particularly the more routine processes, have been decentralized and dispersed among the less populated urban areas. These divergent trends in regional distribution between the administrative and the manufacturing functions result partly from the increasing number of large organizations with regionally dispersed units.

The 250 000 contact-intensive employees, though not a particularly large occupational group, are *a very important group for regional policy*. At least half of them work in the major urban regions and exert there a strong multiplier effect on employment. First, the contact-intensive employees attract other groups of personnel for services, registration and processing of information in their own organizations (A_2 and A_3 in Fig. 9.3). Second, clusters of control units in the major urban regions attract administrative sub-contractors and other types of business services. Third, contact-intensive employees have advanced education and an average income that is four times as high as the average income for all gainfully employed in Sweden. Regional concentration of administration means also a concentration of purchasing power, which lays the foundation for specialized household services and for varied cultural and recreational life. This has accentuated regional inequalities in Sweden in the distribution of income, social structure and education − a trend which is socially undesirable. The question is whether transport economies are a sufficiently strong motive for this clustering of contact-intensive activities.

Transport costs and concentration

Many experts analyse how *transport facilities* and *transport costs* influence the localization of different activities. Researchers have gradually shifted attention away from analyses of facilities for transporting goods to analyses of those for transporting people. Costs incurred in transporting goods vary greatly between plants manufacturing different products: thus 'sensitivity' to differences in regional transport costs varies greatly from one industry to another. Typically installations bound to raw-material sources mainly process heavy, bulky or fragile raw materials into more easily transportable semi-manufactures and finished goods: steelworks, potteries, glass and ceramics works, sawmills, pulp and paper mills, chemical plants and certain food-manufacturing activities. Such plants increased in number in Sweden until the Second World War but have declined since. In 1900 basic industries accounted for most employment in Swedish manufacturing; today, less than 20 per cent of industrial labour works in such plants. The locational limitations exercised by transport costs on this category has lessened in parallel with this trend. Other industries have their mobility restrained by markets: the spatial form and size of their markets often affects the scale and localization of production in various places. Technological and economic trends also have lessened the comparative importance of transport costs, and production has gradually been concentrated into larger and fewer units, causing decreased employment in many regions.

Many plants are *mobile* relative to transport costs: factors other than costs of goods transport are usually of far greater importance for expansion and location in textiles, plastics, machinery, electrical, transport equipment and engineering industries. Many include primarily assembly plants, consuming semi-manufactures and finished components from a long chain of sub-contractors in Sweden and abroad and producing goods of high marketable value relative to transported weight and volume. The majority of new and relocated plants or those established as new industrial branches in Sweden since 1945 belong to this footloose group and today employ approximately half the manufacturing labour force. The same conclusions emerge from foreign studies of industrial mobility. Till now, though, the term 'transport costs' has been defined too narrowly as costs of freight handling. Future studies should broaden the definition of the term, and examine more closely such factors as inter-regional disparities in time consumption and in regularity of deliveries of materials and products.

The connection between transport costs and industrial concentration poses two major questions. First, from the distributing costs viewpoint, what is the optimum location of 1, 2, 3 ... *n* facilities (factories or warehouses) within a spatially-dispersed market, taking account also of the transport costs of all facilities? Second, how large should the different facilities be and how should they divide up the market between themselves to ensure that total distribution costs will be minimized? Together, these two questions form a problem block within which several variables are allowed to play. Since a clear analytical answer is difficult, a heuristic technique has been developed (Törnqvist *et al.*, 1971) which implies but does not prove that the optimum solutions are global.

The example chosen involves a light porous building material, sold in Sweden under the trademark 'Ytong' or 'Siporex'. The empirical point of departure is the

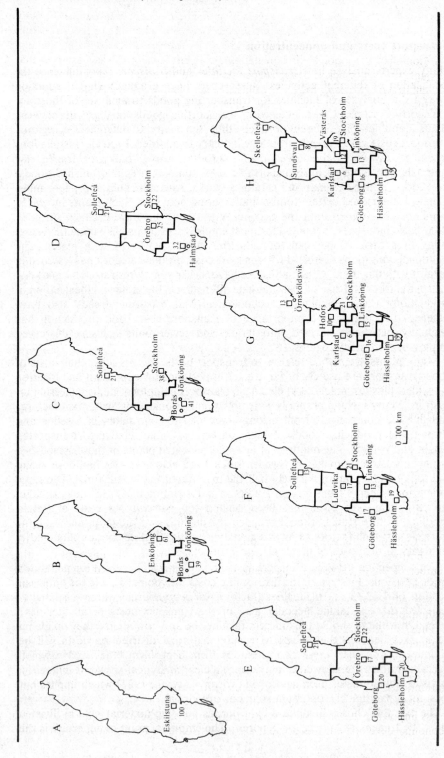

Fig. 9.7 Optimal locations, capacities and market areas for 1–8 plants (warehouses).

sale distribution of this product a decade ago. The market corresponded broadly to population distribution and exports were very low. Then the optimum (within the reservations above) locations of 1–8 units were calculated from the distribution–cost standpoint. In calculating transport costs, it was assumed that carriage was by truck or train depending upon the route and terminal costs prevailing ten years ago. Figure 9.7 illustrates the findings. Map A shows the best transport–cost location for a single plant supplying the entire market. Map B shows the best location of two plants, one accounting for 61 per cent, the other for 39 per cent, of supplies. Maps C to H show the optimum location combination, sizes and distribution areas of 3–8 units. Plants should be situated centrally in the market to minimize transport distances, while being simultaneously spread as far as possible from each other to serve the whole market. These two requirements counteract each other so the optimal locations worked out represent a compromise between them.

As production is allocated among an increasing number of dispersed units, transport costs decline (Fig. 9.8) from about 35 million Swedish Kroner for one plant to about 23 million Kr. for eight plants, while aggregate production costs rise, as scale economies are lost in sub-dividing production among smaller and smaller units which causes duplication of required labour and hence higher labour costs of repairs and maintenance, administration and capital investment per unit of capacity. Assumptions on variations in unit-costs are applied to the plants of varying sizes given in the alternatives A–H (Fig. 9.7), yielding total production costs (excluding transport costs) for 1–8 plants as shown by the middle curve in Fig. 9.8. The upper curve indicates the total costs, i.e. the sum of the transport and production costs for 1–8, to be at a minimum of 5 plants (alternative E in Fig. 9.7). Variations in total costs which occur when the number of plants is altered from 2 to 8 are comparatively slight because transport costs and production costs in these alternatives more or less 'compensate' one another. If we observe the *general rise* in transport costs while holding unit-costs constant, the curve of total costs in Fig. 9.8 demonstrates that the transport cost minimum goes down as this minimum tends to shift towards the right. Also, the location pattern in Fig. 9.7 changes somewhat.

Assume now *a changed relationship between transport costs and other production costs*. Though transport costs are assumed to remain unchanged from the preceding example, technological and other scale economies have increased: unit costs are now assumed to vary between plants of different sizes as illustrated by curve C–D in Fig. 9.9. These assumptions result in the curves shown in Fig. 9.10. The bottom transport costs curve is unchanged. Production costs rise as the number of plants increases, according to the function, illustrated by the middle curve in the diagram. The total costs curve at the top of the figure is quite different in this situation from that in the preceding example. It now appears to be economically advantageous to concentrate production in two units.

Thus, in a society where transport costs decline in *relative* importance – production costs per unit produced rise more rapidly than transport costs per unit transported – there is a strong incentive to concentrate production in bigger and fewer plants even in industries that are closely tied to their markets. Such concentration leads to increases in total transport effort and consequently total transport costs to society as a whole. That total transport costs rise while they also become a less important factor in location decisions is not paradoxical. Technological and economic development has created a situation today where practically in all in-

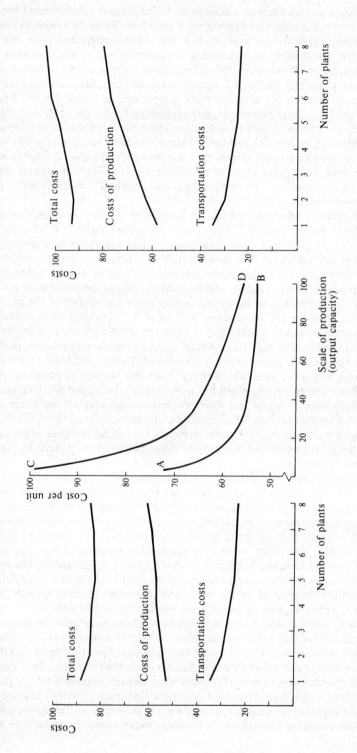

Fig. 9.8 Cost curves for different number of plants on the national market.

Fig. 9.9 Unit–cost curves.

Fig. 9.10 Cost curves for different number of plants on the national market.

dustries unit costs are lowered by greater concentration of facilities. Reduced operation costs probably constitute by far the strongest motive force behind the transformation of production structure. The questions that obviously arise here are whether the rate of structural change and its orientation (the location of new instruments) are the most desirable.

Personal contacts and location: micro-analysis

That Sweden has a highly advanced economy is indicated by high per capita provision of infrastructure like railways, roads and power lines: but this also expresses the substantial economic burden of long distances. Fortunately, progress in transport techniques has practically neutralized the constraints exerted by distance, yet one fact – fundamentally important in the role played by transport in production and social interaction – is that whereas goods and messages are divisible into small parts and stored easily for short or long periods, people must be transported as whole entities and be supplied with a vast range of services both in transit and in situ. Thus whereas distance has practically ceased to be an obstacle to freight transport, its constraint on the transit of persons is, and will remain, substantial. This difference is a fundamental factor underlying urbanization: people functioning in day-to-day contact with each other must live fairly close together.

Contact studies show how organizations located in various places are linked together by direct personal contacts. Contact-dependent employees are greatly involved in contact activity (travel and meetings). Companies and organizations spend much money on such information transmission and the time these contacts take is burdensome for individuals. Manufacturing or service enterprises and public administrations all depend on information transmission via direct personal contacts or telecommunications. A method has been developed for calculating how a changed location affects the scale and orientation of contact activity (Persson, 1974) and facilitates evaluation of regional variations in passenger transport costs. The units studied may be individual employees, departments, workplaces, entire organizations or groups of organizations.

Thus it is now possible to quantify and distribute by region the number of journeys and telephone calls necessary for maintaining contacts. Matrices depict these distributions and the degree of accessibility in the real transport system. As the concept 'accessibility' has different implications for different individuals, both an economic and a time measurement are used to assess contact activity. The actual telephone system is described from the economic point of view. Matrices are compared to evaluate the contact activity of the organizations in the location under review. Together with data concerning the time spent on contacts (length of meetings and calls) matrices can then be prepared indicating the total time spent and the total costs incurred by organizations on maintaining their contact relationships. When the real location has been described and evaluated, the organizations are moved around to a number of hypothetical locations. Relocation is simulated, making assumptions (based on empirical evidence) about the 'new' reality confronting the organizations and the probable effect on contact activity.

Using a simulation technique, several model experiments are performed to test the effects of various changes in the travel and telephone-call patterns. Account is taken of the adaptation of contact behaviour (i.e. contact frequency, choice of counterparts, meeting places and types of contacts) to the hypothetical locations. Parallel with these experiments, a simulation technique is used to create hypothetical transport and communication systems including new air routes, new timetables and a new telephone network. In the latter telephone charges are changed and new media introduced (like conference television).

This method has been used to study the effects on contacts of moving public administration agencies out of Stockholm. An example is the Swedish Telecommunications Administration which, in the model, was relocated to ten different centres around the country (Fig. 9.11). In every centre the Administration's employees were allowed to perform a 'contact programme' designed on the basis of information collected about actual contact activity by the Administration. Findings are presented as variations in transit time between different location alternatives. Throughout the tests, results are compared with the outcome for the actual location (place of location = Stockholm). Transit time is calculated either from actual timetables for transport by bus, train and air and assume use of the fastest single or combined means of transport or from a certain average car speed on roads (here 70 km.p.h.). Contacts are presupposed during office hours only (09.00–17.00), so maximizing the stay time available at eight hours and thus conditioning the number of contacts possible during a day visit.

Relocation to different places (Fig. 9.11) is tested partly with a contact behaviour which is (1) completely unchanged and (2) adapted to the new contact situation in which the Administration finds itself. In the latter case, the aim is not to reconstruct average behaviour – variations in human behaviour are too great for such an exercise – but rather to indicate a possible *scope of action* within the framework of restrictions that actually exist. This is then allowed to influence travel in the 'new' location.

The first component factor in adapting contact behaviour implies that journeys are arranged so that actual meetings take place at one participant's operational base. Second, service contacts made in consultant work, various office services, deliveries and maintenance of equipment are assumed to occur in most A-region centres (the seventy major urban centres in Sweden): thus such service contacts are not tied to the original location but can be transferred to the 'new' location, so limiting the increase in time spent on contact travel. Third is the possibility of using telephone communication instead of face-to-face contact to reduce travelling. A fourth factor included in the assumptions for model testing is the possibility of 'saving up' contact requirements so that more than one contact can be made per journey.

Figure 9.11 shows the effects of relocation *both with unchanged* contact behaviour and with adapted contact behaviour. The values shown reveal that travel time increases very sharply – by an average of all places by 500 per cent – if contact behaviour is assumed to remain unchanged (the upper figure at each place). In absolute figures, this is an increase from about 2300 travel hours to 14 000 travel hours per week. Of all alternative locations, Uddevalla gives the highest increase (c. 750 per cent) because of its 'poor' position in the national transport system regarding travel time. Other northern Swedish towns also show high values: Sollefta, Östersund and Luleå. Moving the administration to the cities of Malmö and Gothenburg results, too, in substantially increased transit time. The weakest relative increases are recorded by Norrköping (c. 300 per cent) and Örebro (over 400 per cent), which are situated fairly centrally and well served by

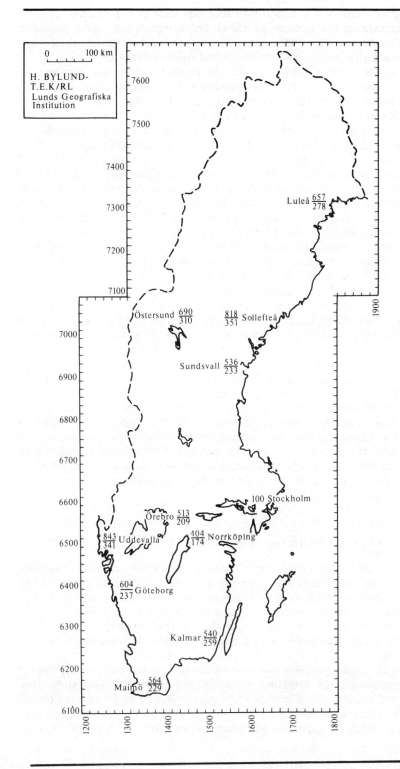

Fig. 9.11   The effects of relocation of the Telecommunications Administration. Unchanged and adopted contact behaviour.

land transport. Proximity in transit time to the Stockholm region determines the relative increase in the number of travel hours consequent upon relocation because the Administration has close ties with various contact sources there: most journeys made after relocation are thus to and from this region.

If contact behaviour is adapted to the new contact environment, however, increases in transit time are much less (the lower figure for each locality in Fig. 9.11). The percentage difference between the result for unchanged and for adapted contact behaviour average 60 per cent over all localities. The assumption that a meeting is generally held at one of the participant's base accounts for threequarters of this difference. Relocation with adapted contact behaviour results in an average increase (all localities) of about 5700 travel hours, or roughly 160 per cent compared with the Stockholm location. The regional results for adapted contact behaviour correspond with the results obtained when contact behaviour was unchanged. The greatest increases in transit time result at the Solleftea, Uddevalla and Östersund locations (respectively by 255, 245 and 213 per cent). The major cities, Gothenburg and Malmö, however, are now much more competitive alternatives than other locations, but Norrköping and Örebro still offer the best locational environment in transit time, with increases of 74 and 109 per cent respectively over the location in Stockholm.

The length of travel time between two towns also affects the duration of stay time. This determines whether it is possible to plan more than one contact per journey to reduce the total number of journeys. The shorter the transit time, the longer the stay time and thus the greater the potential reduction in the number of journeys. Another explanation of regional disparities is the variation in possibilities for satisfying the need for contacts with specialized services in the 'new' locality. Quite apart from the particular choice of location, the amount of travel performed by an organization very much depends on both the contact and travel pattern of the organization and the transport system serving it. In Sweden, the three major cities have good connections with, and greater accessibility to, other centres. Given this transport system, the travel input of an organization is largely determined by whether the travel pattern of the relocated organization generates journeys between the 'new' location and Stockholm or other centres. In the latter case, many 'across-the-grain' journeys are necessary, requiring very high travel inputs.

The Swedish contact landscape: macro-analysis

The whole Swedish system of cities may be tested by the contact studies based *not* on the individual organization or company unit and their 'unique' contact situation in varying locations, but on the urban region. The intentions are (1) to show how the total number of possible contact combinations varies between different regions in Sweden and (2) to study regional balance between the supply of, and demand for, travel facilities. The principle on which such studies are based in shown in Fig. 9.12.

Analysis of contact facilities available to towns or urban regions uses data of contact requirements in economic activities and public administration, their locations, and travel facilities available between the seventy major regional centres of Sweden. Data was derived from earlier studies of contract requirements calculated by value per capita, by job functions, job levels and types of economic activity. To determine the total contact requirement of each region, the number of employees in each job function, job level and branch of economic activity there has been multiplied by the per capita value. The total contact requirement of all job functions present in a region constitute the contact-requirement value of a region (see the Demand side of Fig. 9.12).

The study of travel facilities has been limited to communications between the seventy major regional centres in Sweden. Data includes times of departure and

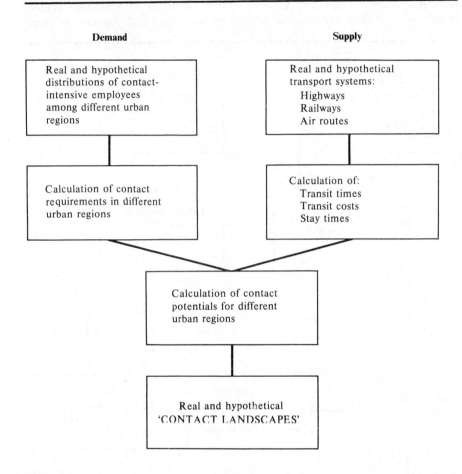

Fig. 9.12   Diagrammatic representation of calculations used in a study of the regional balance between contact requirements and travel facilities.

arrival, and fares, obtained from timetables for railways and domestic airlines, giving travel facilities between each pair of A-region centres at all times of day or night. The road network has been converted into transit time by car. Transit times, stay times and transit costs of journeys between each pair of A-region centres have been calculated by computer. Optional restrictions can be built into the computer program which can also be used to test changes in timetables and route networks (Supply side of Fig. 9.12). Details of these macro-studies are published elsewhere (Pred and Törnqvist, 1973; Engström and Sahlberg, 1973).

Synthesis

Figure 9.13 depicts a process of *adjustment between changed organization of work and changed transport facilities.* Earlier, changes in a modern activity system were studied where the degree of specialization and division of labour

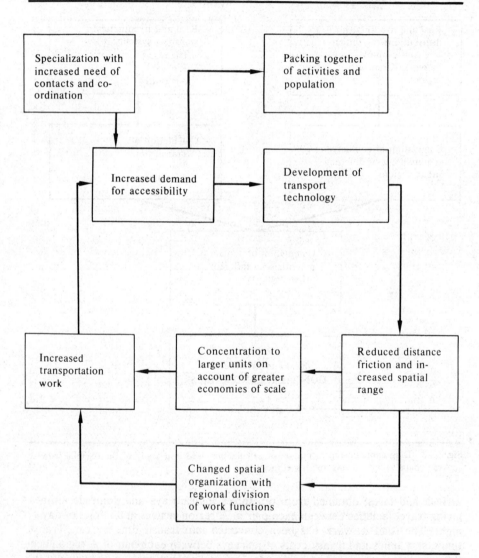

Fig. 9.13   Process of spatial reorganization (cf. D. G. Jannelle: *Spatial Reorganization: a Model and a Concept,* AAAG 59, 1969).

between various job functions is very high. As a result of this change in work organization, activities have gradually become far more interdependent, and society cannot function without the constant transport of goods, people and messages. Study of contact patterns both for the individual organizations and for entire urban regions showed the present degree of this interdependence in Sweden. Figure 9.13 assumes that interdependence leads to demand for greater accessibility. One method of satisfying this demand is to locate workplaces and housing in close proximity. Regional concentration in just a few major urban regions, mainly of those activities which are dependent on direct personal contacts, has been a well-tried method of limiting long-distance transport.

Demand for increased accessibility can, however, also be satisfied by improved transport technology (Fig. 9.13). Steamships, railways, cars, electric-power transmission and pipelines have all altered transport supply since 1800. Telecommunications and aviation have further reduced the constraint exerted by distance in industrial and post-industrial societies. Parallel to these advances manufacturing has become increasingly a matter of cooperation within vast production systems in which work is divided between many specialized component units. So far, though, calculations have only incorporated costs of actually handling the goods. It is necessary to study also the time element involved: the time deliveries take and their regularity affect production conditions, rapid deliveries preventing stoppages, flexibility in delivery schedules influencing warehousing needs and costs.

Figure 9.13 shows that as distance constraints are reduced and, consequently, regional range is extended, it becomes possible to intensify *the division of work functions between localities* even further. Simultaneously, companies often can derive scale economies from concentration of the handling of goods and services in *larger and fewer units*. In the service sector a 'shifting of the cost burden' takes place between different sectors or interest groups in society. When planning services at the national, regional and local levels, the scale and location of various units is often determined by the efficiency criterion and costs estimates of the business world. When costs to consumers and other expenses resulting from more extensive transport are not included in these estimates, scale economies have an enormous impact, as transport costs no longer exert restraint. The result is rapid concentration of social and commercial services in larger and fewer units.

These processes of change demand increased transport which affect the private business and public sectors. Then development has gone the full circle shown in Fig. 9.13. When faced with possibly repeating the cycle again, recall how little is known about the future of energy resources. The rationing of motor fuels and rapidly rising oil prices have shown that modern society is extremely sensitive to changes in transport economics which may result from a continuing energy shortage. The possible effects on the spatial organization of society of such changes are very difficult to foresee. The linkages and the interplay between the location of residential areas, services and workplaces on the one hand, and changes in transport facilities on the other, are very complicated. *Various courses of development are feasible in a society that is short of energy.* These are not mutually exclusive and could very well function alongside one another. Given the components depicted in Fig. 9.13, the following alternatives are feasible.

Alternative 1: Raised transport costs and reduced mobility may lead to decentralization of workplaces and services, while exploitation of scale economies decreases relatively. The lower part of Fig. 9.13 illustrates this process of adjustment if 'reduced distance friction' is changed to 'increased distance friction' and 'concentration to larger units' is replaced by 'division into smaller units'. This would yield a more dispersed location pattern for market-bound industries, decreased concentration in retail trade and a more equalized regional distribution of various service institutions, provided that population distribution is little changed.

Alternative 2: Another alternative exists for an energy-scarce society (Fig. 9.13, top left). A high degree of specialization demands greater transport and rising energy consumption. A society short of energy may have to organize work in an activity system which involves largely self-supporting individuals and production units less dependent on interaction and cooperation. Thus, a change in the modern production system could bring about *increased integration of work operations within independent workplaces instead of intensified division of work between workplaces.*

Alternative 3: Energy shortage and reduced mobility may have effects like those depicted by the top right square in Fig. 9.13. In a low-energy society with a highly differentiated distribution of work, the transport economy is well served by clustering activities and population close together. Increased concentration at national, regional and local levels is very possible. As a result of mutual personal contacts, the interregional traffic between organizations diminishes. Manufacturers and wholesalers may find it beneficial to locate their activities in closer proximity than they do now. It may become so expensive for members of individual households to reach services and their workplaces that these costs influence housing patterns within various regions and localities.

Alternative 4: Future trends in transport technology are a key question in the entire discussion of Fig. 9.13. These may be minor adjustments, such as transition from energy-intensive means of transport to vehicles with low energy consumption. Yet possibly changes could be very radical — technological innovations which completely transform transport facilities in society as they did in the nineteenth century. Alternative 4 is thus a situation where, with the help of technology, development goes the full circle depicted in Fig. 9.13 a few more times, even in a low-energy society.

Undoubtedly in an economically advanced country like Sweden, transport facilities have improved substantially *for the whole country*, but how far have trends *reduced regional inequalities* in transport supply? Studies of direct personal contacts *do not* indicate that development has noticeably reduced inequality at the national level: people in some areas have much greater difficulty in maintaining contacts than those working elsewhere. Often transport improvement has increased regional inequalities by benefiting primarily places with initial advantages, bringin little improvement to places with initially poorer transport supply: such trends are global (Pred and Törnqvist, 1973).

Figure 9.14 depicts four abstract and simplified versions of a 'Löschian landscape' (Lösch, 1944; Haggett, 1965). Workplaces and settlements are assumed to be located in forty-five places which are evenly spread over a surface and linked by transport routes; otherwise the surface is entirely uniform (isotropic). Version A depicts a situation in which all places are of equal size and are offered equal facilities by the transport system. Version B assumes that fifteen of the forty-five places have become larger than the others and have a better traffic base, so justifying a transport supply system superior to that in A. Transport is now improved in aggregate, but the degree of accessibility in the system changes

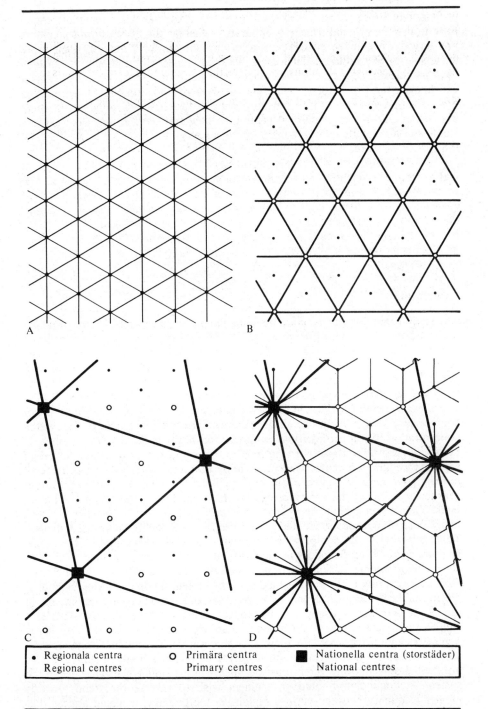

•	Regionala centra	o	Primära centra	■	Nationella centra (storstäder)
	Regional centres		Primary centres		National centres

Fig. 9.14 Transport routes in a hypothetical system of cities.

in favour of those places called the primary centres: the thirty regional centres have to use the original transport apparatus, whereas the fifteen primary centres are served by a more effective transport system *as well*, making them more accessible to one another. Differences between places will gradually increase as new activities are concentrated in places with better transport. This process is a causal cycle (cf. Fig. 9.13) with interplay between the location of activities and the gradual improvement of the transport system. In version C (Fig. 9.14), three places have grown into national centres as new transport routes (like express trains and airlines) have developed: now there are three levels of accessibility in the system of places.

Version D brings the different levels together. Traffic capacity (road quality and width, service frequency and public transport capacity) is always highest on the routes linking a small place with a larger place. Places at the lowest level are assumed to have better connections with centres at the highest level than with places at the intermediate level, when these are the same distance away (see the pattern around the three major centres). Empirical examples illustrating these developments using Fig. 9.14 can be taken from various modes of transport.

Conclusion

The study began by analysing the regional balance between travel supply and demand in Sweden in 1960, 1965 and 1975, demonstrating great differences between urban regions in their possibilities for maintaining direct personal contacts. The main purpose of model experiment was to test how different measures of regional policy – through the interplay of changes in employment structure and in the transport system – may increase or reduce regional inequalities in the future. These experiments provide the following conclusions. Regional concentration of contact-dependent activities results in a more efficient national contact system: the concentration of contact-intensive employees, primarily in Stockholm, makes contacts easier both for those working in the capital and for those located in urban regions throughout Sweden. Decentralization of contact-development activities – moving governmental agencies out of Stockholm – cannot be achieved without drastically reducing the ability of employees to maintain their face-to-face contacts. The reason is that the interregional transport system in Sweden, as in so many other countries, is adapted to the needs of a strongly centralized society. This transport system comprises a hierarchical network with primary centres serving as nodes. Some nodes, particularly the capital, enjoy a high degree of accessibility: people working there have no difficulty in contacting each other or their colleagues working in other nodes of the system. People working in smaller nodes can easily keep in contact with functions which are concentrated mainly in the capital, but not so easily with employees in other smaller nodes. In parts of southern and central Sweden, where nodes are clustered close together, the car is a good means of transport for maintaining contacts. When longer distance contacts are necessary, requiring train or air travel, facilities between smaller nodes are limited and journeys often must be made via the major central nodes in the system – Stockholm. Should government wish to reverse the trend towards greater inequality between various regions in the country, it would appear that proper measures taken in the transport sector would render regional policy more effective.

References

Engström, M. G. and Sahlberg, B. (1973), 'Travel demand transport systems and regional development', *Lund Studies in Geography*, Series, B, **39**.

Haggett, P. (1965), *Locational Analysis in Human Geography*, Arnold, London.

Lösch, A. (1944), *Die raumliche Ordnung der Wirschaft*, Jena.

Persson, Ch. (1974), *Kontaktarbete och frantida lokaliseringsforandringar*, Gleerup, Lund.

Pred, A. and Törnqvist, G. (1973), 'Systems of cities and information flows: two essays', *Lund Studies in Geography*, Series B, **38**.

Törnqvist, G. (1970), 'Contact systems and regional development', *Lund Studies in Geography*, Series B, **35**.

Törnqvist, G. *et al.* (1971), 'Multiple location analysis', *Lund Studies in Geography*, Series C, **12**.

Chapter 10

Influences on the spatial behaviour of manufacturing firms in Southern Ontario

John N. H. Britton

The 1970s have been a turning point for Canadian manufacturing. Productivity has been increasing in a wide range of activities, but from the late 1960s medium and high technology industries have responded to recession conditions by reducing employment, especially in research and development and administration. The short-run significance of this result is to emphasize the 'failure' of manufacturing to employ a stable share of a growing labour force (Science Council of Canada, 1971). Foreign ownership of manufacturing in Canada (56 per cent in 1972) has made this problem worse: first, because it has been easy for foreign corporations, especially those owned in the United States, to reduce white-collar employment in their Canadian subsidiaries, and second, because the trade policy of the United States has been directed towards reducing foreign direct investment and encouraging exports (Fayerweather, 1974). Measures taken by the United States coincided with saturation being reached in the foreign ownership of some medium- and high-technology activities (such as machinery, electrical products and transportation equipment) which already had proved sensitive to the recession.

Publication of the Gray Report (1972) meant not only that a new industrial policy was being sought officially but that a review and interpretation of previous writing on Canadian industry was accomplished. Some of this work is quite dated, but more important than the problems introduced by time is that the behaviour of industrial plants in space was not reviewed in the Gray Reports – presumably because of the lack of research concerned with spatial behaviour and the geographic significance of foreign ownership in Canada.

Although Canada is confronting major growth in the tertiary labour force, and the change in the sectoral emphasis of jobs seems to suggest the economy is emerging into the post-industrial era (Economic Council of Canada, 1972), there is no reduction in the pressure to uncover the workings of the industrial space-economy. Despite sectoral changes in employment, manufacturing is still the pre-eminent component of the urban economy: half of Canadian cities over 10 000 population boast manufacturing as their dominant economic activity (Ray et al., 1976). Increased productivity in manufacturing means greater economic significance for each industrial job and for the multiplier effects that derive from industrial demands. These results of linkage are registered directly in manufacturing itself and in more labour-intensive activities such as transport, warehousing, office activities, research and other 'tertiary' services. Where will the employment (and income) multiplier effects occur – locally or internationally? What are the main economic and geographic determinants of the linkage (especially backward linkage) patterns of Canadian manufacturing? These

110

questions are central to this research on Southern Ontario but the particular approach adopted owes much to the gaps that appear in the spectrum of recent industrial research in general.

Issues in industrial geography

It is easy to become frustrated with non-geographic approaches to the study of *organizational* structures if only minor reference is made to economic or locational aspects of behaviour (Brooke and Remmers, 1970). Flows within organizations have been studied (Törnqvist, 1970) and inferred (Pred, 1975, 1976) but there has been little consideration of either differences in the propensity of firms to maintain close corporate connections or the locational significance of distant rather than close parent–subsidiary relations. Similarly, the locational expansion of corporations, especially giant multinationals, has been studied (McNee, 1974) but, with few exceptions, the impact on the regional environment in which the firms have settled has not been a major issue. Orientation of research has been to the organization not the region; economists, to a lesser extent geographers, in 'host' economies provide the nearest to an exception to this generalization (Paquet, 1972; Fayerweather, 1974). Even then, with only very recent momentum to geographic research on multi-locational firms, it is location patterns that have been studied more than economic interactions (behaviour) that are associated with particular sites (Ray, 1971; Hamilton, forthcoming, 1978).

Of basic concern is the degree to which questions in industrial geography depend on location theory: these ideas promote the importance of location selection as the essential questions, although at any one time the majority of plant managements are sufficiently content to not contemplate a locational shift. To most, 'industrial location' elicits reference to both a collection of elegant, deductively derived theories and some empirical reports which usually are unimpressive in their insights. Perhaps the problem with this latter approach has been that over the past two decades empirical work has been concerned with illuminating theory, and too little in the way of model building has been attempted from an inductive basis. By contrast, programming models, making operational some aspects of location theory, have attained substantial success.

However, it is possible to view most plants as having fixed locations (in the short and medium term) and the research problem becomes one of how plants *function* in a specialized economic world. Of particular geographic importance is how plants interact with others and with firms in other sectors. Classical location theory helps pose the problem of industrial interdependence through its simplistic treatment of agglomeration, and while temporal and spatial uncertainty provide important additions to ideas on the origin of agglomeration the basic issue remains that most industry while locationally static is involved in operating – not locating.

Location theory generally provides a more or less successful economic rationalization of location, after the event, but recent geographic work (Hamilton, 1974) questions the behavioural basis of this type of explanation of *location*. This project was begun in the belief that parallel developments of similar depth must occur in research on how plants *operate* given that their locations are fixed for the foreseeable future. Of particular geographic importance are patterns of interaction of industrial firms with firms in the same and other sectors.

The long history of studies on industrial linkages is characterized by concentration on the assumed incidence of external economies to explain urban clustering. But procedures developed for the analysis of industrial complexes have influenced thinking in this field. In particular, a larger spatial frame is usually involved when considering the nature of a complex, the inter-sectoral investment strategy is a pre-eminent line of enquiry, and evaluation of input–output (technical) relationships a major task. Some recent studies, however, identify a wide range of circumstances in which the local linkage *hypothesis* is of much less importance than suggested by location theory and these doubts derive from work at the interregional level, on metropolitan regions, and within urban areas (Britton, 1969; Karaska, 1969; Taylor and Wood, 1973; Gadd, 1975; Mock, 1976). A number of factors – technological change (e.g. increased vertical integration), organizational growth and improved communication and transport systems – have either freed much manufacturing from local inter-firm dependence or never allowed it to be important. This problem is particularly relevant given the large producing scale of vertically-integrated modern firms, the mobility of skills, information and goods and the locational influences exercised by government. Whereas classical least-cost location theory has focussed attention on complex industrial linkages as an urban consideration (compared with the regional significance of major inputs) contemporary conditions demand that these major and/or minor links be investigated also at the inter-urban regional scale (the level at which planning has adopted growth centre and related ideas).

Research design

Concern with Canadian problems and industrial research in general have influenced the structure of the research reviewed here. The following represent the main components of that research design. First, with the location of each firm fixed, spatial behaviour may be observed most clearly in economic interactions with other business establishments. Such flows incorporate the element of choice between sources in various locations. Material flows are an obvious variable and although there are other inputs whose arrangement has locational impact – for example, the size of a plant's demands on the local electricity utility – only inter-industry flows embody real choice. Even then alternatives may be more apparent than real (Gilmour, 1974), especially when intra-firm linkages are considered. Second, the manner in which plants are connected with service establishments also has been studied. The services of interest are those required by each plant's office and enquiry has been restricted to 'planning' and mainly 'programme' activities. Contacts that might have been related to new capital investments ('orientation' activity) are generally the province of head offices, and thus do not generate linkages for many establishments reviewed or are not comparable with the 'routine' nature of material linkages (Thorngren, 1970). The ease of overcoming distance through various forms of communication ensures that industrial linkages of this type will reflect the organizational power of corporate head offices, main plants or metropolitan centres.

Third, the research uses a cross-sectional mode of analysis and necessary assumptions underlying this approach are that most plants/firms attain a boundedly rational pattern of connections. This depands on the view of firms as adaptive systems that adjust their linkages so that they may be maintained in routine fashion for as long as possible.

Fourth, given the small number of industrial firms enquiry should preserve, in large measure, the identity of each firm; locationally this means using data for plants. Explicit enquiry into the differences in connections of single-plant firms and branches belonging to multi-locational firms is possible with this sort of data. Generally the aim is to seek importance of organizational differences in the development of linkage patterns. Concern with multi-locational firms is intended to supplement, not detract from, the better-known behaviour of uni-locational firms. Variations are found, too, in their degree of self-sufficiency and thus their total linkage patterns: inner-metropolitan locations, for example, are believed particularly suitable for the survival of minimal-scale firms. More distant locations are possible if greater complexity of functions is accepted but longer-distance linkages may substitute for functions that cannot be performed internally or locally.

Fifth, the project has parallels with some other studies (Pred, 1973) but rather than demonstrating the structural dependence of the urban system on the functional form of organizations it seeks to identify industrial responses to urban differences. The inter-urban context of the study is important when distances between nodes are relatively small and when there is a large range in their size. The first factor promotes inter-urban industrial flows and the second means that a variety of *urban-industrial* environments occur within the one region and existing plants will respond to local conditions – in the sense of input demands, for example – according to organizational and economic considerations.

Data

To analyse plant-linkage behaviour, a stratified sampling method was used to ensure inter-plant variation in a range of 'structural' characteristics. Attention concentrates on activities with substantial backward linkages, especially those in the *metal fabrication–engineering industrial complex* concentrated in Southern Ontario. Selection of industries (wire products-SIC 305; auto parts-SIC 325; machinery and electrical goods-SIC 331, 2, 4) was based on: (1) technical homogeneity, industrial distinctiveness regarding type of product (components, low and high value domestic goods or industrial equipment) and process (assembly, or fabrication); (2) scale of development (5 per cent of Ontario's manufacturing employment), and (3) wide distribution.

Toronto is the pre-eminent location of plant, product and office services and wholesaling and it is expected that smaller centres rely on these central services, in hinterland fashion. The sample industries, however, are concentrated in a large number of centres at the western end of Lake Ontario. Their locational diversity within the region reflects the possibility of both local dependence (like Toronto and Hamilton) and extreme independence of the local industrial environment (peripheral towns). Four environmentally-distinct locational strata were used in sampling. These are: Toronto, Lakeshore, Southwest Ontario and the Periphery (Britton, 1974). While these are not exhaustive of the operating circumstances of industry in Southern Ontario they are indicative of the major environmental differences prevailing in the region.

To capture sources of industrial variation a random procedure was used in conjunction with location, industry and plant size (by industry) strata and differential sampling fractions for industries. An overall response rate of 79 per cent (87 interviews) was obtained: 63 'branch' plants (18 being Canadian, 41 US and 4 European-owned) and 24 uni-locational firms supplied data. Interviews (1970–1) using a set of standard questions produced data on (1) the proportion composition of material inputs by commodity and origin in their value of total material inputs and (2) the 'usual' location and nature of the firm from which office services are obtained.

The behaviour of industrial plants in southern Ontario

Material linkages

Although there have been numerous enquiries into the connection patterns of manufacturing, generally it has not proved possible or productive to attempt to identify behavioural differences between plants. Nevertheless, the value of this view of plant operations is illustrated here because by using data describing the spatial, organizational and economic characteristics of linkages, basic *dimensions of linkage behaviour* (from factor analysis) have been identified. The structure of the flow patterns of the sample plants may be expressed in six dimensions – complexity, commodity value, linkage frequency, corporate dependence, long distance-company linkage and wholesalers *vs.* manufacturing supplier. When these are evaluated using structural information on the sample-plants a wide range of dominant associations is found that are illustrated by the following selection: simple flow patterns for wire and many auto-parts plants; high value of inputs for electrical goods producers and American-owned auto-parts manufacturers; long-distance flows of branches compared with single-plant firms; and plant size differences accounting for variation in wholesale/manufacturing dimension.

The scores of each plant on the linkage dimensions provide evidence for testing the impression that plants 'independent' of corporate ties are localized in Toronto and the Lakeshore. A search for types-of-behaviour, however, can only come from a statistical grouping of observations based on their positions on the linkage dimensions. There are in the sample branches whose 'dependence' is indicated by long-distance corporate flows and 'independent' businesses that, by contrast, generally have short-linkages with other firms.

Two distinct groups are of an *independent* type. Small to medium-sized machinery plants in Toronto or the Lakeshore are found to establish short-distance flows, mainly from wholesalers. Of considerable importance is that half the plants in this group are branches owned in the United States! In the same regions, a similar group of single-plant firms (especially in the wire industry) is identified but their inputs dominantly flow directly from other steel wire industrial plants.

Groups defined as *dependent* are distinguished by their major flows generally being from within the corporation. These links tend also to be from distant sources (United States ownership) and of high value. Auto-parts plants dominate one group showing the effect of the Canada–United States Automotive Trade Agreement (Beigie, 1970). These groups of strongly dependent subsidiaries of US corporations add spatial detail to the notion of the 'truncated subsidiary' (Gray Report, 1972) that describes the limited capacity of some branch-plants to become as dependent on the industrial environment of their location as is generally necessary for similar domestic plants.

Some plant-groups are classified as *intermediate* in linkage pattern. Differences in degree of complexity and frequency of input shipments distinguish those groups which contain plants from industries (except wire) that are strongly identified with both independent and dependent groups, although there is no simple arrangement of these types occurring among structural characteristics. Yet wire plants, for example, are strongly independent, but if the remaining industry groups are considered together, a gradient of increasing proportions of corporate dependence is found to be associated with the level of urbanization in different sample regions. Peripheral towns have the highest proportion of 'dependent' branches while in the south-west there is, proportionally, a large number of plants classified in 'intermediate' groups because of longer linkages both within Southern Ontario and to the United States.

Of particular importance is the very wide range of plant types found in and around Toronto. Wholesale services are available at their best in the metropolitan region; both simple and complex patterns of input-assembly are associated equally with this location. Toronto even contains an equitable proportion of dependent plants. A wide range of plant-linkage types, however, is found throughout industry and locational strata and is attributable to organizational factors which determine, for example, the membership of 'dependent' or 'intermediate' groups for any industry or location. Nevertheless, within peripheral areas the proportional importance of 'dependent' branches is not to be underestimated. Their independence from the supply side of the regional economy has perpetuated the relative underdevelopment of these areas by means of corporate and spatial substitution in the flow of industrial inputs.

Office linkages

Nowhere is the importance of corporate organization more likely to be observed than in the way office functions are arranged for each unit of the firm. Since many business services involve the use of professionals, technicians and other skilled workers, these office inputs may be considered analogous to 'high value goods'. There is a relative underdevelopment of knowledge on contact linkages, particularly business-service linkages, and although some studies have made use of personal contact-diaries (Thorngren, 1970; Goddard, 1973; Gadd, 1975) others have evaluated simpler data (Törnqvist, 1970; Engstrom and Sahlberg, 1973): this project has closer affinities with the latter type of study.

Substantial variation occurs in the 'value' of services and this is illustrated by the day-to-day financial service supplied by a local bank and by specialized legal advice (licences, production rights, patents, etc.). Low-value services probably have small spatial range largely because of their broad market structure: the source of demand includes businesses and individuals, so differentiating them from goods.

The relationship of each sample plant to the company's structure in Canada provides a clue to the geographic possibilities of its office linkages. The question to be answered, however, is to what extent the location pattern of the head-office establishes the spatial pattern of a branch's linkages? One would hypothesize, from face-to-face linkage studies, that: (1) joint production-and-head office units tend to be located in Toronto because of the importance to head-offices of the high contact-potential of that city and (2) head-offices, with which separate plants are linked, have a location pattern biased in favour of Toronto. In practice, only two of eleven foreign firms with a joint Canadian head office and branch location occur in Toronto, while locational behaviour of Canadian firms supports the hypothesis. Simple foreign branches, however, are strongly represented in Toronto as are the head offices of sample plants that have other locations. There is, therefore, a high propensity for foreign branches to obtain office inputs from Toronto. The same pattern is found for Canadian branch plants.

While metropolitan bias appears in the location of head offices, it remains to be shown whether sample plants maintain strong service connections with Toronto. There are alternatives. Local sources of various functions may be quite satisfactory or they may be obtained from outside Southern Ontario either within the firm or from a source arranged by head office. For the sample it was expected that influences on input sources would depend upon: whether it is a branch-plant, the degree of branch autonomy, the spatial availability of each office function, whether the service is normally one obtained from another firm, and plant-location reflecting variations in local service infrastructure and metropolitan access. The specific aims of the enquiry were to identify: organizational and geographic differences in the ways plants establish office linkages; and associations in the patterns of service connection with industrial location (environment), industry and plant size.

The services chosen for enquiry were Bookkeeping and Banking for plant operations (e.g. payroll) – the lower-order services – and Legal, Auditing, Other financial and Banking services in connection with loans for capital equipment or expansion, the higher-order services. These vary considerably in geographic range from Bookkeeping (usually undertaken within the plant) to Legal and Auditing which are notably metropolitan-oriented. The effects of organizational and locational differences have been evaluated by simultaneously using two divisions of the plants – branches and single-plant firms – and metropolitan Toronto and other locations.

There is little geographic variation in the source of lower-order services between the four analytical groups. Local sources also dominate the origins of higher-order services for Toronto branches and single-plant firms. Other branches obtain inputs from their town or region, Toronto, and other external sources, in roughly equal proportions while single-plant firms in non-metropolitan locations have weaker connections with Toronto although longer-distance links are minor. Possibly these simpler firms need fewer specialized higher-order office services but also they cannot develop longer-distance linkages within the firm. Single-plant firms appear to be influenced less by a perceived need to maintain metropolitan connections and more by the belief that local service forms will call on *their* metropolitan associates when required.

Probably, however, non-metropolitan *single-plant firms* receive lower quality of service inputs, especially as in less accessible locations high-order service inputs are supplied by low-order businesses to firms unaware of the opportunities available in nearby towns (Goddard, 1975, p. 13). When the sample locations are compared, *branch* plants in the Lakeshore tend to be well connected with Toronto; in the southwest longer-distance linkages replace those that might have been with Toronto, and plants in the periphery show the strongest inter-regional and international connections. These latter instances provide evidence of spatial substitution in the arrangement of linkages that is associated with the form of corporate organization and type of location.

Branches obtain high-order services in one-third of all cases from 'company' rather than 'external' sources. There are industry-cum-organizational differences, however; more wire and machinery branches maintain 'external' connections while the majority of auto-parts and electrical goods branches depend on 'company' arrangements for high-order services. Proximity to Toronto, though, does appear to be inversely related to the degree to which within-company service links are substituted for external connections.

'Control'

From an organizational perspective, administrative control of subsidiary operations can be maintained by service as well as material dependence and there are probably scale economies that derive directly from the operation of central service units or contracts. When flows of this type occur in Canada, they frequently cause an economic linkage to cities in the USA because of both the number of branches whose head-offices are in, and the proximity of, American cities.

Linkages were restricted to those occurring *within the company* over any distance, and those external connections (international or other region) that were potentially *company-organized* links. More than half the branches (thirty-four out of sixty-three) obtain some high-order service linkages in a way which reveals the location of other corporate offices. Within this group, two-thirds (twenty-six) have at least one of their connections with a city in the United States. Generally such 'control' linkages are strongest in the auto-parts industry while machinery branches enjoy a high level of autonomy. The spatial pattern of these connections, however, follows the urbanization gradient: Toronto has the lowest incidence (three plants owned in United States) while the periphery exhibits company 'control' in every case. These patterns are found for both Canadian- and American-owned plants that have corporate control of service linkages. The enquiry verifies both the importance of the substitution of organizational links for metropolitan access and the extent to which substantial leakages are a characteristic of the Ontario economy.

The results

The two analyses reinforce each other: in both spheres of linkage activity environmental differences, ownership, organizational and industrial factors are responsible for patterns of industrial behaviour. However, is there consistency between the two analyses in the way plants have been allocated to behavioural groups?

Single-plant firms are eliminated from the test and of the total of sixty-three branch-plants, fifty-one entered both analyses. When plants are sorted according to the three subjectively-grouped sets of plant-types (material linkages and routine service 'control' *vs.* service independence) the degree of consistency in branch-plant behaviour is statistically significant (Table 10.1a). Branches in the metropolitan centre have considerable influence in reducing the χ^2 value to the level shown in Table 10.1(a): several foreign-owned branches appear to operate autonomously with respect to routine services, reflecting the service-rich character of this type of location. The consistency of the two classifications of behaviour is found to be at an even more significant level when only non-Toronto branches are tested (Table 10.1*b*).

Table 10.1   Consistency of classification of branches ($n = 51$)

Service linkages	Material linkages – plant groups		
	'Independent'	Intermediate	Dependent
(a) All observations			
'Service control'	3	11	9
Independence	14	9	5
	$\chi^2 = 8.07$; significant $\alpha = 0.025$		
(b) Non-Toronto observations			
'Service control'	3	10	9
Independence	10	6	1
	$\chi^2 = 10.69$; significant $\alpha = 0.005$		

Toronto branches are highly independent in their routine service connections, and this may be attributed to the availability of services in the metropolitan centre, the relatively limited significance of office functions for single-branch Canadian-subsidiaries and the probability that 'control' is maintained more directly through production linkages. Production linkages of American branches in Toronto reveal corporate dependence which in turn reflects the economies of corporate production-scale and production-organization obtained by international companies whether the branches are 'miniature replicas' or are continentally-integrated.

Across other locations, however, as metropolitan access declines so does the independence of branch-plants generally, within specific industries, and especially when under US ownership. The peripheral towns demonstrate to the greatest degree the substitution of long-distance corporate flows for regional connections. Southwest Ontario and the Lakeshore are transitional between the periphery and the central region, not only in production inputs, but also since more than half of the American and Canadian branches are not independent in their arrangement of service inputs.

Foreign and domestically-owned branches in the periphery have perpetuated a generally low level of industrial development: industrial and other demands made on local economies by foreign and domestic branches have been minimal and only in the case of Canadian firms have high levels of Provincial purchases been likely. The situation is no better for single-plant firms in non-metropolitan locations whose limited resources are revealed by their satisfaction of higher order (though routine) services in local towns, rather than in larger cities in the Province. The implications of the results are that individual towns in the periphery have far to go to reach even the intermediate level in development found in Southwest Ontario.

Variations in locational behaviour relevant for the formulation of a Canadian industrial strategy have thus been established. Nevertheless, current industrial policy, concerned with increasing the benefits of new investment for Canada, has no geographic terms of reference (for instance on foreign investment) and regional and locational policies in Ontario and Canada are basically concerned with employment and income gains rather than with influencing the economic behaviour of the firms that are subsidized. Until both regional and industrial policies are integrated, however, no official attempt can be made to modify the current trade-off between location and behaviour to increase the locational and economic benefits of new investment.

Concern for the future

The research described here has taken the national and international business environment as a constant. Yet some changes in the economic world are not being treated seriously enough in industrial geography to enable effective predictive and planning work to be undertaken. Three interdependent themes can be outlined.

First, *foreign ownership* is of great importance in the current political atmosphere of 'host countries' like Canada. With few exceptions (see Hamilton, forthcoming, 1978), however, geographers have contributed little to a discussion dominated by economists and business experts. Two pertinent issues are raised by this chapter. How do we progress in coping with the organizational and spatial complexity of multinational (and even smaller) corporations? How is the exercise of foreign economic control to be identified and how is its significance to be assessed within the context of regional economic development or urban programmes? Here operation of multinational/locational companies is viewed from the host regional economy using actual linkage information which permits inference of leakages to the urban system resulting from direct foreign investment. Some of the direct and secondary effects of these international flows are presumed to be revealed in the employment structure of the regional economy and particularly in those urban places where a high level of foreign control is a characteristic.

Second, the dependence of Canadian manufacturing on US capital and control is a consequence of the joint conditions of an economically-dominant neighbour and Canadian tariffs against manufacturing goods. The consequences appear to be low rates of innovation adoption, of productivity increase and of export of the products of secondary manufacturing as compared with other 'advanced' economies. Short production runs, 'miniature replica' plants and generally low comparative efficiency seem closely related to the high level of foreign control of industrial firms. If tariffs were reduced significantly, or eliminated (bi-laterally with the United States or on a multi-lateral basis) would increased production run lengths and efficiency through product specialization be realized? By which activities?

Tariffs have been lowered in recent decades (GATT) and in the mid-1960s trade in automobiles and parts between the USA and Canada was liberated extensively under agreed conditions. The major change in vehicle-assembly in Canada has been the specialization in product-line by plants that now supply the whole North American market. In components-production in aggregate shift in location has probably occurred in Southern Ontario towards the median centre for North American assembly plants. Recently, though, components-producers are operating in the USA under greater security of production contracts and there has been a diversion of decision-making, and related jobs, to head offices in American cities (Fayerweather, 1974).

The seriousness of the more general question is indicated by the support The Economic Council of Canada (1975) gives to free trade. Other economic writings also advocate this position (Daly and Globerman, 1976). A full response to the free trade arguments has not been heard; in large measure, the locationally-based risks of such a move have not been appraised adequately, certainly not by the economists preparing these reports. The comparative regional cost argument developed a decade ago using data for the late 1950s (Wonnacott and Wonnacott, 1967) must be updated and the methodology improved. Industrial geography has a vested interest in exploring potential effects of changes in commercial policy on industrial location and mix at the regional level and in clarifying the response that multi-locational, especially multi-national, firms could make to policy measures as significant as a move to free trade.

Third, most corporate *service* leakages from Ontario involve quaternary functions: managerial, administrative, technical and research jobs. Insofar as these jobs are concerned with innovation, information and decision-making their reduction has significance for the present and future occupational structure and viability of Canadian cities. Unfortunately, however, information on the present urban *job* (*vs.* industry) distribution is an appreciable gap in the output of industrial geography. The significance of this situation is influenced greatly by the rapidity with which Canada as much as any other part of the developed world has embraced changes leading to a post-industrial structure of employment (Britton, 1976). With productivity rising much more rapidly in manufacturing compared with services, forecasts indicate that by 1980, 17 per cent of the Canadian labourforce will be in manufacturing jobs and 69 per cent in the services. Sectoral redistribution of this order should cause some rethinking by geographers on structural models of urban employment growth, and further efforts in modelling the important new and expanded transactions in the non-production part of the economy. Industrial geographers will have to adapt to such economic change and to be able to advise about appropriate occupational mixes that will emerge in cities.

References

Beigie, Carl E. (1970), *The Canada-U.S. Automotive Agreement*, Canadian-American Committee, Washington and Montreal.

Britton, John N. H. (1969), 'A geographical approach to the examination of industrial linkages', *Canadian Geographer*, **13**, pp. 185–98.

Britton, John N. H. (1974), 'Environmental adaptation of industrial plants: service linkages, locational environment and organization', in: F. E. Ian Hamilton, ed., *Spatial Perspectives on Industrial Organization and Decision-making*, Wiley, London, pp. 363–90.

Britton, John N. H. (1976), 'The influence of corporate organization and ownership on the linkages of industrial plants: a Canadian enquiry', *Economic Geography*, **52**, pp. 127–141.

Britton, John N. H. (1976), 'Patterns of business linkages: the significance of foreign ownership and economic change in Canada', in: F. E. Ian Hamilton, ed., *The Organization of Spatial Industrial Systems*, London School of Economics and International Geographical Union, London, pp. 77–83.

Brooke, Michael Z. and Remmers, H. Lee (1970), *The Strategy of Multinational Enterprise: Organization and Finance*, Longmans Limited, London.

Daly, D. J. and Globerman, S. (1976), *Tariff and Science Policies: Applications of a model of nationalism*, Ontario Economic Council, Toronto.

Economic Council of Canada (1972), *The Years to 1980*, Information Canada, Ottawa.

Economic Council of Canada (1975), *Looking Outward. A New Trade Strategy for Canada*, Information Canada, Ottawa.

Engstrom, M.-G. and Sahlberg, B. W. (1973), 'Travel demand, transport systems and regional development: models in coordinated planning', *Lund Studies in Geography*, Ser. B, **39**.
Fayerweather, John (1974), *Foreign Investment in Canada*, Oxford U.P., Toronto.
Gadd, Gunter (1975), *Toronto's Central Office Complex: Growth, Structure and Linkages*, unpublished Ph.D. dissertation, University of Toronto.
Goddard, J. B. (1973), 'Office linkages and locations', *Progress in Planning* (1).
Goddard, J. (1975), *Office Location in Urban and Regional Development*, Oxford U.P., London
Gray Report (1972), *Foreign Direct Investment in Canada*, Government of Canada, Ottawa.
Hamilton, F. E. I., ed. (1974), *Spatial Perspectives on Industrial Organization and Decision Making*, London, Wiley.
Hamilton, F. E. I., ed. (forthcoming 1978), *Industrial Change; International Experience and Public Policy,* Longman, London.
Karaska, G. J. (1969), 'Manufacturing linkages in the Philadelphia economy: some evidence of external agglomeration forces', *Geographical Analysis*, **1**, pp. 354–69.
McNee, Robert B. (1974), 'A systems approach to understanding the geographic behaviour of organizations, especially large corporations', in: Hamilton, op. cit., pp. 47–76.
Mock, Dennis R. (1976), *Agglomeration and Industrial Linkages: Case Studies of Metropolitan Toronto.* Unpublished Ph.D. dissertation, University of Toronto.
Paquet, Gilles, ed. (1972), *The Multinational Firm and the Nation State*, Collier-Macmillan, Don Mills, Ontario.
Pred, Allan R. (1973), 'The growth and development of systems of cities in advanced economies', *Lund Studies in Geography*, Ser. B (38).
Pred, Allan R. (1975), 'On the spatial structure of organizations and the complexity of metropolitan interdependence', *Papers, Regional Science Association*, **35**, pp. 115–42.
Pred, Allan R. (1976), 'The inter-urban transmission of growth in advanced economies: empirical findings versus regional-planning assumptions', *Regional Studies*, **10**, pp. 151–71.
Ray, D. Michael (1971), 'The location of United States manufacturing subsidiaries in Canada', *Economic Geography*, **47**, pp. 389–400.
Ray, D. Michael et al., eds. (1976), *Canadian Urban Trends National Perspective*, Vol. 1, Copp Clark Publishing, Toronto.
Science Council of Canada (1971), *Innovation in a Cold Climate*, Science Council Report, **15**, Ottawa.
Taylor, M. J. and Wood, P. A. (1973), 'Industrial linkage and local agglomeration in the West Midlands metal industries', *Transactions Institute of British Geographers*, **59**, pp. 129–54.
Thorngren, B. (1970), 'How do contact systems affect regional development?', *Environment and Planning*, **2**, pp. 409–27.
Törnqvist, Gunnar (1970), 'Contact systems and national development', *Lund Studies in Geography*, Ser. B, **35**.
Wonnacott, R. J. and Wonnacott, P. (1967), *Free Trade Between the United States and Canada, The Potential Economic Effects*, Harvard U.P., Cambridge.

Chapter 11

Linkage and manufacturer's perception of spatial economic opportunity

Brenton M. Barr and Kenneth J. Fairbairn

The analysis set out here stems from research which was aimed at three objectives: first, to measure provincial inter-industry linkages of individual manufacturing firms; second, to describe the spatial behavioural environment of manufacturing entrepreneurs and managers; and third, to determine whether manufacturers' perceptual environments express such measurable attributes of their firms' size as manufactured inputs consumed, sales volume and intensity of intra-regional inter-industry linkages. The study of manufacturing linkages now comprises a significant share of research in industrial geography in the United Kingdom, the United States and Canada and is assuming increasing importance in the German Federal Republic, France, New Zealand and elsewhere. More attention is also now being paid to individual firms to probe the relationships between industrial connectivity, behaviour and such features as the nature of corporate organization, ownership patterns, type of manufacturing, acquisition processes, firm size or the importance of intra-urban plant location (Hamilton, 1974).

Manufacturing and linkages in Alberta

Inter-industry manufacturing linkages in Alberta as analysed from 503 questionnaires completed by manufacturers are reviewed extensively elsewhere (Barr and Fairbairn, 1975). Only a brief summary is given here, therefore, as a background to entrepreneurial perception of regional economic opportunity. When Albertan manufacturing is measured by the 'selling value of factory shipments', three groups make an overwhelmingly dominant contribution to the generation of manufacturing wealth in the province (Table 11.1): food and beverages based on processing farm commodities; metal and engineering; and petrochemicals – the latter two being related to the oil industry. Except for manufacturers of wood and paper, producers in all industrial groups as measured by 'value-added' are heavily concentrated in Edmonton and Calgary which clearly dominate the spatial pattern of all secondary industry in Alberta.

At present the province has a weakly-developed regional industrial complex. Provincial inter-industry linkages are relatively greater in number than in value. In the assembly and light manufacturing industries, supply ties with extra-regional producers are much stronger than those within the province. The strongest backward linkages occur in food and beverage industries and among non-metallic mineral producers (Table 11.2). Manufacturers in these industries rely heavily on semi-processed goods and on packaging materials (paper, paperboard, plastics

Table 11.1   The structure of manufacturing in Alberta, 1970

Industrial group*	Establishments No.	%	Value added $ × 10⁶	%	Shipments $ × 10⁶	%	Calgary and Edmonton Establishments No.	%	Value added $ × 10⁶	%	Shipments $ × 10⁶	%	Relative share of Calgary and Edmonton in Alberta manufacturing, by industrial group % of Establishments	% of value added	% of shipment
1 Food and beverage	463	24	185	27	764	40	180	17	131	28	483	38	39	71	63
2 Petrochemical, coal and synthethic textile	93	5	114	17	318	17	79	7	65	14	246	20	85	57	77
3 Non-food and general manufacturing	592	30	117	17	204	11	439	40	97	21	170	14	74	83	83
4 Wood, paper and allied industries	374	19	77	11	168	9	92	8	35	8	79	6	25	45	47
5 Primary metal, engineering, transportation industries	324	16	134	19	347	18	251	23	93	20	205	16	77	69	59
6 Non-metallic mineral products	110	6	63	9	102	5	52	5	45	9	73	6	47	71	72
Total	1956	100	690	100	1903	100	1903	100	466	100	1256	100	56	68	66

Source: Alberta Bureau of Statistics, Industry and Commerce (1973), *Industry and Resources 1973*, pp. 25–33; Missing data have been estimated from other sources.

* The composition of each industrial group is listed in Appendix I.

and glass). Similarly the petro-chemical industry makes significant local purchases of packaging materials but its relatively weak backward manufacturing linkages appear to reflect the purchase of chemical-based and related materials from producers outside of Alberta.

The remaining three groups also exhibit weak backward manufacturing linkages within the province. Non-food and general manufacturers clearly rely on sub-components produced in central Canada and foreign industrial regions since, at the end of the production chain, they assemble finished goods for sale to final personal or industrial consumers. Thus the Albertan economy is consumer-oriented. Wood, paper and allied industries similarly rely heavily on lumber and paper from other provinces. Glues and inks originate from elsewhere. Linkage strength would be greater if Alberta had a finished paper industry but in 1972 the province had only one pulp mill which shipped its entire output to other provinces for conversion into paper. The major purchases by these industries of Alberta manufactured goods involve commodities which neither enter directly into the production process nor comprise a significant share of the final product. Enterprises engaged in primary metals, engineering and transport also purchase most manufactured inputs outside the province but differ from firms in group 2 because the components they buy within the province do enter into their final product and are not an adjunct to the main manufacturing process. The backward linkages of both groups 3 and 5 reveal how dependent Alberta is on manufacturing processes and enterprises in other parts of Canada or the world.

Although the proportions of manufactured goods purchases within Alberta vary from one group to another, most firms – except in non-food and general manufacturing – make some purchases of manufactured goods within the province. The data in Table 11.2 also suggest that linkage between Alberta manufacturers and consumer-forward linkages involves more firms (496) than those associated with backward linkages (417). In fact only 206 out of 503 respondents gave conclusive evidence – even though 496 claimed in interviews that they shipped to other Albertan manufacturers. Thus the number of backward linkages is actually double that of forward linkages with provincial manufacturers. Yet the gross dollar value of deliveries to secondary industries in Alberta, $168 million, is approximately two-and-a-half times greater than the backward linkages. The number of provincial backward linkages of Alberta manufacturers is high but their average dollar value is low; and in fact the average value of forward provincial linkages is roughly four times greater than that of provincial backward links. This confirms that the Alberta industrial economy functions as part of wider Canadian or world manufacturing and that local producers are mainly at the end of the production chain, the prior links of which are not found primarily in Alberta.

Attitude scaling

Though existing linkages among manufacturers can be identified, little is currently known about the correspondence between the location and linkage patterns of manufacturing firms and the perceptual environments of the entrepreneurs who create and sustain the spatial economy. The subject does not seem to have been investigated at all in Alberta (Task Force on Urbanization, 1975). Behavioural studies have usually been based on some form of open-ended interview schedule in

Table 11.2   Aggregate industrial linkages of Albertan manufacturing plants

| | Purchase of manufactured materials and supplies | | | | | Selling value of factory shipments | | | | | |
| | Total purchase | | From Alberta manufacturers | | Alberta purchases as a % of total purchases by industrial group | Total shipments: | | Shipments within Alberta | | Alberta shipments as a % of total shipments by industrial group |
Industrial group	No. of establishments	Value $ × 10⁶	No. of establishments	Value $ × 10⁶		No. of establishments	Value $ × 10⁶	No. of establishments	Value $ × 10⁶	
1 Food and beverage	89	36.3	81	23.7	·65	89	300.0	85	127.1	42
2 Petrochemical, coal and synthetic textile	23	20.5	18	3.5	17	23	98.8	23	39.2	40
3 Non-food and general manufacturing	190	56.8	139	4.6	8	190	146.4	189	80.8	55
4 Wood, paper and allied industries	36	26.6	33	6.2	23	36	60.7	36	34.2	56
5 Primary metal, engineering transportation industries	134	125.9	118	21.3	17	134	212.6	132	138.6	65
6 Non-metallic products	31	15.7	28	8.9	·57	31	40.2	31	31.3	78
Total	503	281.8	417	68.3	24	503	858.7	496	451.2	52

Source: Questionnaire survey, May–August 1972

which entrepreneurs and managers have been asked to provide information pertaining to their processes of locational decision-making (see Stafford, in Hamilton,
1974). Such investigations attempt to identify factors and processes common to
particular types of firms located in special industrial environments. Because of
time and cost constraints, many analysts are forced to draw direct conclusions
from specific pieces of information provided consciously by the interviewee. Such
data obviously assist in interpretation but they do not usually facilitate rigorous
statistical analysis especially if collected verbally. The objective of most interviews
has been to obtain information rather than *to test* the interviewee or his information for specific attributes.

Thus, having identified the backward and forward provincial inter-industry
linkages of 503 Alberta manufacturers, the authors approached the 382 respondent firms in Calgary and Edmonton with a list of statements designed to elicit entrepreneurial attitudes toward salient aspects of the economic milieu of Alberta.
On these, 233 firms agreed to cooperate. The technique of attitude scaling
(Edwards, 1957) offered the possibility of testing entrepreneurial perception of
Alberta's economic milieu and to obtain consistent results for all industries in both
major cities.

The attitude survey (Appendix II) consisted of fifty statements divided into two
sections and nine groups. The first section (four groups and twenty-three
statements) sought to determine attitudes toward the function of all manufacturing industries in Alberta. The second section (five groups and twenty-seven
statements) measured attitudes toward the interviewee's own firm or industry. The
key objectives of the authors were related to location, urban influences, manufacturing mix, structure, and function, the role of government, access to suppliers and
customers, and the importance of transport. The goal of the attitude survey was to
have each interviewee react to statements associated with each of the nine groups.
Hence the authors were less interested in the specific response to any one statement but rather more in the consistency shown in the responses to all statements
within a group. Small variations within a group suggests that the statements are a
valid indication of general attitude; sizable variation suggests that the statements
are probably contradictory and that great care should be taken in interpreting attitudes toward the problem implied by the group title.

Each interviewee was offered the choice of responding in one of seven ways,
excluding 'yes' or 'no' responses since these hardly conveyed any attitude. Acceptable responses were 'strongly agree', 'agree', 'disagree', 'strongly disagree',
'undecided', 'do not possess sufficient information on this matter to pass
judgement', and 'not relevant in my case'. The interviewee was presented with the
list of statements and asked to respond verbally. The interviewer then made an appropriate entry on a code sheet. Unknown to the interviewee, the interviewer also
recorded if the response to each statement was fast or slow, positive or hesitating.
Responses could then be converted to a numerical scale and punched on computer cards for machine processing. The average time required for each interview
was approximately fifty minutes. The number of statements thus reflected not only
the type of information required for the research, but also the reluctance or inability of most entrepreneurs to devote more than one hour to meetings unrelated to
their normal business.

Perception: the results

Spearman rank-order correlation coefficients were computed for ninety pairs of economic and perceptual variables (Table 11.3). Spearman's r_s is non-parametric and thus does not depend either upon a normal distribution or on the metric quality of interval scales, but it does require variables which have numeric values and can be ranked. Two of the five behavioural variables *Positive* (Pos.) and *Negative* (Neg.) are amalgamations of attitude responses. *Positive* comprised the responses 'strongly agree' and 'agree' where either response suggests a positive attitude toward the Albertan economy. Where agreement would be with a negative statement about the economy (statements 4, 5 and 6), the *Positive* variable is comprised of the responses 'strongly disagree' and 'disagree'. *Negative* has been calculated in exactly the opposite manner. Thus, the raw response data were transposed for relevant reactions to statements 4–6, 24, 32, 36–38, 40, 41, 43, and 49 (Appendix II). Positive and negative phrasing of the statements provided variety in the total list and a check for consistency of response. The complete titles of the other three behavioural variables, *Undecided* (Un.), *Insufficient* (Ins.) and *Not Relevant* (Nr.), are given in Table 11.3; these variables each represent one possible type of response and have not been recorded or transposed in any way.

The numbers 50, 23 and 27 associated with each behavioural variable indicate whether responses to all statements (50), responses from Part I of the list of statements (23) or responses from Part II (27) were analysed. Economic data could be correlated in this manner with perception of the entire or aggregate milieux (5), the general milieux common to all manufacturers (23) or the specific milieux of each manufacturer (27). Positive coefficients suggest that the strength of response is directly correlated with the size of firm or size of linkage; negative coefficients imply that the strength of response is inversely correlated with the size of firm or size of linkage.

The nature of manufacturers' perception of their spatial economic milieux (Table 11.3) is not generally associated significantly with the *size of firm* or size of the firm's aggregate intra-regional industrial linkage. Weak negative coefficients between the 'not relevant' response to the aggregate and specific milieux suggest a tenuous inverse relationship between perception of relevant conditions and the size of firms which corresponds to the weak direct relation between positive attitude toward the aggregate and specific environments of the firm and the size of firm; smaller firms appear to have narrower aggregate and specific behavioural environments than larger organizations, whereas larger firms seem to feel more confident toward the specific and aggregate milieux in which they operate. Does, then, perception of the economic environment vary with the nature of commodities purchased or sold by the firm or with the location of manufacturers?

When the strength of specific *inter-industry linkages* is correlated with attitudes toward the environment, the number of significant coefficients continues to be as sparse, but the positive or negative strength of many coefficients increases. The strength of relationship between responses of any type and the size of specific inter-industry linkages does not vary consistently throughout the three behavioural milieux. Strong positive feelings toward the aggregate and general milieux by those with small backward inter-industry food and beverage linkages, for example, are not matched by the attitudes of those same firms toward their specific industrial milieux. Firms, however, with direct correlations between positive feelings towards the aggregate economic milieux and backward linkage

Table 11.3 Relationship between economic and perceptual attributes of the firm: Metropolitan Alberta (Spearman correlation coefficients)

Economic variables	Behavioural variables														
	Aggregate					General					Specific				
Size of inter-industry linkage	POS 50	NEG 50	UN 50	INS 50	NR 50	POS 23	NEG 23	UN 23	INS 23	NR 23	POS 27	NEG 27	UN 27	INS 27	NR 27
Firm size															
Input 1					−0.22*						0.19*				−0.23*
Output 1	0.16†				−0.17†						0.24*				−0.18†
In/Out 1	0.15†				−0.19†						0.24*				−0.19†
Input 2					−0.32*						0.23*				−0.32*
Output 2	0.15†	−0.13†		0.12‡	−0.16‡						0.23*				−0.16‡
In/Out 2															
Backward															
Qu 91	−0.51†			0.54†		−0.38†			0.53†						
Qu 92		0.26‡	0.45†					0.47†			0.42*			−0.48†	−0.54†
Qu 93		0.18‡			−0.45*						0.28*				−0.44*
Qu 94					−0.31†						0.20†				−0.30†
Qu 95					−0.33†										−0.35†
Qu 96															

Forward

Qu 101					
Qu 102					
Qu 103	0.31†				
Qu 104		−0.30‡	0.58†		
Qu 105		0.28‡	−0.27†		
Qu 106					

Aggregate

Qu 131				
Qu 132				
Qu 133				
Qu 134			−0.19†	
Qu 135				
Qu 136	−0.30†			−0.33* 0.25†

Source: Derived from Authors' Questionnaire Survey May–August 1972, and Authors' Survey of Manufacturing Opinion, Calgary and Edmonton, 1973.

* Significant at 99 per cent confidence level.
† Significant at 95 per cent confidence level.
‡ Significant at 90 per cent confidence level.

Table 11.3 (continued): Explanation of variable names

Variable title	Full name of variable
	Economic variables: size of firm
Input 1	Value of purchased manufactured commodities
Input 2	Value of purchased commodities manufactured within Alberta
Output 1	Selling value of factory shipments
Output 2	Value of factory shipments to all Alberta customers
In/Out 1	Combined total value of purchases manufactured commodities and factory shipments
In/Out 2	Combined total value of purchased commodities manufactured within Alberta and factory shipments to all Alberta customers

Full name of variable	Variable title	Backward	Forward	Aggregate
	Economic variables: size of inter-industry linkage			
Type of	Foods and beverages	Qu91	Qu101	Qu131
inter-industry	Petrochemicals and	Qu92	Qu102	Qu132
linkage with	synthetic textiles			
Alberta	Non-food and general	Qu93	Qu103	Qu133
manufacturers	manuf'd. products			
of:	Wood, paper and allied	Qu94	Qu104	Qu134
	products			
	Primary methods, engineering	Qu95	Qu105	Qu135
	and transportation eqt.			
	Non-metallic mineral	Qu96	Qu106	Qu136
	products			

Variable title	Full name of variable
(Prefix)	Behavioural variables (combinations of prefixes and suffixes listed below)
POS.,	Positive attitude toward the economic milieu
NEG.,	Negative attitude toward the economic milieu
UN.,	Respondent's attitude is undecided
INS.,	Respondent does not possess sufficient information to assess the statement
NR.,	Statement is not relevant to respondent's industry
(Suffix)	or firm
... 50	Response to total set of 50 statements
... 23	Response to subset of 23 statements pertaining to the milieu of all manufacturers in Alberta (Part 1 of list of statements)
... 27	Response to subset of 27 statements pertaining to the milieu of respondent's own firm (Part 2 of the list of statements)

with petrochemical or non-food general manufacturers, display even stronger relationships within the milieux of their own firm, but none of the coefficients between their positive attitude toward the general milieux and their backward linkages is significant.

Generalization of relationships between attitude and size of linkage is truly difficult using the coefficients presented in Table 11.3, but two features do emerge. First, positive attitudes towards the specific milieux of the firm or industry tend to be related directly to size of firm, general regional linkage or some specific types of backward industrial linkage. Second, the extent to which environmental characteristics are considered irrelevant to individual firms seems to vary inversely with the size of firm, its general regional linkage and its specific inter-industry backward linkage. Coefficients between attitudes and forward or aggregate inter-industry linkages are far too inconsistent to permit generalization.

The relationships between environmental perception and *firm size* shown in Tables 11.4 and 11.5 differ between the two metropolitan centres. Calgary manufacturers show modest direct relationship between their positive attitudes toward the aggregate and specific industrial milieux and the size of their firms, and a modest inverse relationship between what they consider relevant to their specific firms and the size of their operation. These statements cannot be made for manufacturers in Edmonton where, furthermore, the coefficients between attitudinal response and aspects of firm size cannot be generalized.

Attitude and inter-industry linkage are weakly interrelated and also differ between the two cities. The extent to which Calgary manufacturers are undecided about their attitude towards the aggregate economic environment varies directly in a rather strong manner with some of their backward linkages; the opposite is suggested by the same pairs of coefficients for Edmonton firms. Consistently in Calgary and, to a lesser extent in Edmonton, the feeling that aspects of the general environment are not relevant has a strong inverse relationship with the size of backward linkages.

Positive attitudes toward aggregate economic environments are inversely correlated in Calgary with the size of forward linkage, whereas undecided attitudes in Edmonton are strongly and directly related to size of forward linkage. A positive attitude, however, is modestly inversely related in Calgary, but not in Edmonton, to the aggregate size of inter-industry linkage. Significant coefficients between the behavioural and economic variables of firms in the two Alberta metropolitan centres are few in number and are uniform neither in direction nor in strength.

Significant coefficients pertaining to relatively few pairs of behavioural and economic variables do suggest that important differences exist among the six *industrial groups* analysed. The coefficients were derived for metropolitan centres in aggregate rather than for each individually because of the limited number of respondents in some industries in either centre. Yet they suggest that managements in different manufacturing activities neither utilize space nor perceive spatial opportunity similarly to each other. Though many pairs of behavioural and economic variables have not provided significant correlation coefficients, the relationships identified (but not listed here because of space limitations) strongly suggest that manufacturers in different industrial groups cannot be expected to respond in a uniform manner toward economic policies or other stimuli designed to modify the existing structure of regional economic space.

Discussion

No apparent general relationship exists between the nature of manufacturers' perceptual economic environment and the size of the firm or its intra-regional, inter-industry linkages when measured across the spectrum of Alberta metropolitan manufacturers. The large number of cases studied (233) and the analytical procedure employed further suggest that the results merit careful consideration in behavioural studies. The findings on relationships between firm size and manufacturers' spatial perception are constrained not by variations in entrepreneurial perception, nor by the wide variety of industries surveyed, but rather

Table 11.4 Relationship between economic and perceptual attributes of the firm: Edmonton (Spearman correlation coefficients)

Economic variables	Behavioural variables														
	Aggregate					General					Specific				
Size of inter-industry linkage	POS 50	NEG 50	UN 50	INS 50	NR 50	POS 23	NEG 23	UN 23	INS 23	NR 23	POS 27	NEG 27	UN 27	INS 27	NR 27
Firm size															
Input 1			0.19‡												
Output 1											0.15‡				
In/Out 1															
Input 2					−0.22‡						0.17‡				
Output 2			0.21‡	0.18‡					0.18						
In/Out 2															
Backward															
Qu 91	−0.52†														
Qu 92			0.53†		−0.50†			0.52†	−0.39†					0.41†	−0.50†
Qu 93					−0.32†	−0.25†	0.34†								
Qu 94															
Qu 95			0.39†												
Qu 96			0.56†											0.93†	

Forward							
Qu 101					−0.38‡		
Qu 102	0.48†						0.68†
Qu 103		−0.45‡	0.36‡				0.73†
Qu 104	0.45†						
Qu 105	−0.37†	0.38‡			−0.45*		
Qu 106	0.61†	0.63‡	0.64†				0.89†
Aggregate							
Qu 131				−0.40‡			
Qu 132							
Qu 133						−0.29‡	0.36†
Qu 134							
Qu 135							
Qu 136						−0.37†	

Source: Derived from Authors' Questionnaire Survey, May–August 1972, and Authors' Survey of Manufacturing Opinion, Calgary and Edmonton, 1973.

* Significant at 99 per cent confidence level.
† Significant at 95 per cent confidence level.
‡ Significant at 90 per cent confidence level.

Table 11.5 Relationship between economic and perceptual attributes of the firm: Calgary (Spearman correlation coefficients)

Economic variables	Behavioural variables														
	Aggregate					General					Specific				
Size of inter-industry linkage	POS 50	NEG 50	UN 50	INS 50	NR 50	POS 23	NEG 23	UN 23	INS 23	NR 23	POS 27	NEG 27	UN 27	INS 27	NR 27
Firm size															
Input 1	0.21†				−0.28†						0.31*				−0.31†
Output 1	0.26†										0.38*				
In/Out 1	0.25*										0.37*				−0.24†
Input 2					−0.40†						0.29*				−0.43*
Output 2	0.25†		−0.25†								0.35*				
In/Out 2	−0.24†			0.21†		−0.19‡			0.24†						
Backward															
Qu 91				0.86†					0.89*						
Qu 92					−0.69*										−0.73*
Qu 93		−0.42†			−0.56*						0.33†				−0.57†
Qu 94					−0.37†	−0.28†	0.28†				0.31†				−0.37†
Qu 95			−0.36‡		−0.43†					−0.37‡					−0.49†
Qu 96															

Forward

Qu 101	−0.36‡							−0.64*		
Qu 102								−0.53†		0.30‡
Qu 103	−0.39†	0.34†			−0.37†					
Qu 104	−0.41‡									
Qu 105										
Qu 106			−0.60‡	0.63†				−0.93*		

Aggregate

Qu 131					−0.38†					
Qu 132					−0.39†					0.28‡
Qu 133										
Qu 134							0.29†			
Qu 135				0.24‡	−0.30†	−0.28‡				0.25‡
Qu 136	−0.42†								−0.29‡	

Source: Derived from Authors' Questionnaire Survey, May–August 1972, and Authors' Survey of Manufacturing Opinion, Calgary and Edmonton, 1973.

* Significant at 99 per cent confidence level.
† Significant at 95 per cent confidence level.
‡ Significant at 90 per cent confidence level.

by the specific input and output relations of individual firms. Important variations in linkage patterns within the six major manufacturing groups in Alberta might be associated with other variables such as ownership characteristics or multi-plant firms, and clearly merits further study.

The research technique – attitude scaling – is a crude instrument for measuring perception, not permitting interviewees to qualify or to justify their responses: it cannot show whether another set of statements might have been more effective. Yet it is efficient in time and processing costs while providing information not otherwise available. It can place people first into broad groups, correlating their responses with other variables, like linkage and secondly, on a continuum relative to each other in their responses to selected problems. When related to firm size or linkage attitude scaling cannot be analysed in terms of cause and effect, although strong correlations might suggest that some processes create strong relationships between a firm's size or linkage and manufacturers' attitudes. Like all tests of behaviour analysis, the technique must rest on the assumptions that those interviewed are crucially involved in the spatial decision-making process and that decisions are taken in similar ways in all firms: in reality these are difficult to sustain.

Conclusion

Though this research has not identified a strong and comprehensive relationship between economic and perceptual data, the findings suggest that economic variables such as firm size and inter-industry linkage incorporate varying degrees of associated behavioural elements which must be considered in regional development policies. For example, Albertan government inducements to deglomeration from Calgary and Edmonton probably should be based on an understanding of crucial components of the aggregate general, and specific regional economic milieux of manufacturers in those industrial groups and urban places which are the foci of government industrial policy. Yet the problems are numerous in verifying many of the general 'theories' on the composition of decision-makers' behavioural environments that are prevalent in current industrial geography.

References

Barr, B. M. (1975), 'The importance of regional inter-industry linkage to Calgary's manufacturing firms', in: B. M. Barr, ed., *Calgary: Metropolitan Structure and Influence*, University of Victoria, Department of Geography, Victoria, pp. 1–50.

Barr, B. M. and Fairbairn, K. J. (1975), 'Inter-industry manufacturing linkages within Alberta', in: B. M. Barr, ed., *The Themes in Western Canadian Geography: The Langara Papers*, Canadian Association of Geographers, Western Division, **21**, pp. 37–65.

Barr, B. M. and Fairbairn, K. J. (1976), 'Regional inter-industry linkages in Edmonton's manufacturing economy', in: P. J. Smith, ed., *Economic and Urban Analyses of Edmonton*, University, Western Geography Series, Victoria.

Beyers, W. B. (1974), 'On geographical properties of growth centre linkage systems', *Economic Geography*, **50** (3), pp. 203–18.

Britton, J. N. H. (1969), 'A geographical approach to the examination of industrial linkages', *The Canadian Geographer*, **13**, pp. 185–98.

Campbell, J. (1974), 'Selected aspects of the inter-industry structure of the State of Washington 1967', *Economic Geography*, **50** (1), pp. 35–46.

Edwards, A. L. (1957), *Techniques of Attitude Scale Construction*, Appleton-Century-Crofts, Inc., New York.

Gilmour, J. M. (1971), 'Some considerations of spatial separation between linked industries', *The Canadian Geographer*, **15** (4), pp. 287–94.

Gilmour, J. M. and Murricane, K. (1973), 'Structural divergence in Canada's manufacturing belt', *The Canadian Geographer*, **17** (1), pp. 1–18.

Hamilton, F. E. Ian, ed. (1974), *Spatial Perspectives on Industrial Organization and Decision-Making*, Wiley, London/New York.

Karaska, G. J. (1971), 'Manufacturing linkages in the Philadelphia economy; some evidence of external agglomeration forces', in: I. S. Bourne, ed., *Internal Structure of the City*, Oxford U.P., London/New York, pp. 256–67.

Leigh, R. and North, D. (1975), *Industrial Location Research Project*, Middlesex Polytechnic, various Working Papers.

Lever, W. F. (1972), 'Industrial movement, spatial association and fundamental linkages', *Regional Studies*, **6**, pp. 371–84.

Moseley, M. J. (1973), 'The impact growth centres on rural regions', *Regional Studies*, **7**, pp. 57–75.

Moseley, M. T. and Townroe, P. M. (1973), 'Linkage adjustment following industrial movement', *Tijdschrift voor Economische en Sociale Geografie*, **64** (3), pp. 137–44.

Murricane, K. (1975), 'Inter-urban industrial linkages in Montreal's hinterland', Unpublished Master's thesis, McGill University, Montreal.

Oppenheim, A. N. (1966), *Questionnaire Design and Attitude Measurement*, Basic Books, New York.

Richter, C. E. (1969), 'The impact of industrial linkages on geographic association', *Journal of Regional Science*, **9** (1), pp. 19–28.

Schmidt, C. G. (1975), 'Firm linkage structure and structural change: a graph theoretical analysis', *Economic Geography*, **51** (1), pp. 27–36.

Steed, G. P. F. (1970), 'Changing linkages and internal multipliers of an industrial complex', *The Canadian Geographer*, **14** (3), pp. 229–42.

Steed, G. P. F. (1973), 'Inter-metropolitan manufacturing: spatial distribution and locational dynamics in Greater Vancouver', *Canadian Geographer*, **17** (3), pp. 235–58.

Steed, G. P. F. (1974), 'The Northern Ireland linen complex, 1950–1970', *Annals, Association of American Geographers*, **64** (3), pp. 397–408.

Task Force on Urbanization (1975), *Index of Urban and Regional Studies, Province of Alberta 1950–1974*, Edmonton.

Taylor, M. J. (1973), 'Local linkage, external economies and the ironfoundry industry of the West Midlands and East Lancashire conurbations', *Regional Studies*, **7**, pp. 387–400.

Appendix I

Composition of industrial groups in this study*

GROUP DESCRIPTION

Group Number	(Component Industries Described According to the Standard Industrial Classification)	S.I.C. Group Code
Group 1: Food and beverage industries		
	Meat products industries	101, 103
	Dairy products industries	105, 107
	Fruit and vegetable canners and preservers	112
	Grain mills	123, 124, 125
	Bakery products industries	128, 129
	Other food processors	131, 133, 135, 139
	Beverage manufacturers	141, 143, 145
	Agricultural implement industry	311
	Artificial ice manufacturers	3998

Group 2: Petrochemical, coal and synthetic textile industries

	Rubber industries	163, 169
	Synthetic textile mills	201
	Petroleum and coal products industries	365, 369, 371, 373, 375, 376, 378, 379

Group 3: Non-food and general manufacturing industries

	Leather industries	172, 174, 175, 179
	Woollen mills	193
	Textile industries (excluding synthetic textile mills)	213, 221, 223, 229
	Knitting mills	239
	Clothing industries	243, 246, 247
	Furniture and fixture industries	261, 264, 266
	Printing, publishing and allied industries	286, 287, 288, 289
	Machinery industries (excluding agric. implement industry)	315, 316
	Electrical products industries	335, 336, 337, 338, 339
	Miscellaneous manufacturing industries – including the following:	
	Scientific and professional equipment manufacturing;	381
	Jewellery and silverware manufacturing;	382
	Broom, brush and mop industry;	383
	Venetian blind manufacturing;	384

*Note: Industries listed in the S.I.C. Code which have not established in Alberta are omitted.

General plastic fabricators;	385
Sporting goods and toy industry;	3931
Fur dressing and dyeing industry;	395
Signs and displays industry;	397
Model and pattern manufacturing;	3985
Fountain pen and pencil manufacturing;	3989
Stamp and stencil (rubber and meat) manufacturers;	3995
Statuary, regalia and novelty manufacturers	3996

Group 4: Wood, paper and allied industries

Wood industries	251, 252, 254, 256, 258, 259
Paper and allied industries	271, 272, 273, 274

Group 5: Primary metal, engineering and transportation industries

Iron and steel mills	291
Pipe and tube mills	292
Iron foundries	294
Non-ferrous metal smelters, refineries, rollers, casters, extruders	295, 296, 297, 298
Metal fabricating industries (excl. machinery industries)	301–309
Transportation equipment industries	321, 324, 325, 328, 329

Group 6: Non-metallic mineral products industries

Manufacturers of:

Cement	341
Lime	343
Gypsum products	345
Concrete products	347
Ready-mix concrete	348
Clay products	351
Stone products	353
Mineral wool	354
Glass	356

Survey of manufacturers' attitudes, metropolitan Alberta

A. All manufacturing industries in the province of Alberta

Group 1: Location of manufacturing and urban areas

1. The discovery and development of oil and gas deposits in Alberta since 1947 has been the prime influence on the growth of Alberta's manufacturing industries.

2. The development of Alberta's oil and gas reserves since 1947 has been greatest benefit to manufacturers in Edmonton and Calgary.

3. The petroleum industry of Alberta has encouraged manufacturing to grow in all major centres of the Province of Alberta (i.e. with over 10 000 people in 1971).

4. The petroleum industry of Alberta has offered more stimulus to manufacturers in the southern half of the Province than in the northern half (Red Deer included in the southern half).

5. Most towns in Alberta have developed important manufacturing industries since the discovery of major oil and gas reserves in Alberta.

Group 2: The mix of manufacturing industries

6. Without the demand generated by the oil and gas industry for goods and services, manufacturing in Alberta would consist primarily of light industry and industries producing consumer goods.

7. The most important manufacturing industries in Calgary are engaged primarily in production of goods for the petroleum industry.

8. The most important manufacturing industries in Edmonton are engaged primarily in the production of goods for the petroleum industry.

9. Although the number and size of manufacturing establishments in Albertan urban places have grown in the past twenty-five years, the nature of the goods they produce has not changed very much.

10. Most manufacturing industries in Alberta do not produce goods for the oil and gas industry.

11. Manufacturing industries in Alberta are chiefly engaged in the production of goods and products not directly associated with the petroleum industry.

Group 3: The function of manufacturing industries

12. Most of the materials (raw and manufactured) used by the manufacturing industries in Alberta are produced within the Province.

13. Manufacturing industries in Alberta chiefly produce goods which are sold to other manufacturers.

14. Manufacturing industries in Alberta chiefly produce goods which are further processed by their customers.

15. The volume of demand by manufacturers in Alberta is strong enough to warrant greater production of their material supplies within the Province.

16. Products of Alberta manufacturers are uncompetitive in regions outside the Province because of high transportation costs.

17. The Canadian western Arctic and other regions in the Yukon Territory and the Mackenzie district of the N.W.T. offer important although limited potential demand for products manufactured in Alberta.

18. Manufacturers in Alberta should strive to purchase materials and supplies whenever possible from producers within Alberta.

Group 4: Government and manufacturing industry

19. The Albertan Government's attempts to encourage manufacturing industry to locate within the Province are proving successful.

20. The Albertan Government's programme for developing markets outside the Province for Albertan manufacturers is not very successful.

21. Government at all levels is right to provide financial assistance to new manufacturing industry in less prosperous areas of the Province.

22. The Albertan Government keeps the federal Government aware of the needs and problems of Albertan manufacturers.

23. It is wise for government at all levels to provide assistance to manufacturing industries experiencing economic difficulties.

B. Influences on my manufacturing industry

Group 5: General location within Alberta

24. This firm could not profitably conduct its business if it were located in another place in Alberta.

25. All major urban places in Alberta (i.e. over 10 000 people in 1971) offer the same opportunities for conducting a profitable business enterprise.

26. This firm could locate in one of the intermediate size (15 000–45 000 population) urban places of Alberta and not suffer any economic disadvantages.

27. This firm would enjoy the same or better volume of business if located in Edmonton (or Calgary, if firm is in Edmonton).

28. This city has become less satisfactory as a location for our firm during the last twenty-five years.

Group 6: Influence of supply factors on location

29. This firm's *present* location is chiefly determined by the need for proximity to raw materials and other material inputs.

30. This firm is closely linked to enterprises within the immediate urban area for raw materials and sub-components.

31. This firm requires close proximity to suppliers of material inputs.

32. This firm purchases material inputs from suppliers outside Alberta although similar, but unacceptable, materials are available from Albertan suppliers.

33. The labour requirements of this firm are adequately met at this location.

Group 7: Influence of demand factors on location

34. This location offers my firm good geographical proximity to our major customers.

35. The local area offers a good market for our products.

36. The location of the major market for goods produced by this firm varies considerably from one year to another.

37. Given the location of the demand for the products manufactured by this firm, the firm could conduct a more profitable business by relocating in another Albertan urban area.

38. Because the market location for products of this firm has changed since the firm was established in this location, the firm could now operate more profitably by relocating outside the Province of Alberta.

Group 8: Transportation and location

39. Transportation costs favour the assembly of materials at this location.

40. Transportation costs from this location to our major markets are too high.

41. Transportation costs impose severe geographical constraints on the size of our market area.

42. The forms of transportation available in this urban place favour the present location of our firm.

43. Transportation costs on shipment of our good are unfair compared to costs of transportation on similar goods manufactured in other Albertan places.

44. At any other location in Alberta, our firm would incur higher total transportation costs.

Group 9: Location and the general environment

45. Alberta is a good province to carry out manufacturing of our goods.

46. Our urban area is better than other Albertan urban places for this type of manufacturing enterprise.

47. Manufacturers in this industry are quick to sense new opportunities for sales and product development.

48. Other local businessmen feel our well-being is important to the success of their own operations.

49. The general business community in this urban area is not as progressive as business groups in other Canadian industrial regions.

50. The civic government is helpful to our business enterprise.

Chapter 12

Spatial competition and the sales linkages of Auckland manufacturers

Michael J. Taylor

The strength of material linkages between Auckland manufacturers and the consumers of their products elsewhere in New Zealand are measured here to assess the impact of spatial competition within the country's space economy and to determine how far it affects different types of industry and of organization. Two simple interaction and linear transport models are used. These generate patterns of sales linkage and sales decay-curves with which to compare equivalent patterns and curves constructed from empirical survey data for Auckland manufacturers.

Previous studies in the United Kingdom and New Zealand have provided partial insight into the role of industrial linkage in the operations of manufacturing firms. Iron foundries in the West Midlands and East Lancashire conurbations are shown to have stronger local links in the sale of castings for the general engineering market than would be expected from a simple interaction model which builds in the large market size for these products in either conurbation (Taylor, 1973) while it is almost completely absent in the section producing castings for automobiles. This suggests that strong local linkage yields behavioural, rather than monetary, benefits to agglomerated manufacturers: reduction in risk and uncertainty rather than cost-reducing local external economies. McDermott (1974) has shown similar patterns of stronger-than-expected local sales linkage to exist in five of New Zealand's secondary population centres; Whangarei, Napier, Wanganui, Nelson and Timaru. Such linkage, which Taylor terms 'parochialism', was labelled 'spatial monopoly' by McDermott, suggesting limited and imperfect spatial competition whereby firms may exercise an element of monopolistic control over their immediately adjacent market. Indeed, McDermott (1974) demonstrates that the strength of local sales linkage varies from centre to centre, indicating variability in spatial monopoly from place to place. These results, however, were derived from an analysis of highly aggregated data for manufacturing as a whole; this is a major shortcoming (Taylor and Wood, 1973) so that here attempts are made to improve the measurement of 'parochialism' and 'spatial monopoly' by analysing the linkage patterns of seven industrial sectors and eight organizational categories covering ownership type, management type and plant status.

The simulation of sales linkage patterns

The empirical data base for analysis was collected from manufacturers in the Auckland urban area in 1973 by a questionnaire; this had been distributed through the Auckland Manufacturers' Association and had achieved a 30 per cent

144

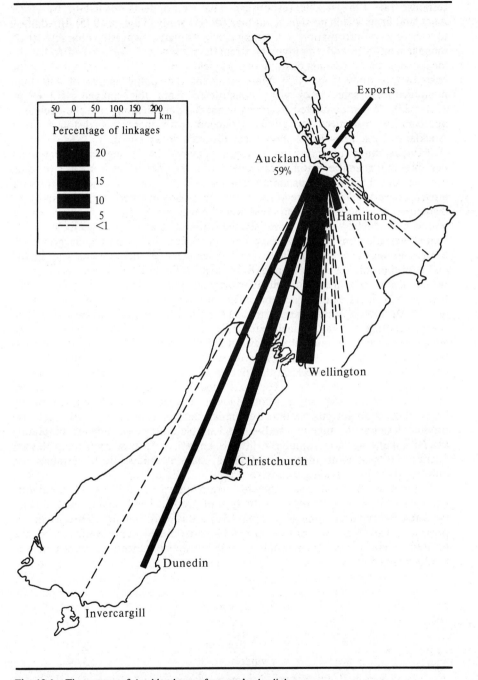

Fig. 12.1   The pattern of Auckland manufacturers' sales linkages.

response rate (259 usable responses). That respondents tended to be larger Auckland firms yields no significant bias for this study (Taylor, 1975). In addition to 'census' type information concerning products made, ownership characteristics, management type and employment strength, respondents were asked to list the locations of their five main customers: this yielded the 1157 sales links that are the basis of this study (Fig. 12.1). Maps depicting the spatial pattern of Auckland manufacturers' sales links were constructed from this linkage data (Figs. 12.1–12.9). When converted to graph form, the data demonstrate the decline in numbers of customers for goods produced, with increasing distance, from Auckland: Figs. 12.5–12.12 show these distance decay curves.

Previous study of industrial linkages (Taylor, 1973) suggested that eight variables influence the spatial arrangement of sales linkages of firms in a production centre: (1) the type of product being sold; (2) the size of production centre for a particular good; (3) the size of market for that good in different localities; (4) the distance separating production centres and consumer locations; (5) competition amongst production centres to satisfy the demand at any consumer location; (6) spatial variation in the price asked by producers for a particular good; (7) ownership ties between producers and consumers pre-determining the spatial orientation of market linkages; and (8) the availability of local external economies, pre-disposing producers to sell to adjacent and nearby consumers. While, theoretically, local external economies should create local sales linkages, Taylor and McDermott's notions argue that the eight variables should be reduced to seven, omitting the last, 'local external economies', since the parochialism to which this variable alludes is a behavioural modification of the fifth, 'spatial competition', variable. The list has to be reduced further because it is difficult to incorporate the price and ownership variables (6 and 7 above) into the analysis. Conceptually, the price variable could modify the size of production centre variable, increasing it as price becomes lower, and vice versa. Since it is virtually impossible to obtain information on spatial variations in prices – for even one product, let alone a range of goods – this variable must be excluded in simulating spatial linkage patterns. Similarly, little is known as to how ownership ties influence the spatial arrangement of firms' sales contacts. Both variables are omitted, therefore, creating unknown error.

The interaction model used, therefore, employs variables 1 to 5 in simulating linkage patterns, with variable 1 – the type of product being sold – being accommodated by separate runs of the model. In this way, linkage patterns in the presence of spatial competition can be approximated. The model, originally devised by Huff (1960) for estimating shopping-centre trade-areas, is used here in the following form:

$$E_{ij} = \frac{\dfrac{S_j}{D_{ij}^a}}{\sum\limits_{j=1}^{n} \dfrac{S_j}{D_{ij}^a}} \cdot C_i$$

where:

E_{ij} is the expected number of customers at consumer location 'i' patronizing producers at production location 'j'

S_j is the size of production centre 'j'

C_i is the size of consumer location 'i'

D_{ij} is the distance separating consumer location 'i' and production centre 'j'
a is a parameter reflecting the friction of distance.

The model emphasizes consumer choice, the decision being which of several alternative production centres a consumer will patronize. Competition amongst the producers is incorporated in the model as a probability term which is dependent upon the sizes of the competing production centres and the distances separating them from any particular consumer location.

Simulations of market linkage patterns from which spatial competition is excluded are made with a simple linear transport cost minimization model. Such models are described by Cox (1965) but the solution employed here was proposed by Ford and Fulkerson (1956). Only the size of production centres (S_j), the size of consumer location (C_i) and the distance separating the two (D_{ij}) are built into the model, the type of product being sold (variable 1) being accommodated once more by successive runs of the model.

Published statistics have been employed to calibrate the linear transport and the interaction models. The sample survey of Auckland manufacturers, which yielded the empirical data, was divisible into seven manufacturing sectors (sectors 2 to 8 in Table 12.1). Estimates were required of the appropriate spatial distributions of supply and demand (S_j and C_i respectively) to simulate the patterns of sales linkage for each manufacturing sector. The demand estimates were produced in two stages. First, the seven industrial sectors were used to construct a fourteen-sector input–output table (Table 12.1) from the national figures for 1959–60 (New Zealand Department of Statistics, 1966), the intermediate output and final demand sectors being updated to 1966 by data from Gillion and Frankel (1967). The table was then used to estimate relative sectoral demand for each industry's production. Second, 1971 employment data for thirteen sectors (New Zealand Department of Labour, 1972, 1973), and population data (New Zealand Department of Statistics, 1972) for the fourteenth – as an estimate of the distribution of final demand in New Zealand – were used to distribute the sectoral demand proportions amongst seventy-five regions. These regions (Fig. 12.2) comprise individual counties, or amalgamations of counties, with a single railway station accounting as their focus. Railway stations were used as the regional foci since broadly all freight hauled more than 40 miles is the sole preserve of the New Zealand Railways Department, except where it is too bulky, uneconomic or involves certain primary products like livestock and timber. Employment numbers for each of the seven manufacturing sectors (New Zealand Department of Labour, 1972, 1973) as distributed amongst the same seventy-five regions, provided measures of the distribution of supply, i.e. the size of production centres.

Transport costs data for 1971 measured the distance separating consumers and producers. The basis of the matrix of transport costs was the cost of shipping one ton of class C goods from one railway station to another. However, when, according to the Holme Shipping Co., it was cheaper to transport goods between two regions by coastal freighter, the cost per ton was taken to be that appropriate for coastal shipping (McDermott, 1972). Road transport costs – calculated as the cartage rates for the distance between the two most separated centres with more than 1000 inhabitants in each region – were used to measure intra-regional movement. The transport cost estimates have not been modified by any exponent as was suggested for the interaction model since that parameter 'a' can only be interpreted as a behavioural modification of the friction of distance as measured by

Table 12.1 Input–output matrix of the New Zealand economy

	1	2	3	4	5	6	7	8	9	10	11	12	Total intermediate output	Exports 13	Local final demand 14	Totals
1 Farming, hunting, fishing and forestry	86.20	191.05	2.90	11.75	0.75	0.45	0.00	1.80	9.00	6.70	0.30	1.20	312.10	98.25	37.95	448.30
2 Food, drink and tobacco	4.70	30.90	1.20	0.00	1.25	0.00	0.00	0.05	0.00	11.20	0.85	0.40	50.55	179.15	139.65	369.35
3 Textile, clothing and leather	1.20	0.55	8.35	0.30	0.20	0.35	0.00	0.20	0.10	0.55	1.05	0.65	13.50	2.65	80.70	96.85
4 Wood, furniture, paper and printing	4.50	8.25	2.15	25.00	3.10	1.40	0.70	1.60	25.20	5.45	10.80	2.00	90.25	7.95	18.15	126.25
5 Capital products and rubber	18.05	0.85	0.80	1.35	3.25	2.70	0.45	0.65	6.75	2.85	1.30	1.85	40.85	1.95	14.60	57.30
6 Metal, machinery and transport equipment	10.45	2.90	0.55	1.50	2.25	12.20	1.10	0.65	12.65	2.15	1.60	13.95	19.75	2.10	66.75	130.80
7 Electrical goods	0.50	0.10	0.10	0.10	0.00	0.55	1.20	0.05	1.65	0.25	0.05	0.40	4.95	0.10	10.45	15.50
8 Miscellaneous mfg. (incl. non.met. prods.)	2.40	1.90	0.30	0.45	0.55	0.60	0.20	2.00	12.20	1.80	0.10	0.10	22.65	0.10	13.80	36.50
9 Building and construction	4.35	0.85	0.30	0.75	0.25	0.45	0.05	0.30	43.75	12.35	4.00	2.95	70.35	0.05	189.65	260.05
10 Services	9.80	5.50	2.95	4.65	2.05	3.80	0.40	1.70	4.95	44.45	13.10	4.05	117.40	8.50	300.20	426.10
11 Trade	17.80	8.75	5.65	6.20	3.60	6.75	1.15	2.70	18.90	6.15	3.75	3.60	85.00	12.20	183.10	280.30
12 Transport	15.40	11.90	4.25	7.40	3.65	4.90	0.60	2.35	11.45	8.55	10.60	17.05	98.10	25.50	48.60	172.20
Total intermediate inputs	175.35	263.50	29.50	59.45	20.90	34.15	5.85	14.05	146.60	102.45	67.50	48.20	925.45	338.50	1113.50	2419.50
13 Imports	17.90	17.80	17.85	12.70	15.75	32.65	3.85	5.35	12.85	11.00	5.95	9.60	163.25	1.65	115.00	270.90
14 Other inputs	255.05	88.05	49.50	54.10	20.65	64.00	5.80	17.10	100.60	312.65	206.85	114.40	1288.75	0.90	52.10	1341.75
Totals	448.30	369.35	96.85	126.25	57.30	130.80	15.50	36.50	260.05	426.10	280.30	172.20	2419.50	341.05	1280.60	4041.15

Sources: New Zealand Department of Statistics, *Inter-Industry Study of the New Zealand Economy, 1959–60,* Wellington, 1966.

Fig. 12.2   The regions employed in the study.

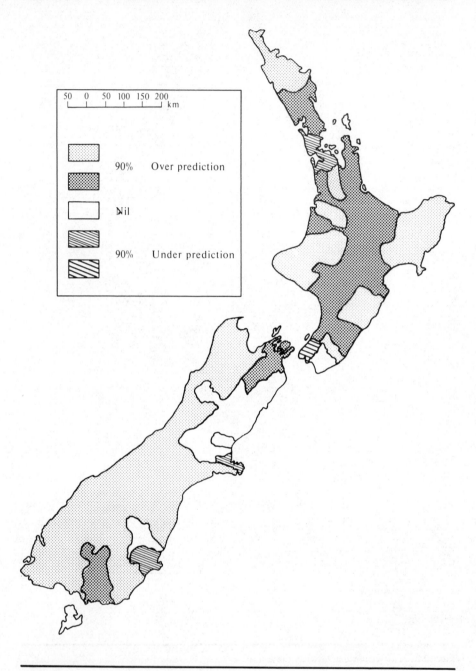

Fig. 12.3 Residuals from the comparison of the actual sales linkage patterns and their equivalent predicted by the interaction model.

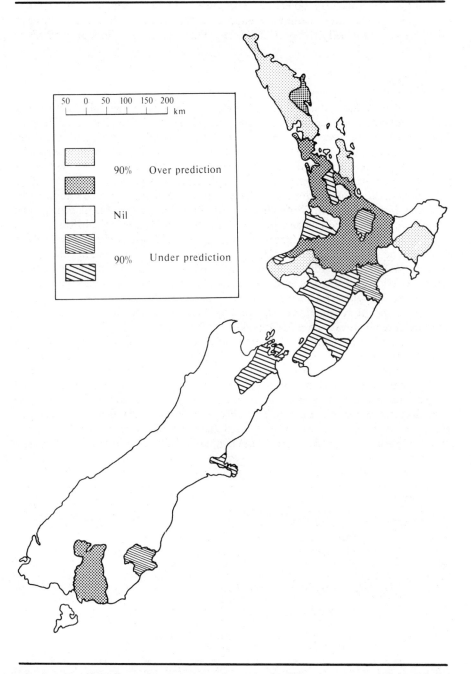

Fig. 12.4 Residuals from the comparison of actual sales linkage patterns and their equivalent predicted by the transportation model.

transport costs. Given the objective to produce rational estimates of sales linkage patterns in an attempt to isolate the effect of competition, the use of an exponent other than '1' to modify the cost–distance estimates would be inappropriate.

The results

Comparisons of the simulated linkage patterns and their empirical counterparts, for all Auckland manufacturers, are mapped in Figs. 12.3 and 12.4; the difference between empirical and predicted degrees of sales linkage between Auckland manufacturers and consumers in any of the seventy-five regions is expressed as a proportion of the predicted figures. Obviously, the interaction and transport models predict sales linkage patterns very differently. The former under-predicts local linkage and the amount of linkage between Auckland manufacturers and consumers in Wellington, Christchurch, and Dunedin (Fig. 12.3). Elsewhere, the model over-predicts, especially in the more peripheral areas of Northland, the East Coast of North Island, Taranaki, and the West Coast, and southern half of South Island. The transport model, however, over-predicts linkage in those areas adjacent to Auckland (Fig. 12.4) but, at a distance and for all major population centres outside Auckland, it under-predicts manufacturers' sales contacts. There is an apparently greater accuracy of prediction by the transport model throughout large parts of South Island, but this reflects the few industrial consumers located there outside Christchurch and Dunedin.

To present fuller results of simulation and to compare them with empirical sales linkages, the seventy-five regions were aggregated to nine cost–distance zones centred on Auckland. Zone 1 contains only the Auckland region (region 7 in Fig. 12.2), within which it costs less than $NZ10.00 per ton to ship manufactured goods; the remaining zones incorporate regions into successive $NZ5.00 cost–distance bands to a maximum of $NZ50.00 per ton, which is only slightly in excess of the actual cost of shipping manufactured goods from Auckland to the remoter West Coast of the South Island (Table 12.2). To facilitate the comparison

Table 12.2   New Zealand regions grouped into cost–distance zones

Cost–distance zone	Cost per tonne ($NZ)	Regions
1	0.00–10.00	7
2	10.01–15.00	3, 5, 6, 9, 10, 11, 13, 14, 17
3	15.01–20.00	1, 2, 4, 8, 12, 15, 16, 18, 19, 24, 28
4	20.01–25.00	20, 23, 25, 26, 27, 29, 30, 31, 32, 33, 34, 37, 38, 39, 40, 42
5	25.01–30.00	21, 22, 35, 36, 41, 43, 44, 45, 46, 61, 65, 67, 71
6	30.01–35.00	48, 58, 59, 62, 64, 66, 73
7	35.01–40.00	49, 50, 54, 57, 60, 63, 70, 72, 74, 75
8	40.01–45.00	47, 53, 55, 69
9	45.01 and over	51, 52, 56, 68

of the two simulated and one empirical sets of linkage data each set has been standardized, the number of links between Auckland and a particular distance zone being expressed as a proportion of the appropriate net total. This procedure allowed drawing comparable distance decay curves (Figs. 12.5–12.12).

The curves of aggregate sales links of all manufacturers in Auckland, irrespective of the products they make or the form of organization they possess, are shown in Fig. 12.5. The actual sales decay curve shows a strong local bias to linkage (59.6 per cent), the proportion of total sales links falling sharply in all other zones, except in zone 5 where it swings up to 26.5 per cent. The explanation is that all the main urban centres in New Zealand outside Auckland, namely Wellington, Christchurch and Dunedin, lie in cost–distance zone 5 as do also the secondary centres of Napier, Hastings, Camaru and Taimaru. Indeed, zones 1 and 5 contain 86.1 per cent of the counterparts in Auckland manufacturers' sales links, demonstrating high polarization of the country's space economy.

The aggregate sales decay curves produced by the interaction model (Fig. 12.5) is broadly similar to the actual sales curve, but differs from it in several important respects: it dramatically underestimates both local sales linkages (only 41.2 per cent of sales links being with customers in zone 1) and the number of sales contacts between Auckland manufacturers and customers in zone 5 urban centres (only 18.5 per cent), yet it overestimates the number of customers that Auckland manufacturers find in zones 2 to 4 closest to them.

The sales decay curve produced by the linear transport model is again different (Fig. 12.5), closely approximating reality in zone 1 but overestimating both local sales linkage at 64.7 per cent and with zones 2 to 4, and grossly underestimating linkage with zone 5 (4.4 per cent).

How can these three distance decay curves be reconciled one with another? It can be argued for distance zone 1 that the more closely the actual situation approximated the transport model prediction, the weaker is competition in the local market and the greater the degree of parochialism and spatial monopoly. The more closely reality approximates the interaction model prediction, however, the stronger is spatial competition and the more rational are manufacturers. Thus Fig. 12.5 suggests a large measure of spatial monopoly and parochialism in aggregate Auckland manufacturing. In zone 2 and particularly 3, the simulation models over-predict the frequency of linkage with Auckland manufacturers, implying that some mechanism prevents firms obtaining customers in these zones. That mechanism is spatial monopoly wielded by producers in Whangarei (as McDermott, 1974, confirms) and Hamilton in zone 2 and Tauranga and Rotorua in zone 3.

Spatial monopoly also explains the general under-prediction of linkage between Auckland firms and the market for manufactured goods in zone 5. Clark (1974) shows that as firms grow and develop in New Zealand, their spatial expansion path progresses into the main population centres of Auckland, Wellington, Christchurch and Dunedin, and that, from whatever location they begin, they establish and acquire sales offices, warehouses, branch plants and subsidiaries in these centres. Thus, strong linkage between Auckland manufacturers and zone 5 can be anticipated from ownership ties between Auckland firms and their branches, or between Auckland branches and their parent firms. Recall that it was impossible to build this variable into either simulation model. Branches of an Auckland company might be used to distribute Auckland-made goods in adjacent markets to exercise monopolistic control over them. Corporate expansion can thus be conceived to operate within a spatial monopoly framework. Under-prediction by the interaction model, which already predicted a large volume of sales between Auckland firms and firms in zone 5 because of the large size of the market they present, confirms that organizational and ownership traits may be an

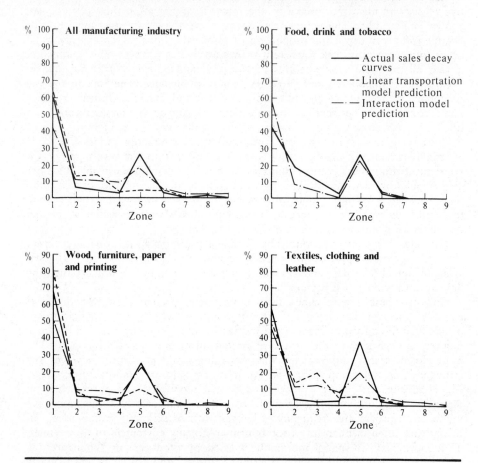

Figs. 12.5–12.12   Actual and predicted sales decay curves for Auckland manufacturers.

important determinant of spatial linkage, for not all Auckland firms are multi-plant concerns operating at more than one location and many are no more than small scale, single-plant concerns.

So Figs. 12.6–12.12 disaggregate the situation for each of seven industrial sectors, and expose how the situation between industries differs from that for aggregate manufacturing. All industries demonstrate some consistency in the relationship of the empirical to the predicted sales decay curves in cost–distance zones 2 to 9. Both models tend to over-predict in zones 2, 3 and 4 except in zone 2 for Miscellaneous Manufacturing industry (Fig. 12.12) and in all three zones for the Food, Drink and Tobacco industry (Fig. 12.6). Apparently Auckland's food, drink and tobacco industries are closely tied to the North Island regional market. Varying degrees of under-prediction are the rule for zone 5 for all industries, except Miscellaneous Manufacturing industry (Fig. 12.12), although interaction model predictions are very close to reality for the Wood, Furniture, Paper and Printing industry (Fig. 12.7) and the Metal, Machinery and Transport Equipment

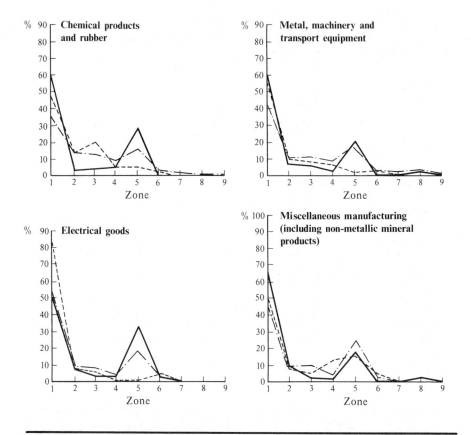

industry (Fig. 12.10). Both models over-predict linkage with zones 6 to 9 despite the very small numbers involved.

There is, however, very little consistency for zone 1 (the Auckland region) between the actual proportions of local sales linkage and the predictions produced by the two simulation models (Figs. 12.6–12.12). Conceptually, the transport model should have provided an upper limit to the volume of local linkage where spatial competition was absent, the interaction model a lower limit to the volume of local linkage where competition was intense but rational; reality was expected to fall somewhere between these two. Only one industry – the Wood, Furniture, Paper and Printing industry (Fig. 12.7) – approximates this arrangement, though it is also so for aggregate industry (Fig. 12.5). For four industries – Textiles, Clothing and Leather (Fig. 12.8), Chemical Products and Rubber (Fig. 12.9), Metal, Machinery and Transport Equipment (Fig. 12.10) and Miscellaneous Manufacturing (Fig. 12.12) – local linkage is even more intense than the transport model would predict. This might indicate that parochialism is much more than an imperfect form of spatial competition. And yet, for the remaining two industries, Food, Drink and Tobacco (Fig. 12.6) and Electrical Goods (Fig. 12.11), the complete opposite is the case, local sales linkage being weaker than even the interaction model would suggest, which could be interpreted as depicting

Table 12.3   Deviations of simulated sales decay curves from their empirical counterparts for zones 1 and 5 by organizational type

| Organizational type | Deviations from empirical sales decay curve | | | |
| | Interaction model | | Transport model | |
	Zone 1	Zone 5	Zone 1	Zone 5
(a) Management				
Boards of directors	−16.64	− 8.66	+ 7.42	−22.90
Owner-operators and				
partnerships	−20.74	− 5.84	+ 0.13	−19.78
(b) Ownership				
Public	− 7.01	−10.66	+19.72	−25.43
Private	−20.92	− 7.17	+ 1.04	−21.33
(c) Plant status				
Single-plant	−20.15	− 6.66	+ 1.65	−20.77
Multi-plant	−15.76	− 9.37	+ 9.02	−23.56
Main production centres	−16.71	− 9.20	+10.53	−24.25
Subsidiaries and				
branch plants	−10.30	− 9.00	+10.49	−23.20

stronger-than-rational spatial competition in these two industries in New Zealand.

No allowance has yet been made for differences in organizational structure between industries in constructing the curves for separate industries. To determine the influence of organizational features on spatial linkages, the results from each simulation model for individual industries have been aggregated according to the contributions of an industry to the total of surveyed links for a particular organizational type. Eight organizational categories have been recognized (Table 12.3). An ownership criterion facilitates division of firms into publicly- and privately-owned. A management criterion facilitates segregation of firms run by owner-operators and partnerships from those run by boards of directors. A plant status criterion enables division of firms into single-plant and multi-plant operations, the latter being divided further into branch plants and those which are main production units of larger firms.

The results for each organizational type show high consistency in over-predicting reality in the relationship of actual and simulated linkage volumes between Auckland manufacturers and zones 2 to 4 and 6 to 9. But interesting variations occur in zones 1 and 5. To expose them, figures for the deviations of both the interaction and transport model predictions from the empirical figures for cost–distance zones 1 and 5 are presented in Table 12.3. In zone 5, both models under-predict, but in zone 1 the transport model estimate of local linkage is invariably greater than reality while the estimate from the interaction model is invariably smaller: the models do provide an upper and lower limit to local sales linkage as postulated.

Significantly, actual estimates of local sales linkage tend towards either these upper or lower limits, depending upon organizational type. Local linkage for owner-operators and partnerships tends towards the transport model estimate much more than does local linkage for firms run by boards of directors, suggesting stronger 'parochialism' and 'spatial monopoly' among the simpler management type. Even more dramatic is the way in which the degree of local sales linkage for publicly-owned firms closely approximates the interaction model estimate while that for privately-owned firms even more closely approximate the transport model estimate. Table 12.3 also demonstrates a similar relationship for single-plant and multi-plant firms, hinting at a generally stronger spatial monopoly amongst main production units than amongst branch plants and subsidiaries. Clearly, privately-owned, single-plant firms with simple management structures are far less influenced by spatial competition in their sales linkage arrangements and far more dependent upon spatial monopoly and parochial attitudes than are larger, publicly-owned, multi-plant organizations run by boards of directors.

Conclusion

The models and the empirical data used in this study have many limitations which detract from any conclusions which might be drawn. Yet the results are clear enough to suggest that organizational type, much more than industry, is an important determinant of the spatial arrangement of manufacturers' sales linkages. Larger, more complex organizations are more frequently involved in interregional trade and interregional competition within New Zealand, although corporate expansion through the establishment and acquisition of branches may involve some spatial monopoly. But some types of firms – irrespective of the kind of product they make – have few interregional sales links and their ability to deal almost exclusively with their local market would seem to be important for their continued survival.

References

Clark, T. C. (1974), *The patterns of expansion of large manufacturing companies in New Zealand*, unpublished MA thesis, University of Auckland.

Cox, K. R. (1965), 'The application of linear programming to geographic problems', *Tijdschrift voor Economische en Sociale Geografie*, **56** (6), pp. 228–36.

Ford, L. R. and Fulkerson, D. R. (1956), 'Solving the transportation problem', *Management Science*, **3** (24), pp. 24–32.

Gillion, C. and Frankel, Z. (1967), 'Data for input–output analysis', *New Zealand Institute of Economic Research*, Technical memorandum 13.

Huff, D. L. (1960), 'A topographical model of consumer space preferences', *Papers and Proceedings, Regional Science Association*, **6**, pp. 159–73.

McDermott, P. J. (1972), *Industrial Location Theory and the Distribution of Manufacturing in New Zealand*, unpublished MA thesis, University of Auckland.

McDermott, P. J. (1974), 'Market linkage and spatial monopoly in New Zealand manufacturing', *New Zealand Geographer*, **30**, pp. 1–17.

New Zealand Department of Labour (1972, 1973), Industrial Information Bulletin, *Labour and Employment Gazette*, **22** (4), **23** (1), (2) and (3).

New Zealand Department of Statistics (1966), *Inter-Industry Study of the New Zealand Economy 1959–60*, Wellington.

New Zealand Department of Statistics (1972), *N.Z. Census of Population and Dwellings 1971*, Wellington.

Taylor, M. J. (1971), *Spatial Linkage and the West Midlands Ironfoundry Industry*, unpublished Ph.D. thesis, University of London.

Taylor, M. J. (1973), 'Local linkage, external economies and the ironfoundry industry of the West Midlands and East Lancashire conurbations', *Regional Studies*, **7**, pp. 387–400.

Taylor, M. J. (1975), 'The industrial linkages of Auckland manufacturers', *Proceedings of the International Geographical Union Regional Conference and Eighth New Zealand Geography Conference*, pp. 203–17.

Taylor, M. J. and Wood, P. A. (1973), 'Industrial linkage and local agglomeration in the West Midlands Metal Industries', *Transactions of the Institute of British Geographers*, **40**, pp. 129–54.

Chapter 13

Acquisitions in British industries: implications for regional development

Roger Leigh and David J. North

Acquisitions (takeovers and mergers) are common in capitalist business. The incidence of takeovers undoubtedly varies from year to year, yet in Britain in 1973 – a 'moderate' year (compared to the late 1960s peak and the mid-1970s trough) – at least 465 UK industrial firms were acquired by other UK companies (*Business Monitor*, 1973). Between 1955 and 1960 a British manufacturing firm had up to 25 per cent chance of being taken over, depending on its size, while the most common reason for the 'death' of a publicly-owned company was acquisition – 75 per cent *versus* 10 per cent for liquidation (Singh, 1971). Not surprisingly, acquisition activity has been extensively studied by economists and management scientists to assess the contribution of takeovers to the concentration of production in certain industries (Hart, Utton and Walshe, 1973) and the factors that influence the financial success of takeovers (Ansoff *et al.*, 1971; Kitchen, 1974). Yet there is only one spatial study of acquisition (Brue, 1971), though some researchers refer to it in analyses of location decision-making (Keeble, 1971; Rake, 1972; Hamilton, 1974; North, 1974).

The lack of geographical studies is surprising given that acquisition has rather obvious spatial aspects: it may be an alternative to relocating and extending plants or to opening new ones. It may involve spatial searching for candidates. Post-acquisition integration may entail locational adjustments. Acquisition is probably far more frequent than the sorts of business behaviour traditionally investigated (plant relocation or the establishment of branch plants) and hence potentially more relevant to understanding changing industrial location patterns (Rake, 1972) and their regional impact. Acquisitions and mergers play a major role in the growth of city systems (Pred, 1974), suggesting a link between acquisition activity and urban and regional development. Certainly acquisition is a process leading to corporate reorganization with implications for regional development. It has been contended, with some support (Parsons, 1972; Rake, 1972; Brue, 1971), that (1) acquisition concentrates certain corporate functions and exacerbates regional differences; (2) when a previously independent firm is brought within a larger organization, its performance and viability is evaluated on different (group) criteria and this may not favour facilities in peripheral or depressed regions. These observations, if confirmed and elaborated, have implications for government regional policies, which so far have concentrated on influencing regional development by a system of allowances and controls applied to particular places and not by measures directed at the process of corporate development and reorganization.

Methodology, concepts and definitions

A 'behavioural' approach is adopted here. Emphasis is on the direct investigation of the behaviour of industrial organizations, particularly their investment decision-making processes as these are conceived and carried through by firms interacting with their complex and dynamic environments. Spatial changes are seen as consequences of purposeful or adaptive corporate behaviour. The advantages of this approach (Leigh and North, 1975) are that it is flexible, dynamic, holistic and empirically-useful, involving no limiting assumptions and clearly relating spatial effects to what actually goes on inside the firm. It is inductive, and uses a conceptual framework as a guide to data collection, and aims at creating models of types of acquisition-related spatial change via the grouping of extended case studies. For regional study, the methodology is in the emerging style of 'micro-level' analysis of regional development, analysing the behaviour of business organizations within a region characterized as a system of individuals, enterprises and organizations (Firn, 1975). It essentially complements the traditional 'macro' or structural approaches which emphasize the role of industrial sectors, external markets and regional resources.

The conceptual framework that structures the study is summarized in Fig. 13.1. Acquisition processes begin in a firm when either goals are set or problems arise which demand appropriate investment policy response. It is one possible strategy by which to achieve an identified investment policy. Once having moved on to the acquisition path, a firm may identify more specific objectives to be achieved by acquisition and begin a process of search for, and evaluation of, candidates. This process varies greatly between firms in the degree of planning and care in execution. Sometimes the 'decision to acquire' is taken as unexpected opportunities arise rather than as a result of carefully evaluated policy. After takeover the acquired firm is integrated into the new parent, various spatial readjustments being implicit in this process. Some are direct and expected consequences of takeover, others follow later as the enlarged firm makes adjustments to its new environment. Spatial changes do not occur in isolation, but are clearly consequences of a type of corporate behaviour. They, and the regional development trends they generate, must be explained by reference to the behaviour that created them.

By 'takeover' is meant the purchase by one industrial firm (usually a public company) of the shares, assets, stocks, premises, brand names and goodwill of another firm (usually a smaller and often privately-owned company, or a subsidiary of a public company). It excludes 'mergers' between public companies of about equal size, which imply a thorough reorganization of both companies.

'Spatial change' means changes in the geography of the acquired firm (North, 1975b), including: expansion, contraction or change of products manufactured by the factories of the acquired firm; setting-up new factories: factory closure or factory relocations; transfer of product ranges from one factory to another, changes in executive and administrative functions (with or without changes in personnel) at acquired sites; alterations in material and service inputs at acquired sites; changes in the types and locations of markets served from acquired factories.

'Regional impact' relates to the consequences of acquisition on the region(s) in which the acquired firm is located, since acquisition is usually by larger firms located elsewhere. The impact may be 'negative' or 'positive' as measured by various criteria of regional economic expansion and stability. Reduction of output, factory closure and the internalization of service linkages (if these occur) are

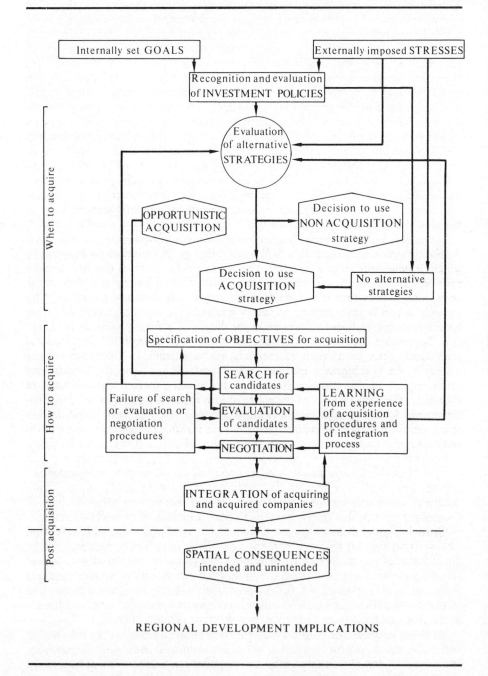

Fig. 13.1 A framework for the interpretation of acquisition behaviour.

'negative' effects, implying a decrease in regional output and employment and reduced local multiplier effects through lost linkages. Similarly, the hypothetical loss of local control over important purchasing, production, sales and investment decisions, and related loss of transfer of administrative staff to 'group' sites, are 'negative' for the region: they imply an increased vulnerability to closure during recession and a loss of certain types of professional employment opportunities in the region. By contrast, the expansion of output, changes of product lines, enlargement of markets, access to large company management and financial resources, are 'positive' for the region, implying enhanced levels of regional output and employment and decreased vulnerability to business cycle fluctuations. Better working conditions and pension plans are other hypothetical benefits of acquisition to a region's labour force. Assessments of regional implications depends upon being able to 'net out' the different types of spatial change.

Data sources and study techniques

Four sectors of British manufacturing industry are studied – chemicals, food, textiles and clothing – because aggregate data of acquisition activity for all sectors of British industry through the 1960s and 1970s showed these sectors to have high and consistent levels of activity: they were neither erratic from year to year nor dominated by large-scale mergers (Table 13.1). Yet the four sectors did differ in their degree of orientation to industrial and consumer markets, their overall growth performance and their basic geographical distribution in the UK and were thus expected to display some contrast in acquisition motive, procedures, consequences and regional implications.

Fortunately an unpublished inventory of UK acquisition activity is maintained by the Department of Industry's Bureau of Economic Statistics, facilitating identification of all firms in the chemical, food, textile and clothing sectors which acquired other named UK firms (in the same or different sectors) in any year between 1968 and 1974. For this project all firms in the four sectors were selected which made acquisitions in 1973 and 1974 as the basic study population. This amounted to 117 firms: 23 in foods, 29 in chemicals, 45 in textiles and 20 in clothing. Since some firms made multiple acquisitions in these two years, the total number of acquisitions was 263: 63 in foods, 70 in chemicals, 88 in textiles and 42 in clothing.

Much data on the acquiring and acquired firms was gathered from secondary sources (directories, company reports and company accounts) to build up a comprehensive picture of the industrial, financial and locational aspects of acquisition activity in each sector (Jackson, 1975; Leigh, 1975; North, 1975a; Parker, 1975). The data indicated a distinction in all sectors between 'active' and 'less active' acquirers (i.e. firms making frequent versus firms making few acquisitions and variations in the incidence of 'horizontal' versus 'diversification' acquisitions, and of 'local' versus 'long distance' acquisitions). Local acquisitions were commonest in clothing and food industries.

However, acquisitions motives and procedures and spatial changes can only be studied by direct interview with involved businessmen, not from public sources. Thus the 117 companies formed a sampling frame, of which 61 cooperated by allowing interviews of their senior executives (usually the chairman or managing director). These comprised 15 firms in foods, 16 in chemicals, 19 in textiles and 11

Table 13.1 Acquisition activity by British manufacturing firms 1969–74 by sector

Acquisition of independent companies	1969	1970	1971	1972	1973	1974
Food						
No.	14	12	13	25	33	10
value (£m)	26.6	5.0	19.9	161.0	23.5	23.2
Chemicals and allied						
No.	36	24	20	20	18	26
value (£m)	85.7	102.6	23.8	66.0	32.4	12.5
Textiles						
No.	60	30	27	52	51	21
value (£m)	36.7	21.2	17.7	30.5	31.8	11.3
Clothing						
No.	30	36	36	40	26	10
value (£m)	9.7	10.6	25.0	41.9	9.4	2.0
All manufacturing						
No.	418	325	278	442	465	192
value (£m)	646.4	585.5	287.6	1199.3	378.0	166.7
Transfers of subsidiaries between groups	1969	1970	1971	1972	1973	1974
Food, drink, tobacco						
No.	6	17	12	10	18	9
value (£m)	10.2	34.4	8.8	25.1	9.6	5.6
Chemical and allied						
No.	4	10	5	6	13	6
value (£m)	28.0	5.1	10.1	2.6	6.6	1.6
Textiles and clothing						
No.	10	23	12	19	29	7
value (£m)	3.9	9.9	3.4	8.7	21.2	5.6
All manufacturing						
No.	63	116	146	134	155	73
value (£m)	70.2	87.8	84.2	92.9	83.5	35.6

Source: *Business Monitor* (M.7) (various issues).

in clothing which respectively acquired 44, 29, 40 and 28 firms (a total of 141 'cases' of acquisition) so that respondent firms differed little from the non-respondent in terms of sector, size of financial characteristics.

Types of spatial change

Since the single acquisition of a multi-plant firm can lead to more than one type of spatial adjustment, there are more cases of spatial change than of acquisitions. Five major types of spatial adjustments are distinguished: in managerial control, expansion of output, changes in products, closure of factories and alterations in external linkages.

Transfer of managerial control

Takeover implies the transfer of managerial control from the acquired to the acquiring company: spatially, control over a region's productive resources can be transferred to another region upon acquisition if the acquirer is headquartered elsewhere, leading to increased 'external control' of local industry for some regions and consolidation of ownership into other regions (Firn, 1975; Dicken, 1976). However, important post-acquisition differences of *degree* occur in the transfer of management responsibilities. Complications also arise because not all acquired companies are independent prior to acquisition: some takeovers transfer subsidiary companies from one group to another.

Senior executives of acquiring companies were questioned about (1) the level of decision-making either left with the acquired company or transferred to the acquirer and (2) the kind of performance standards, budgetary monitoring and control systems that were imposed on the acquired company. In virtually every case – a few reverse takeovers being the exception – top level managerial functions (i.e. responsibility for long-term goal-formation and planning, final approval of major capital expenditures and the establishment of performance rules for subsidiaries or divisions) were transferred to the acquirer. Inevitably the acquired company was expected to submit to the new headquarters regular performance data covering sales, costs, and gross profits. Headquarters involvement followed if monitoring revealed actual or potential deviations from the prescribed course. To this extent all acquisitions involved relocation of senior management functions to the acquirer. Yet, this still left much scope for variations in the degree to which other managerial functions remained with the acquired firms. Indeed, the 141 acquired firms can be grouped into four categories according to their residual management functions and their relationship with the acquiring firm.

1. Forty-four firms (31 per cent of the total) retained 'relatively high' post-acquisition managerial control, a board of directors, for developing existing product lines, production methods, material purchasing, marketing, personnel recruitment and minor capital expenditures (typically under £5000). Such relative autonomy was maintained because the acquired firms were expected to initiate medium- to long-term product and market development plans, but not implement them without central approval. Monitoring of performance by the acquirer was limited to a few strategic variables.
2. Forty-eight firms (34 per cent) retained a 'moderate' degree of post-acquisition managerial control over production, purchasing, marketing recruitment and minor capital spending but were more closely integrated with the acquirer in conventions and practices in all departments and more closely monitored.
3. Thirty-eight acquired firms (27 per cent) retained a 'low degree' of post-acquisition managerial control of low-level, routine management responsibilities over short-term production planning and material purchasing, and becoming, in effect, branch plants of the acquirer. Setting production targets, marketing decisions, and operating procedures were decided by the new divisional or central headquarters.
4. The final category comprises eleven firms (8 per cent) which were liquidated after acquisition, their assets being sold or distributed among other subsidiaries or division of the acquiring company.

Strong and consistent patterns and relationships between the three types of post-acquisition managerial control (relatively high; moderate; low) and attributes of the acquiring company are hard to identify, yet some generalizations do emerge. Acquisitions by clothing firms most frequently allowed the acquired firm a high degree of post-acquisition control (52 per cent of all surviving acquisitions by clothing firms), because managers need intimate knowledge of products with high demand elasticities and decentralized decision-making aids rapid adjustment to a frequently changing market. At the opposite extreme, acquirers in the chemical sector permitted less autonomy to their acquisitions (41 per cent of cases were in the lowest autonomy category, only 19 per cent retaining a high degree of management control). These are the more obvious sectoral contrasts. Table 13.2 suggests others.

Table 13.2   Post-acquisition management control and industrial sector of acquiring company

Sector of acquirer:	Level of post-acquisition management control retained by acquired company						
	High No	Sector (%)	Moderate No.	Sector (%)	Low No.	Sector (%)	Totals
Food	16	40	11	27.5	13	32.5	40
Chemicals	5	18.5	11	40.7	11	40.7	27
Clothing	13	52	4	16	8	32	25
Textiles	11	28.9	21	55.3	6	15.8	38
	45		47		38		130*

* Excludes 11 firms liquidated post acquisition.

Diversification acquisitions tended to leave the acquired company with at least a moderate degree of managerial control (46 per cent of diversification acquisitions) and reduced the acquired company to branch status much less often (23 per cent). When a firm moves into new product lines via takeover, it normally values the expertise and know-how of the acquired management and thus leaves the existing management in charge with retained responsibilities. Horizontal acquisitions were most likely to lead to the lowest level of managerial control: 36 per cent of horizontal acquisitions and accounted for two-thirds of acquired firms keeping only low-level control. This reflects opportunities for close integration of firms in similar lines of business and the scope for involvement by the acquiring management already familiar with the technology, product types and markets of the acquired concern (except in the clothing sector, for reasons cited above).

A large acquiring company (with a turnover exceeding £50 million per annum) tended to leave the acquired firm with a moderate rather than a low degree of managerial control (42 per cent, compared to 19 per cent respectively). Small acquiring firms (below £5 million per annum turnover) permitted low levels of managerial control (30 per cent moderate, 37 per cent low). However, this reflects the coincidence between small-sized acquirers and horizontal acquisition, rather than some independent influence of acquirer size on post-acquisition management integration procedures.

The pre-acquisition status of the acquired company was also related to the degree of management autonomy it retained after takeover. A subsidiary of another firm at the time of takeover would most likely retain only low-level control: 35 of the 141 acquired firms were such subsidiaries and 15 (43 per cent) of them reverted to branch plant status after takeover. Relationships between acquisition procedures and the level of post-acquisition managerial control were less clear: there was no correlation between planned and unplanned takeovers or the extent of searching for acquisition candidates and levels of post-acquisition management integration. Yet when initiative for takeover came from the acquired company, there was less tendency for the level of management autonomy to be low subsequently (16 per cent), compared to those takeovers where the acquirer took the initiative (31 per cent). Apparently it is easier to distinguish the common characteristics of cases where the acquired firm retains a low level of control (as a branch plant) than it is to differentiate the circumstances that led to relatively high or moderate control levels. Low levels of autonomy resulted more often in chemicals and foods industries and associated with horizontal takeovers, small acquirers, acquirer initiative in the takeover process or subsidiary status of the acquired firm. Moderate degrees of autonomy were most common in the textiles sector and related to diversification acquisitions, larger acquirers and acquired company initiative in the takeover process. Much more relevant to the eventual management status of the acquired company may be such factors as the stage of corporate development of the acquirer (for instance in terms of Scott's three-stage model of development) or the organizational structure of the acquirer (in terms of Wrigley's organizational types: see Channon, 1973, Ch. 1). Further research might differentiate the acquiring firms in such terms and explore any relationship with the level of managerial control retained over acquired firms.

What are the implications of such changes in managerial control for economic development in the region of the acquired firm? Most writers argue that the loss of control over resources and the transfer of ultimate decision-making responsibility to another location is detrimental to the region concerned. At present, this essentially expresses *a priori* reasoning rather than empirical evidence of actual behaviour by multi-location firms (Dicken, 1976). However, at least three negative aspects of loss of management control can be suggested: (1) it places a region at greater economic risk; (2) profits are lost by transfer of control to the new region; and (3) high-level executive and administrative job opportunities are lost in the acquired firm's region.

Transfer of managerial control away from the acquired firm and its centralization in group headquarters does increase spatial disparity between control and operating units, strengthening the dominance of core over peripheral regions. Hypothetically, this places the region at greater long-term risk because loss of local control over major decisions may create conflicts of interest between the corporate system and the regional economy which are detrimental to the region. Interviews emphasized that while most acquired firms continued to operate as separate profit centres, all profits were subsumed under group profits and capital allocation decisions between a wider range of competing units (divisions, subsidiaries, and in different locations) were made at headquarters, so confirming loss of local control. Thus a process of profit redirection is initiated reducing regional income, with some secondary multiplier effects. Of course, this may be counterbalanced by access to the acquiring company's larger investment resources: not uncommonly acquirers financed expansion of acquired firms. But the continued success of an acquired firm to attract further capital depends upon its profit performance following initial investments, so in the long-term capital flows from the region of the acquired to that of the acquiring company is more likely.

A significant, unqualified negative result of transfers of managerial control to an acquiring company is reduced executive and administrative white-collar employment and entrepreneurial initiative in the acquired firm's region. This is most severe where a full range of functions is transferred, as when the acquired firm becomes a branch plant, yet fully 40 per cent of the takeovers involved actual transfer of key management staff from the acquired firm to the acquirer's headquarters. Over half the acquisitions studied involved public companies taking over private firms. Often acquirers (and the sellers) ostensibly intended the private entrepreneur to retain an executive position as a director of his former company. Usually, clashes over managerial methods soon resulted in the entrepreneur's departure from the organization. This evidence raises important questions concerning the need to foster entrepreneurship in underdeveloped regions. Do the acquired entrepreneurs establish another company and where? Does the threat of acquisition and increasing industrial concentration deter potential entrepreneurs from setting up, or enlarging, their own business? Qualifying these points are that one quarter of all acquired firms were already subsidiaries before takeover (and thus relinquished less significant management control) and that one-third of the sample firms taken over retained a 'relatively high level' of management autonomy and independence of management procedures.

Although it is more meaningful to differentiate metropolitan centres, the spatial pattern of managerial control transfers was studied at the standard-region scale.

Table 13.3 Regional location of acquired and acquiring companies: transfer of managerial control

Acquiring company	Acquired companies										
	S.E.	S.W.	E.A.	E.M.	W.M.	N.W.	N.	Y.H.	W.	Sc.	N.I.
S.E.	29		3	5		11		3		7	2
S.W.											
E.A.	5									1	
E.M.	1			6					1		
W.M.	1								1	1	
N.W.	3		1	1	1	15	1	3		3	
N.	1										
Y.H.				1		3		7		3	
W.											
Sc.	2			2	1					5	
N.I.											
Totals	42	—	4	15	2	29	1	13	2	20	2	130*

* This table excludes 11 acquired firms that were liquidated after acquisition.

The abbreviations of the standard regions denote: S.E. = South East, S.W. = South West, E.A. = East Anglia, E.M. = East Midlands, W.M. = West Midlands, N.W. = North West, N. = North, Y.H. = Yorkshire and Humberside, W. = Wales, Sc. = Scotland, N.I. = Northern Ireland.

Table 13.3 summarizes the pattern, cross-classifying the 130 cases (where companies survived acquisition) by the respective locations of the acquired firm and the headquarters of the acquirer: the latter is presumed to be the location to which ultimate management control reverts after takeover. Not always did acquisition necessarily result in an inter-regional transfer of control, yet as the table includes acquisitions of subsidiaries of other firms at takeover (26 per cent of all acquired firms) it yields an overall pattern of consolidation and spatial concentration of control resulting from contemporary acquisitions.

Though no differentiation is made in Table 13.3 of management status (i.e.

relatively high, moderate and low), the results are interesting. First, 52 per cent of all acquisitions were made by acquirers external to the acquired firm's region. Not surprisingly, inter-regional acquisitions were less common in the more localized clothing and textiles industries than in chemicals and food. The incidence of inter-regional *versus* intra-regional acquisitions was higher in some regions than in others: certain regions showed a stronger tendency to become subject to external control than others. The proportion of intra-regional acquisitions declined quite markedly away from the South East (73 per cent) through the North West and Yorkshire and Humberside (50 per cent each) to Scotland (25 per cent) and Northern Ireland (zero). Most 'peripheral' or 'problem' regions lost control over more companies than they gained control over in other regions: for them acquisition contributes to their growing dependence on decision-makers based in another region.

Second, firms headquartered in the South East dominated extra-regional acquisitions of firms in peripheral regions, leading to further concentration of this high-order 'control' function in the South East at the expense of other regions. This confirms the spatial growth patterns of senior administrative functions discerned by Parsons (1972) and Westaway (1974). Third, companies based in peripheral regions predominantly acquired other local companies or firms in other peripheral regions: only weakly do they 'invade' the South East to acquire firms headquartered there. Thus no real counter process acts against the growing national centralization of ownership in the South East. Yet intra-regional acquisitions demonstrate an analogous regional centralization process in some regions, notably the North West, where local acquisitions concentrates ownership and control into a major metropolitan area (like Manchester).

Extra-regional acquisitions led to a higher degree of integration than intra-regional ones, but there was no obvious tendency for firms in peripheral regions to revert to branch plant status. Indeed, the regions experiencing the most branch-plant type of close integration were the East Midlands, South East and Scotland (38, 34 and 30 per cent respectively of each region's acquired firms). Rather paradoxically, Scotland also had many cases where the acquired firm retained a high degree of managerial independence (35 per cent of Scotland's acquired firms), mostly when the acquirer was a South East-based firm. Long distance between headquarters and subsidiary necessitated, leaving effective managerial control locally, partially mitigates the negative effect of the growth of external control over the productive resources of peripheral regions by South East firms.

Increased output of existing product lines at acquired factories

Almost half the takeovers studied (62 out of 141, or 44 per cent) led directly to an increased output of existing product lines at one or more of the factories of the acquired company, making this the most common spatial consequence of acquisitions. Usually the expansion occurred soon after the takeover (40 per cent of the cases within one year, 71 per cent within three years, of acquisition). Significant differences were found between the four industrial sectors largely depending on the variation of growth opportunities available to them. Expansion of output was most common in the chemicals sector (62 per cent of the takeovers by chemical firms) which, of the four sectors, had experienced the fastest growth rate in the early 1970s, and least common in the clothing sector (21 per cent of takeovers by clothing firms). Furthermore, post-acquisition expansions were more common if the acquirer was a large firm: 50 per cent of the takeovers by firms with turnovers exceeding £50 million compared to 39 per cent of the takeovers by firms with turnovers below £5 million. This partly resulted from sectoral differences, large and medium-sized firms being more common in chemicals and food industries, small firms dominating the clothing industry.

What was the typical behavioural background to these acquisition-related expansions of production? 'Diversification' acquisitions tended to result in expansion of the acquired company (54 per cent of diversification acquisition did so) as did acquisitions classified as 'backward integration' (60 per cent). In contrast, 'horizontal' acquisitions (i.e. takeovers of firms making or marketing products essentially similar to the acquirer), though numerically the commonest type of acquisition, were much less likely to result in expansion (only 38 per cent). This pattern is understandable given managers' reasons for adopting a strategy of diversification by acquisition: to obtain growth and improve profitability by moving into unsaturated markets or into counter-cyclical product lines. Similarly, for the backward-integration type of takeover the objective was to secure or stabilize a supply of inputs: protection or expansion of the acquired company was expected. Motives behind 'horizontal' acquisitions varied far more and related less predictably to this spatial consequence.

Acquisition led to expansion being 'planned' (69 per cent could be so classified) with the initiative coming from the acquiring company itself (56 per cent) rather than from the acquired company or a third party. Often, acquisition procedure involved formal or informal searching for acquisition candidates. Where no search was apparently conducted, either a large company with an explicit acquisition programme 'knew the field' well enough to pick its acquisition candidates without searching, or firms with reputations as 'active acquirers' received approaches from firms interested in selling out: these would be accepted if they fitted into the required acquisition policy.

Though accurate, the pattern of the procedural background of acquisitions leading the expansion differs little from that of the entire sample of 141 cases studied: the proportions of takeovers characterized by 'planning' were 72 per cent, acquirer initiative (60 per cent), formal searching (31 per cent) and informal searching (18 per cent).

Many acquisitions by chemical firms were of the 'diversification' type: typically, firms explicitly planned to expand into complementary product lines by searching for, and purchasing, proven management, labour and plant. Acquisition was seen as a quicker, less costly solution to their diversification strategy than organic development. Not surprisingly, the factors that influenced search were not geographical but rather a quest for a product range with good growth prospects, satisfactory management and established markets. The search embraced firms ready for 'take-off' through the addition of such capital, management or marketing resources as the acquirer could supply, and certainly not companies requiring a massive 'turn-around' effort to achieve the planned growth. Thus, usually, the acquirer gave the acquired concern a fair degree of post-acquisition autonomy.

Expansionist acquisitions classified as 'horizontal' typified firms in foods and clothing. These included planned acquisitions, expressing expansionist policies to increase the acquirer's market share. Often negotiation was initiated by the acquired company, making search procedure unnecessary. Complete post-acquisition integration was more common than in 'diversification' acquisitions because of the greater opportunities for combining and centralizing similar or linked activities. 'Integration' type acquisitions occurred mostly in the textile sector as planned takeovers generally without a search for candidates. Those unplanned were 'opportunistic' acquisitions of known companies undertaken to protect supplies.

What typical circumstances were associated with such output expansions in the companies acquired? First, in 59 out of 62 cases the acquiring company intended to expand production at all or some of the inherited factories after takeover. Expansion was not a response to opportunities arising after, but was an anticipated and planned consequence of, acquisition. Some firms publicized this intention during takeover negotiations to ensure trade union cooperation, to avoid rumours of closure and to avoid loss of a skilled labour force which had often been the attraction from the outset. Second, although expansion was usually associated with new investment in plant and machinery (82 per cent of cases), the scale of capital commitment by the acquirer was small (a median of £0.2 million). *Most expansion was attributed by acquirers to the application of better management practices and more efficient use of existing assets, rather than to large capital transfers from the acquiring to the acquired firms.* Third, employment increases were even less common than new investment in acquisition-related expansions. New labour was recruited in fewer than half the cases, and in 16 per cent of the cases employment actually declined: indeed the average decreases (median 55) was more than double the average increase (median 22). Nevertheless six expansions did result from significant investment (transferred or guaranteed by the acquiring company) and employment growth in a completely new plant built by the acquired company, usually as part of a strategy to penetrate a new regional market. This may be construed as a 'sub-model' of the acquisition-related expansion model generalized here. One example was a West Midlands firm specializing in refining used industrial oils: the increased capital borrowing power offered after its acquisition by a large chemical company enabled it to open a branch plant in South Wales to tap a new market.

What were the regional implications of acquisition-related increases in output? This spatial change most obviously benefits the region in which the expanded acquired factory is located: increased employment or productivity, income, intraregional linkages and hence multiplier effects. Although usually a 'short-term' immediate consequence of takeover, benefits to the regional economy are sustained in the long term: in 15 per cent of the cases studied, increases in output were a 'continuous' process following acquisition, in another 18 per cent, expansion still occurred two to four years after takeover. Since takeovers typically lead to production expansion via improvements in management quality, expanding firms subsequently operate in a more planned environment with closer scrutiny of investment proposals and some reduction of uncertainties. New management can achieve more efficient resource use and to improve per capita productivity, possibly at the expense of short-term employment reduction. More significant are the implications for long-term stability: the acquired firm will become more competitive in external markets, less vulnerable in economic recession and better able to borrow capital resources within a larger organization.

Such clearly regional development implications must be qualified by an important caveat. Often production expansion at an acquired factory formed only part of wider reorganization of the acquired company's facilities and functions, *the effects of which have been negative in greater vulnerability to the same region that benefits from expansion.* In one quarter of the cases – commonest in foods (5 cases) and chemicals (7) – increased production capacity at a plant was associated with that plant losing all significant management and administrative functions, becoming in effect a branch plant – albeit an enlarged one. Another form of reorganization resulted when expansion at one factory was associated with reduced output at, or closure of, other factories of the acquired company, or even of the acquirer: ten cases fitted this model (see later), typically production capacity being rationalized into a modern or larger factory to raise productivity or to reduce communication costs. Commonly the closed plant was in the same standard region as the expanded one, resulting in lost employment.

Regional distribution of acquisition-related expansion sheds further light on its spatial implication (Table 13.4). An interesting statistic is the proportion of

Table 13.4 Acquisition-related expansions by region of acquired firm's headquarters

Acquiring company	Acquired companies										
	S.E.	S.W.	E.A.	E.M.	W.M.	N.W.	N.	Y.H.	W.	Sc.	N.I.
S.E.	10 31%		2	1	1	9 82%		1		3 37%	1
S.W.											
E.A.	2									1	
E.M.	1			2 29%							
W.M.									1	1	
N.W.	1				1	10 62%		3		1	
N.	1										
Y.H.				1		2		1		1	
W.											
Sc.										4 80%	
N.I.											
Totals	15 34%		2 50%	4 25%	2 50%	21 68%		5 36%	1	12 57%	1

Number in each cell = number of takeovers resulting in expansion.
Percentage figures = proportion of total takeovers per regional cell.

acquisitions made in a region that eventually involved expansion (the percentage figure). When the acquired firm was a multi-plant enterprise, often its expanded factory was not in the same region as its head office. Thus Table 13.5 gives the locations of the acquired *factories* which were expanded and shows the proportion that these form of all acquired factories in each region (percentage figure).

What are the patterns that emerge and what is their significance? The sample is really too small in most regional cells of Tables 13.4 and 13.5 to permit inferences. Comment here is restricted only to those regions in which the total of acquired firms or factories exceeded ten. The North West and South East appeared to benefit most from production expansion with 21 and 15 respectively of their acquired firms being expanded (together, three-fifths of all the expansionist

Table 13.5 Acquisition-related expansions by region of expanded factory

Acquiring company	Acquired factories										
	S.E.	S.W.	E.A.	E.M.	W.M.	N.W.	N.	Y.H.	W.	Sc.	N.I.
S.E.	10 27%	4 80%				10 (1) 59%	1 13%		(2)	7 (1) 58%	1
S.W.											
E.A.	2									2	
E.M.	1		2 20%								
W.M.									1	(1)	
N.W.	1			1		10 44%		3 38%	1		
N.	1										
Y.H.			(1)			1 8%		1 13%		1 14%	
W.											
Sc.										4 36%	
N.I.											
Totals	15 28%	4 67%	3 11%	2 18%		21 39%	1 25%	5 19%	3	16 43%	1

Number in each cell = number of factories expanded.
Percentage figure = proportion of total acquired factories for each regional cell.
Bracketed number = number of new branch factories established post-acquisition.

takeovers). Scotland (12 cases) was third. Yet this somewhat conventional picture alters in relative terms: the North West enjoyed a much higher proportion of expansionist acquisitions than did the South East (68 per cent compared to 34 per cent). The margin is smaller but again favours the North West in the proportion of acquired factories that were expanded (39 per cent and 28 per cent).

The attributes of acquisitions in each region explains the over-representation of the North West and under-representation of the South East. Two-thirds of the 'within region' acquisitions in the North West led to subsequent output expansion by thriving, medium-size, entrepreneurial style firms, chiefly in chemicals and textiles, deliberately expanding their interests both horizontally and vertically by acquiring less successful local companies. Expansion invariably followed takeover by such 'lead firms' and benefits the regional economy for reasons outlined: continued independence of such firms could be of great significance for the North West. Similarly, four-fifths of takeovers of North West firms by South East firms led to subsequent expansion. Without exception, these were made by large national or international companies (though not conglomerates) with London headquarters: two thirds were by textile firms. Large South East companies continually seek either to acquire either well-managed, efficiently-run, smaller firms which flourish in the North West with reputable competitive products or as key suppliers of materials. The high probability of expansion suggests that this acquisition process does little to harm the North West's industrial prospects.

The South East acquisitions are different. Ten of the thirty-two intra-regional acquisitions which led to expansion were in the fast-growing chemicals sector well established there. 'Within-region' acquisitions in clothing and foods in the South East were often followed by closures or no expansion. Clothing takeovers were typically 'horizontal' by wholesaling and retailing companies seeking increased profits from acquiring specialists in high quality garments mostly in Central and Inner London at a time of zero growth. Foods acquisitions mostly involved diversification out of the food sector with little subsequent expansion of the acquired company. Thus the different incidence of expansionist acquisitions between the North West and South East is largely explained in the different sectoral composition of the two regions and in the variations in sector performance during the period studied. From the national perspective, one 'problem' region (the North West) has benefited more from acquisition-related expansion than has the South East region (Fig. 13.2).

Experience in other regions varied. Scotland has an above average rate of expansionist acquisitions (57 per cent of 44 per cent for the whole sample) largely because expansion almost invariably followed intra-regional Scottish acquisitions. Scotland fares better than any other region (except East Anglia) in the proportion of acquired factories which underwent expansion (43 per cent compared to 32 per cent for the whole sample), most plant expansions being made there by South East-based acquirers, indicating an analogous situation to that existing between the North West and South East. Only 11 per cent of the factories in the East Midlands which underwent a change of ownership experienced post-acquisition expansion (even by South East firms) because most were in the stagnant clothing sector.

Two conclusions emerge from the regional incidence of expansionist acquisitions: (1) the peripheral regions have not been disadvantaged by post-acquisition changes in production levels and indeed the North West and Scotland have experienced higher rates of post-acquisition expansion than the South East, East Midlands and West Midlands; (2) a switch to 'external control' of the factories of a region was not subsequently associated with lower levels of production expansion as compared with a retention of 'intra-regional' control.

The change of product at acquired factories

Another type of 'spatial change' occurs where the product range manufactured at the acquired factories after takeover is altered significantly: rationalization may drop product lines or transfer them to, while diversification introduces a new line from other locations in the acquired or in the acquiring group. In the sample, rationalization was marginally more common than diversification: factory re-equipment or different use of existing fixed capital occurred in 21 out of the 141 cases studied (15 per cent), making it the least common – yet significant – spatial consequence. Many attributes of this change resemble those of 'production expansions' but some specific features deserve mention: (1) The timing of product changes after the date of acquisition resembled that of production expansion: 76 per cent occurred within three years of takeover. (2) So, too, was the sectoral breakdown of absolute production changes, being greatest in textiles followed by food, least in clothing. (3) All types of acquisition (horizontal, diversification, integration) were equally likely to lead to post-acquisition changes of product. Horizontal acquisitions usually resulted in phasing out fringe products, marginally profitable or low-volume lines and over-specialized lines which were 'misfits' in the product mix being developed or marketed by the acquirer, so giving greater product standardization. (4) The behavioural background of the acquisitions causing product changes was similar in initiative, planning and searching to those leading to product expansions.

Yet some post-acquisition circumstances were distinctive. First, a high rate of post-acquisition management integration occurred in 13 of the 21 cases: changes of product seem to need (or to reflect) a higher-than-usual degree of involvement by the acquirer in the subsequent running of the acquired company. Second, although 80 per cent of product changes were intended before acquisition, a minority were not and often followed intra-group reorganization of production after another takeover. Third, whilst two-thirds of all product changes demanded some new investment, this was actually less than was associated with straight-forward production expansions and the likelihood of an employment increase was smaller also. This reflects the contrary trend towards both product simplification or rationalization of product lines and additional product lines which could be achieved without extra capital or labour.

Conclusions on the regional distribution of acquisition-related product changes are qualified by the few cases studied. There is no apparent tendency for intra-regional, rather than extra-regional, acquisitions to generate changes and no obvious correlation with peripheral regions. Yorkshire and Humberside region had the highest proportion (36 per cent) of acquisition leading to production changes, resulting from corporate reorganization to concentrate production into the region's modern factories. The regional implications of such spatial change are positive since planned rationalization and phasing out of marginal product lines imply higher productivity and concentration on lines with maximum growth prospects, though this may require a reduced labour force. Changes which involve additional or totally new lines imply diversification or regional output and entry into new markets and hence greater business cycle stability.

Closure of factories of acquired firms

Forty-seven of the 141 acquisitions studied involved closures of 61 acquired factories. This, one-third of acquisitions, is lower than the two-fifths discovered by Rake's study of East Midlands' firms (Rake, 1972). Evidence here is thus a useful corrective to the popular belief that acquisition leads to mass closures, asset stripping and redundancies. In this sample, acquisition has more often resulted in expansion of output from acquired plants. Yet closure was just as immediate a consequence of takeover as was factory expansion when it occurred, in 21 of the 47 cases within a year. Closure was most common in food industries (14 of the 47 cases) but there was limited intersectoral contrast. Surprisingly firms in the slower growth and more cyclical textiles industry showed a slightly lower incidence of plant closures after acquisitions than did the firms in other sectors. Closures were rarest when the acquiring company was large (one quarter of acquirers with turnovers exceeding £50 million made closures decisions) and commonest for medium-size acquirers: two-fifths of acquirers with turnovers between £6 million and £50 million made closures. They resulted more from horizontal (42 per cent) acquisitions in the cyclical clothing industry than from growth-oriented diversification (33 per cent) acquisitions. It also reflected behaviour by acquiring foods firms which expressed purposeful horizontal expansion into related product lines or into new geographical markets through rationalized production. Only 60 per cent of the 47 plant closure cases were intended by the acquiring company before takeover (compared to 95 per cent of production expansions). The other 40 per cent of cases were 'unintended' and were a consequence of altered and adverse post-acquisition economic environment: poor textile and clothing trading conditions in the 1970s. Thus 'industrial sector' not 'poor acquisition procedures' explains most unintended closures.

The typical circumstances associated with plant closure in acquired companies is best discussed by recognizing four distinct types, or sub-models, of acquisition-related closure. First, unintended 'negative' closures (one quarter of the total) made by clothing and textile firms, which made no related compensating expansions elsewhere in the corporate system: it involved the sale of factories and plant, the sacking of labour and occasionally liquidation of the acquired company. Second, was the classic 'asset-strip' with a firm being acquired with the prior intention of liquidating the business and selling apparently under-valued assets to make a quick profit: only three cases, all opportunistic acquisitions not part of some 'search and destroy' policy, suggesting limited spatial implications of such behaviour.

Third, the most common type (two thirds) of closure involved 'closure with rationalization': intended closure of the acquired company's factory was partially offset by expansion of production elsewhere in the enlarged company, typically by rationalizing among several sites and increasing production at more modern or best-located factories. Elimination of overheads and achievement of scale economies were major motive together with profits to be made from selling vacated sites. This process occurred in all sectors and in both horizontal and diversification acquisitions. Closures yielded local redundancies but simultaneously production was expanded either at remaining factories in the acquired company (one third of the cases), at other established sites within the corporate system (two-fifths) or at completely new sites chosen post-acquisition (one quarter). In over half of the cases, machinery was transferred from the closed to the expanded plant, while new investment went into the expanded plant in one-third of the cases. In another third, labour was transferred to the expanded site, mostly key production workers and managers.

A final sub-model is a variation on 'closure with rationalization'. Diversification takeovers of small chemicals and foods firms occurred largely to acquire not existing factories but management skills, trading contacts or products with development potential, subsequent exploitation of which implied their closure.

Acquisition sometimes has a direct negative effects upon the local economy of the acquired firm. The 47 cases studied averaged 95 redundancies per acquisition or 64 per factory closed. Even where closure was associated with transfer of staff elsewhere, a loss resulted of skilled or professional job opportunities locally. Acquisition which transferred a promising new product away from an acquired firm for development and production elsewhere is also arguably negative to the regional economy, representing the loss of its 'seed bed' firms and industries. Three qualifications must be set against these obvious negative effects. First, any factory closure releases regional resources for use in other, productive lines of activity. More definite data was available about the use of released factories and sites: most were sold for other industrial or for residential development. Second, most closed factories were marginal and probably would have been liquidated, particularly in clothing and textiles: acquisition-related closure was thus a better form of adjustment for the regional economy in allowing more orderly rundown of business, transfer of useful stocks, machinery and personnel and more knowledgeable sale of assets. Third, closure with rationalization essentially transferred production (in 70 per cent of cases) to another factory site *in the same region*. Thus, while redundancies at the abandoned site were not fully offset by extra labour employed in production expansion in the same region, the effect on regional output, extra-regional sales, income and linked-industry or final demand multipliers was not wholly negative. However, if the greater productivity was translated into higher profit margins, these would leak out to another head-quarters region for disbursement, so stunting regional multiplier effects.

What was the regional incidence of the sample of acquisition-related closures? Table 13.6 records the locations of the headquarters of the acquired and acquiring

Table 13.6   Acquisition related factory closures by region of acquired firms headquarters

Acquiring company	Acquired companies										
	S.E.	S.W.	E.A.	E.M.	W.M.	N.W.	N.	Y.H.	W.	Sc.	N.I.
S.E.	12 38%			3	1 9%	2				2 25%	
S.W.											
E.A.	1									1	
E.M.				3 43%							
W.M.	1										
N.W.	1					5 31%	1	1		1	
N.	1						1				
Y.H.					1	2		2 29%		3	
W.											
Sc.										2	
N.I.											
Totals	16 36%			6 38%	1 25%	8 26%	4 100%	3 21%		9 43%	

Number in each cell = number of takeovers resulting in closure.
Percentage figure = proportion of total takeovers per regional cell.

companies, and gives the proportion of acquired firms in each region that subsequently experienced closure (percentage figure). Table 13.7 gives the exact regional location of all factories closed and indicating the percentage these form of all the factories acquired in each standard region.

The South East region suffered twice as many closures as any other region (16 firms and 19 factories), followed in decreasing order by Scotland, the North West and the East Midlands. The more realistic proportional figures show that acquired firms headquartered in Scotland (43 per cent), the East Midlands (38 per cent) and the South East (36 per cent) experienced significantly higher rates of post-acquisition closure than did those of the North West (26 per cent) and Yorkshire and Humberside (21 per cent). Since the factories closed were often located in regions different from the acquired firms' headquarters, the most meaningful set of

Table 13.7 Acquisition related closures by region of closed factory

Acquiring company	Acquired factories										
	S.E.	S.W.	E.A.	E.M.	W.M.	N.W.	N.	Y.H.	W.	Sc.	N.I.
S.E.	15 (3) 41%	1		3 (2) 33%		2 12%	2 (1)	2 25%		2 (1) 17%	
S.W.											
E.A.	1 20%									1 (1)	
E.M.				6 (6) 60%						1	
W.M.	2	1			1	1					
N.W.	1			1 (1)		4 (3) 17%	1	4 50%			
N.							1				
Y.H.					1 (1)	2 (1) 8%		2		3 (1) 14%	
W.											
Sc.										2 18%	
N.I.											
Totals	19 (3) 36%	2		10 (9) 36%	2 (1) 18%	9 (4) 17%	4 (1) 100%	8 30%		9 (3) 24%	

Number in each cell = number of closed factories.
Percentage figure = proportion of total acquired factories for each regional cell which were closed.
Bracketed number = number of 'negative closures' (see text).

statistics is the regional breakdown of factory closure rates. From these figures, the East Midlands clearly suffered most from post-acquisition closures (36 per cent), the majority being 'negative', unintended closures by clothing firms facing surplus capacity and shrinking profit margins during the 1973–4 recession. Superficially the South East suffers as badly (36 per cent of acquired factories being closed), but the impact was moderated since 16 of the 19 closures were of the 'rationalization' type, especially among food companies (7 closed factories).

Despite the high proportion of its locally-headquartered firms experiencing post-acquisition closures, Scotland actually had a relatively low proportion of factory closures (24 per cent) relative to the total number of acquired factories located there. The basic reason is that Scotland had a much larger number of acquired factories than acquired firms. Takeovers by non-Scottish firms (especially South East and Yorkshire-based firms) of other non-Scottish multi-plant firms sometimes involved the inheritance of a factory located in Scotland; in these instances, Scottish factories were seldom closed. Furthermore, the five intra-regional acquisitions in Scotland involved eleven acquired factories, only two of which were later closed. Thus Scotland appears to suffer less from closures than

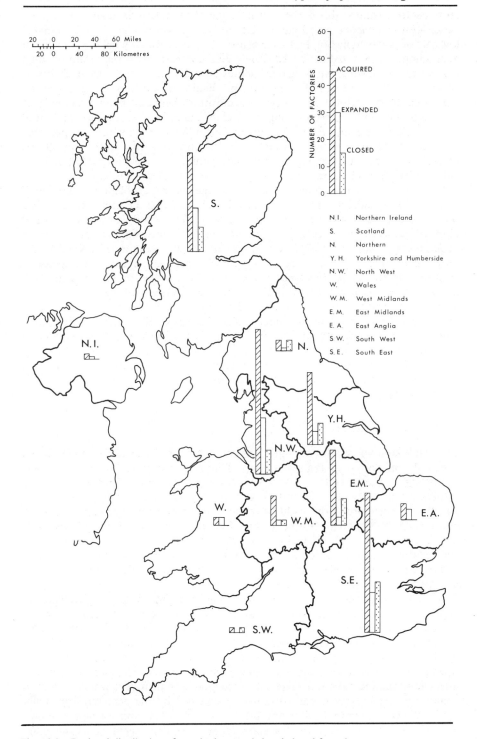

Fig. 13.2   Regional distribution of acquired, expanded and closed factories.

more central regions: this is the mirror image of the relatively high rate of post-acquisition expansions noted earlier. Similarly, the North West had a relatively low rate of post-acquisition factory closures (17 per cent), very few resulting from acquisitions by South East-based firms. This contrasts with the relatively high closure rate following intra-regional acquisitions in the South East itself but is consistent with the pattern discussed for production expansions, being largely attributable to the sectoral differences in acquisitions between the two regions: the closure-prone clothing sector and the rationalizing food sector are both well represented in the South East, whereas the North West benefits from the presence of textile firms with growth potential. Thus takeovers of North West firms, whether by other leading North West companies or by South East firms, invariably led to production expansions, very rarely to plant closures (Fig. 13.2).

Thus no consistent pattern of closures emerges in the 'problem' or 'peripheral' regions. Some had low rates of closure, lower even than central regions, while others experienced high rates. No clear pattern appears either in volume or rate of closures between intra-regional and inter-regional acquisitions: intra-regional acquisitions in most regions more often resulted in closures than did 'long-range', 'external' or 'inter-regional' acquisitions. One can refute, therefore, the hypothesis that acquisition implies increased vulnerability to closure for factories that are nationally remote or are distant in the corporate geography of the acquiring firm. The size and age of plant and product competitiveness were major considerations in closure irrespective of location, while the scale of possible redundancy payments and the opportunities for disposal of the factory site could also influence the choice. Occasionally, when a spatial factor determined closure, it was usually the specific problem of management communication and supervision resulting from long distance separation of an acquired factory from the acquiring firm's headquarters.

Linkage adjustments

The final kind of spatial change considered here is adjustment made to the acquired firm's physical and service (input) linkages and marketing contacts (output linkages) after takeover. *A priori* takeover presents opportunities for linkage rationalization between acquired and acquiring organizations: suppliers and agents of the acquired firm might be replaced by those of the acquiring group, so benefiting large national (relative to small local) businesses, especially if spending decisions become the responsibility of a central buying division. The survey showed that while acquisition often rearranges or consolidates service linkages on to the acquiring company's suppliers, material linkages are little affected directly and usually maintain their pre-acquisition pattern.

In almost 85 per cent of takeovers, service linkages (auditing, banking, legal, insurance, advertising, market advice, transport, security and maintenance services) the established links of the acquired firm were severed and transferred to the acquiring group's suppliers, usually to a large established supplier located in the headquarters region of the acquiring company. If the acquirer was large, then maintenance, legal service and marketing were internalized. Such adjustments immediately followed takeover. The sole exception was transport which tended to continue to be supplied locally and hence managed by the acquired firm. Only when the acquirer ran its own transport fleet which could cater for new demands was there an alteration in transport supply arrangements. Diversification acquisitions by relatively small acquirers account for most cases where service linkages remained local (15 per cent). The regional pattern of service linkage-rearrangement obviously reflected the spatial distribution of the headquarters of acquired firms relative to the headquarters of acquirers. Half the service transfers were intra-regional, often involving a shift from town suppliers to provincial capital suppliers (e.g. to Manchester-based suppliers in the North West, to Leeds-based suppliers in the Yorkshire–Humberside region) which, in turn, were commonly branches of national professional service organizations. Other transfers were inter-regional: the acquired firm was now serviced by professional organizations located in the headquarters region of the acquirer, usually the South East. Such service linkage adjustments reinforce the effects of managerial transfer. The main 'linkage impact' of acquisitions is felt by the local service suppliers of the acquired firm as changes favour the large 'chain' professional service organizations with headquarters in London and branches in larger provincial cities, so generating a cumulative process of falling demand and reduced supply of specialist services in lower-order centres and peripheral regions which is harmful to their structural balance of employment and future growth potential.

Material input patterns were not often (18 per cent) altered directly by acquisitions: most firms regard materials purchase as a middle-to-low management function best left at the level of the acquired firm or factory. Managers then 'shop around' for the 'best buy' and are as likely to maintain traditional, as to develop new, linkages. Yet there is no evidence that takeovers caused any major reorganization of material linkages, centralization of purchases, or shift of trade from small regional to a few preferred bulk material suppliers. The regional implications are thus indeed positive, given that production expansion is a common consequence of takeover, so that established suppliers of acquired companies (including local suppliers) can expect to share in such expansion. Qualifying this, however, some food and chemicals firms are tied to a very limited range of national suppliers and the question of loss or gain of trade for local suppliers does not apply. Material linkages were most likely to be rearranged if the acquirer was a large chemical or food company and if acquired companies maintained only the lowest degree of post-acquisition autonomy: over one third of the 38 acquisitions that left the acquired firm with only 'routine management' functions resulted in significant material input changes which favoured the acquiring companies suppliers compared with only 5 per cent of the cases characterized by a 'high degree' of post-acquisition management autonomy.

Only the broadest generalizations are possible about changes in market (output) linkages: except in cases of liquidation customers of the acquired firm stayed with the enlarged organization. Any change added new customers to the acquired firm's market, usually by extending the geographical range of sales. Rarely were established customers abandoned, or completely new customers or market areas gained – not surprising since most acquisitions were of horizontal or diversification types and made for expansionist motives to acquire a firm's resources, products and markets. A geographical expansion of markets (from regional to national, or national to international levels) after acquisition was usually achieved by integrating the acquired company's sales force and marketing effort into the larger marketing system of the acquirer, allowing the acquired firm's products to be 'carried into' market areas already served by the acquirer, alongside existing products, and rapidly penetrating new markets. The regional implications are clearly positive: enhanced sales volumes and more diversified market outlets via larger and probably more efficient marketing organizations. Major reorganization or concentration of markets was uncommon except in a few clear-cut circumstances. Some 'backward integration' acquisitions involving textile firms resulted in the acquired firm forfeiting all its former customers to become a supplying unit within an integrated textile combine. Horizontal acquisitions by foods firms occasionally led to market-area rationalization, customers distant from the acquired plant being served at lower transport costs for another nearer plant in the parent group. When a multi-product company was acquired commonly the acquirer would rationalize the product mix by dropping low volume, low profit or difficult-to-market items. In the medium term at least, such product rationalizations enhance the economic stability of the acquired firms and seem to benefit the regional economies involved.

Regional implications: synthesis and conclusions

That the immediate consequence of acquisition for the acquired firm's region is more often positive than negative is a conclusions based on only 141 case studies and such optimism may be biased by responses from more successful firms involved in acquisition activity. Acquisition commonly generated output expansion by improving management practices and investment at the acquired site. Additions to local product lines and sectoral or geographical expansion of markets were also common, having immediate negative impacts, counteracted however by some 'closures-with-rationalization' localizing production at other factories in the same region. More uncertain for the long-term prospects of a region are the negative effects of the transfer of managerial control and staff and internalization of service linkages. The former results in external control over the redistribution of profits and major investment decisions and local losses of top-level job and entrepreneurial opportunities. The latter reduces some local multiplier effects, atrophies local services so that they cannot become a significant external economy attraction to other enterprises. All such changes imply a less healthy environment for sustained regional growth. Nevertheless, some provincial regions (such as the North West) enjoyed more encouraging short-term experience than the traditional growth region of the South East, at least for the four industrial sectors studied. Yet significantly the 'home' region of active acquirers making extra-regional acquisitions, the South East, derives the long-term benefits from the transfer of management control and the internalization of service linkages. Scotland, Wales and the Northern region suffer net losses from this transfer process and hence from increasing dependence on the core region. This is strongest in those peripheral regions that have no active acquiring firms of their own to compensate for the loss of their local firms.

References

Ansoff, H. *et al.* (1971), *Twenty Years of Acquisition Behaviour in America*, Cassel, London.
Brue, S. (1971), *Local Economic Impact of Corporate Mergers*, Unpublished Ph.D. thesis, University of Nebraska.
Business Monitor (1973), *Acquisitions and Mergers of Industrial and Commercial Companies*, Government Statistical Service, HMSO, London.
Channon, D. F. (1973), *The Strategy and Structure of British Enterprise*, Macmillan, London.

Dicken, P. (1976), 'The multi-plant business enterprise and geographical spaces: some issues in the study of external control and regional development', *Regional Studies,* **10.**

Firn, J. (1975), 'External control and regional development: the case of Scotland', *Environment and Planning,* **7.**

Hamilton, F. E. I. (1974), 'A view of spatial behaviour, industrial organizations and decision-making', in: F. E. I. Hamilton, ed., *Spatial Perspectives on Industrial Organization and Decision-Making,* Wiley, London.

Hart, P. E., Utton, M. and Walshe, M. (1973), *Mergers and Concentration in British Industry,* Cambridge U.P., London.

Jackson, R. (1975), *A Profile of Acquisitions in the Textiles Sector 1973,* Middlesex Polytechnic, Industrial Location Research Project, Working Paper 5.

Keeble, D. E. (1971), 'Employment mobility in Britain', in: M. Chisholm and G. Manners, eds., *Spatial Policy Problems of the British Economy,* Cambridge U.P., London.

Kitchen, J. (1974), 'Why acquisitions are abortive', *Management Today,* November, pp. 82–7.

Leigh, R. (1975), *A Profile of Acquisitions in the Clothing Sector in 1973,* Middlesex Polytechnic, Industrial Location Research Project, Working Paper 6.

Leigh, R. and North, D. J. (1975), *A Framework for the Study of the Spatial Aspects of Acquisition Activity in Manufacturing Industry,* Middlesex Polytechnic, Industrial Location Research Project, Working Paper 1.

North, D. J. (1974), 'The proces of locational change in different manufacturing organizations', in: F. E. I. Hamilton, ed., *Spatial Perspectives on Industrial Organization and Decision-Making,* Wiley, London.

North, D. J. (1975*a*), *A Profile of Acquisitions in the Chemicals Sector in 1973,* Middlesex Polytechnic, Industrial Research Project, Working Paper 4.

North, D. J. (1975*b*), *Acquisitions and Spatial Change,* Middlesex Polytechnic, Industrial Location Research Project, Working Paper 8.

Parker, D. J. (1975), *A Profile of Acquisitions in the Food Sector in 1973,* Middlesex Polytechnic, Industrial Location Research Project, Working Paper No. 3.

Parsons, G. (1972), 'The giant manufacturing corporations and balanced regional growth in Britain', *Area,* **4** (2), pp. 99–103.

Pred, A. (1974), *Major Job-Providing Organisations and Systems of Cities,* Commission on College Geography Resource Paper No. 27, A.A.A.G., Washington.

Rake, D. (1972), *Economic Geography of the Multi Locational Firm,* unpublished Ph.D. thesis, University of Nottingham.

Singh, A. (1971), *Takeovers: their Relevance to the Stock Market and the Theory of the Firm,* Department of Applied Economics, Monograph No. 19, Cambridge U.P.

Westaway, J. (1974), 'The spatial hierarchy of business organisations and its implications for the British Urban System', *Regional Studies,* **8,** (2), pp. 145–55.

Chapter 14

Location, urban size and industrial productivity: a case study of Brazil

Sergio Boisier

The significance of spatial differentiation of both productivity and industrial wages in Brazil is examined for the period 1967–69. Relationships between industrial productivity and urban size are also quantitatively analysed for over 200 Brazilian cities, using information theory. In Brazil, spatial variation is more important for wages than for productivity, but technology is still very important in explaining divergences between productivity and wages. Yet there are increasing returns between productivity and urban size for medium-sized cities, decreasing returns for cities of larger size. Certain crucial inferences are derived regarding the content of national regional-development policy.

Basic questions on regional development

Recent literature amply comments on regional development regarding the change in the *scale of operation* in regional planning which has evolved from the intra-regional towards an inter-regional approach (Kuklinski, 1967; De Mattos, 1970; Hilhorst, 1971; Stöhr, 1972; Boisier, 1972). Leaving aside conceptual problems, in operational terms the new approach has meant a growing tendency towards the adoption of national regional-development policies which are conceived as steering and controlling the economic and social change process in the entire regional system. As often happens in social sciences, this new outlook for action has appeared surrounded by an aura of respectability which exceeds its possibilities. For economic planners, who are always disillusioned, the national concept of regional planning is 'exactly what was lacking for planning to function in reality'. This dialectical process of illusion–disillusion in the development field is well described by Utria (1972) from Latin American experience. Unfortunately national regional-development plans – though fashionable in Latin America – are quite superficial because they lack the backing of theoretical and empirical knowledge of economic–spatial processes. Most plans *suppose* certain types of behaviour on the basis of slogans, dogmas or simply intuition. If the variables actually behave differently from that supposed, the inter-regional approach will be officially declared obsolete a few years hence and a new hope sought in monotonous, tiresome repetition of something *déjà vu*.

Plans usually assume that some regional underdevelopment problems are solved by simple (but sometimes costly) creation of labour opportunities in the poorest areas. Few formulate in advance the unavoidable question of whether the local labour is unemployed through lack of work opportunities or through poor nutrition, health and training conditions which prevents its access even to the non-

182

specialized labour market. Worse still, all national regional-development plans implicitly start with extremely simple structures and activity levels in each of the regional sub-systems: they assume that some regions are *overall* more or less developed than others, i.e. 'region A is three times more developed than region B'. Seldom is it recognized that regional socio-economic structure is a complex network of relationships between developed or modern elements (sectors, social groups, activities) and underdeveloped or primary elements. Consequently, the policies for each region (within the inter-regional scheme) are formulated in highly homogeneous, generalized terms as if the problem were to lift the *entire* region to another level.

Alternatively, development plans suppose that space acts as a differentiating element in all economic processes and variables. Naturally this encourages advocacy of regional disaggregation of the global plans and policies – a legitimate procedure in many cases but completely counteractive in others (Kuklinski, 1974). In short, a national regional-development plan should be conceived 'between the men and the median', i.e. with a flexible combination of global policies in certain cases and for certain regions, and of regionalization of global and sectoral policies in other cases, plus purely global, non-spatial handling of other variables.

The research (Boisier, 1973) for this chapter attempts to analyse quantitatively the spatial conduct of two important economic variables: industrial productivity and industrial wages. The main justification for their selection is this. The spatial structure of a country is the result of interaction between natural elements (the supply and distribution of resources, topographical accessibility, climate, land) and a series of political, sociological, economic and cultural processes. 'Economic landscape' is largely the fruit of societal impact on the environment. At some stage of development, the spatial structure begins to conflict with a society's values and objectives, most usually between the consequences of spatial economic concentration and the egalitarian objectives of society. This explains the upsurge of regional development policies as attempts at a social response to the problem. In Brazil the huge size of the country and the existence therein of enormous empty spaces are additional justifications for the need to devise a national regional-development policy. If such policy intends to modify the 'spatial structure' it should specifically concentrate attention upon those components of the spatial structure which are most susceptible to locational control and steering. Hence the emphasis on the industrial sector since manufacturing, aside from its multiplier effects, offers considerably greater freedom than do most other activities.

Thus a major instrument of conscious regional development effort should be a *spatially-defined* industrialization policy, designed to both locate and relocate industries within the nation. Structural and functional knowledge is a *sine qua non* requisite for identifying the instruments of control as the efficacy of a policy significantly depends on the level of knowledge of the process on which the policy will act. Neither the objectives nor the means can be efficiently selected without such knowledge – yet in many countries spatial industrialization policies take the simplistic form of a set of incentives to location with no clear perception of the merits of either such incentives or of other correlative variables whose behaviour should be influenced if industrialization is really going to produce positive results in a given geographical area.

Productivity and wages are both key parameters in an industrial location policy which, in turn, is a key element in a regional development policy. Are some regions less productive than others? What degree of spatial differentiation should be introduced into a wage policy or into a productivity promotion policy? What is the relationship between urban size and industrial productivity? What is the threshold on which agglomeration diseconomies reflect themselves on productivity levels? Can 'concentrated deconcentration' be quantitatively justified in cities of medium size? In Latin America there are few efforts to answer these questions quantitatively, except in Columbia (Manrique, 1970) and Venezuela (Centro de Estudios del Desarrollo, 1969).

Information supply and methodology

Selection of the period 1967–9 was conditioned by the availability of information on the overall behaviour of the Brazilian economy in that relatively 'normal' period of expansion. Most statistical data were from an annual survey of industry, *Produçao Industrial*, by the Brazilian Institute of Geography and Statistics. This analyses some 36 000 industrial units employing 2 million people or 85–90 per cent of all Brazilian industry.

To examine relationships between urban size and productivity, all the municipalities were selected with more than 75 per cent of their population in urban areas and with more than 95 per cent of their urban population living in the municipal centre. Adjustments were made in defining the large urban agglomerations of São Paulo, Rio de Janeiro, Recife, Belo Horizonte and Porto Alegro. Such procedure facilitated study of 222 urban centres with varying sizes from 1000 to over 6 million inhabitants. Work was also carried out for: 24 regional units (the States, the Federal District and the group of Roraima Amapa and Rondonia Territories); 21 industrial sectors (two digits of the IBGE classification); and 8 size-strata of industrial establishments. Urban data were also re-grouped into 9 urban size categories.

No sample is perfect, yet in no country in Latin America is it possible to count on such an abundant (and quick) supply of information about industry as in Brazil. There are, though, limitations to the data. First, the level of aggregation (two digits) prevents greater depth of analysis, though this is not serious for policy purposes. Second and more important, the published data do not allow calculation of the net value-added to factor cost nor do they give man-hours: thus productivity is estimated by simply comparing gross value added to market price with employment. Third, what the survey shows as 'wages' corresponds rather to the cost of employed personnel, only includes monetary payments, and does not differentiate between manual and office employees. These limitations do not noticeably affect the results: all figures are expressed in fixed 1969 prices.

The research is essentially descriptive and positive rather than normative, combining static analysis with the analysis of comparative statics. The operational methods used are derived from standard econometric analysis and information theory (Theil, 1967). The first research stage sought to quantify the relative importance of spatial distribution in explaining total heterogeneity deviations from the mean value of the variable of both productivity and industrial wages between sectors, states and cities and between sizes of establishments. The second examined the empirical functional association between urban size and productivity. Since current econometric methods are sufficiently well known, the use here of the entropy concept is merely summarized.

If data on productivity are examined by different categories of analyses (observe the possible matrices that are formed with the categories 'sectors', 'states' and 'sizes'), substantial variations become visible around the mean. The analysis seeks to examine the relative importance of differences 'between sectors', 'between states' (and between cities) and 'between establishment sizes' in explaining the total differences. 'Entropy' is the mean or expected content of the information, and for 'n' events with ex-ante probabilities $x_1, \ldots, x_n$, which are transformed by a message into *ex-post* probabilities $y_1, \ldots, y_n$, the entropy can be described by the expression:

$$I(y:x); \sum_{i}^{n} y_i \, \log \, y_i / x_i \tag{1}$$

If the notion of probability is replaced by the participations, both in employment (P_{ijk}) and in the value of industrial transformation (q_{ijk}), of establishments of size i localized in state (or city) j and belonging to sector k, the expression $I(q_{ijk}:p_{ijk})$ continues to be a measurement of the entropy whose maximum value (log $\cdot$ n) is reached when all the participants are equal. To obtain a measurement of inequality, expression (1) can be subtracted from its maximum value.

Now, considering any sector k localized in state j, the differences in productivity (or wages) existing among the several sizes i of establishments can be measured. The formula is given by the expression:

$$I_{ijk} = \sum_{i} \frac{P_{ijk}}{P_{jk}} \, \log \, \frac{P_{ijk}/P_{jk}}{q_{ijk}/q_{jk}} \tag{2}$$

being

$$p_{jk} = \sum_{i} p \quad \text{and} \quad q_{jk} = \sum_{i} q_{ijk} \tag{2}$$

Within any sector k the differences of productivity (or mean wages) between the different territorial units correspond to:

$$I_{kj} = \sum_{j} \frac{p_{kj}}{p_{\cdot k}} \, \log \, \frac{p_{kj}/p_{\cdot k}}{q_{jk}/q_{\cdot k}} \tag{3}$$

being

$$p_{\cdot k} = \sum_{i} \sum_{j} p_{ijk} \quad \text{and} \quad q_{\cdot k} = \sum_{i} \sum_{i} q_{ijk}$$

The differences of productivity (or wages) between industrial sectors only, once the influences of the differences between states (or cities) and sizes have been eliminated, are given by:

$$I_k = \sum_{k} p_{\cdot k} \, \log \, \frac{p_{\cdot k}}{q_{\cdot k}} \tag{4}$$

Now, expression (1) can be broken down as follows:

$$I = I + \sum_{k} p_{\cdot k} \, I_{kj} + \sum_{k} \sum_{j} p_{jk} \, I_{ijk} \tag{5}$$

or else

$$\sum_{i} \sum_{j} \sum_{k} p_{ijk} \, \log \frac{p_{ijk}}{q_{ijk}} = \sum_{k} p_{\cdot k} \, \log \frac{p_{\cdot k}}{q} +$$

$$\sum_k p_{..k} \sum_d \frac{p_{.jk}}{p_{..k}} \log \frac{p_{.jk}/p_{..k}}{q_{.jk}/q_{..k}} +$$

$$\sum_k \sum_j p_{jk} \sum_i \frac{p_{ijk}}{p_{.jk}} \log \frac{p_{ijk}/p_{jk}}{q_{ijk}/q_{.kj}} \tag{6}$$

In the foregoing expression, the first term on the right side measures that part of the total differences of productivity (or wages) that results from inter-sectoral differences that can be explained by differences of geographic distribution, within one and the same sector; lastly, the third term measures that part of the total differences that is explained by differences of size of establishments.

Table 14.1 Analysis of the differences observed in industrial productivity (State level)

Differences of productivity	1967		1968		1969	
	Abs.	%	Abs.	%	Abs.	%
Total heterogeneity	0.156 97	100.00	0.146 62	100.00	0.147 55	100.00
Breakdown A						
Between sectors	0.070 56	45.00	0.066 59	45.47	0.064 42	43.71
Between states within each sector	0.039 72	25.35	0.036 74	25.10	0.040 09	27.79
Between sizes within states and sectors	0.046 68	29.78	0.043 28	29.56	0.042 21	28.59
Breakdown B						
Between states	0.022 91	14.64	0.023 21	15.88	0.024 81	16.86
Between sectors within each state	0.087 37	55.71	0.080 12	54.69	0.080 54	54.63
Between sizes within sectors and states	0.046 68	29.78	0.043 28	29.56	0.042 19	28.64
Breakdown C						
Between sizes	0.015 14	9.69	0.017 02	11.65	0.020 19	13.73
Between sectors within each size	0.087 31	55.66	0.079 85	54.50	0.077 17	52.35
Between states within each sector and size	0.054 53	34.78	0.049 76	33.98	0.050 18	34.06

Source: CEPAL/IPEA: *Estructura Espacial y Productividad Industrial*, Rio de Janeiro, 1972.

Spatial variability of productivity and wages

The tables show the results of applying this methodology to the *state* data (Tables 14.1 and 14.2), and to the *urban* data, on productivity and wages (Tables 14.3 and 14.4). The first general observation derived from Table 14.1 is that the total heterogeneity tends to *diminish* between 1967 and 1969: differences in industrial productivity tend to lessen. Second, this results from the operation of several factors. Differences in productivity *between sectors* diminish in both absolute and relative values while differences in productivity *between states* increase both absolutely and relatively as do also differences in productivity *between sizes of establishments*. Thus the figures reflect one facet of the industrial concentration process that Brazil is currently experiencing.

Third, differences are in fact, less important than differences between sectors but are more important than the differences between strata of sizes of establishments in explaining total differences in industrial productivity. For example, the first breakdown (A) indicates that differences in productivity between petrochemicals and metallurgy are more significant than the differences between petrochemicals (metallurgy) in São Paulo and petrochemicals (metallurgy) in Bahia. The second breakdown (B) shows that differences in productivity between petrochemicals and metallurgy either in São Paulo or Bahia are more influential than the differences in average productivity between São Paulo and Bahia.

Highly significant conclusions emerge from Table 14.1. Specialized literature and political debate commonly magnify the effects of external regional economies in explaining both the higher productivity of certain regions and the persistent tendency for private entrepreneurs to locate investments in developed regions. Though the above figures do not measure externalities, they suggest less validity for this argument at the state level in Brazil. Regions cannot be more productive than others *per se*: what really exist are *regions with differing industrial mixes*. An efficient policy to promote productivity or to reduce the differences between productivity levels, could be conceived in *purely sectoral terms* with no evident need for spatial discrimination: intra-sectoral issues are more crucial than spatial problems of productivity. Regional planners should thus recognize the selective nature of a national regional-development policy, i.e. that the spatial behaviour of different processes may vary greatly and that the intra-regional behaviour of some variables may differ from their inter-regional behaviour.

Table 14.1 also infers the type of industrial growth that occurred between 1967 and 1969, though in rather generic terms. Differences in productivity between States increased by 8.3 per cent, while the differences between sectors diminished by 8.8 per cent and those between sectors within States fell by 7.2 per cent. These results suggest that increased industrial production between 1967 and 1969 occurred in large-scale establishments, chiefly in activities with relatively low productivity and located in States whose productivity level was slightly above average. The territorial division of Brazil into States is completely arbitrary from the economic viewpoint so that the geographic factor has little relevance in explaining total productivity differences: Table 14.1 confirms this. But stated another way, the fact that the *inter-State* differences in productivity have relatively little importance within the total does not mean that this is also true at the inter-regional or inter-municipal levels. Thus a real analysis of the *spatial sensitivity* of the differences in productivity was made between various geographical units for 1969.

Six divisions of Brazil were considered for that year in studying the 'spatial sensitivity' of inter-State differences in productivity as an explanatory hypothesis of total differences of productivity. Each represents a possible geographical division of the country, defined as aggregates of two or more States. The first comprises two areas: the State of São Paulo and the remainder of Brazil. The second partitions Brazil into four units according to their industrial homogeneity. The third delimits five units to coincide with the natural regions of Brazil. The fourth division comprises eight spaces randomly defined by the twenty-four basic areal units with which the project has worked. The fifth one defines eleven spaces according to industrial homogeneity. Finally, the sixth division contains twenty-four spatial units defined by calculations set out in Table 14.1.

The quantitative analysis – which is not set out here – yielded several facts. Total heterogeneity increases steadily as the number of spatial units in the analysis is raised. Next, differences in productivity between 'spaces' are relatively invariable, oscillating around 15 per cent, though the range of spatial units is quite high. In theory, the spatial sensitivity of any variable can be measured by the value of the slope of the straight line fit between the number of spaces and the differences between spaces. The logic of such a procedure rests on the premise that, if the variable is independent on any territorial division, the fit in question will show a straight line parallel to the X-axis. This method makes it possible to overcome some problems related to ecological correlation and is thus particularly apt for making international comparisons.

Table 14.2   Analysis of the differences observed in mean industrial wages (State level)

Wages differences	1967		1968		1969	
	Abs.	%	Abs.	%	Abs.	%
Total heterogeneity	0.087 99	100.00	0.086 88	100.00	0.098 13	100.00
Breakdown A						
Between sectors	0.045 51	51.77	0.044 49	51.25	0.052 24	53.29
Between states within each sector	0.023 92	27.23	0.023 78	27.42	0.027 12	27.69
Between sizes in each state and sector	0.018 56	21.14	0.018 61	21.47	0.018 75	19.11
Breakdown B						
Between states	0.032 42	36.89	0.033 81	38.97	0.038 61	39.40
Between sectors within each state	0.037 01	42.11	0.034 45	39.70	0.040 75	41.57
Between sizes in each sector and size	0.018 56	21.14	0.018 61	21.47	0.018 75	19.16
Breakdown C						
Between sizes	0.024 00	27.32	0.025 17	29.02	0.029 74	30.36
Between sectors within each size	0.039 98	45.49	0.037 06	42.71	0.042 60	43.47
Between states in each sector and size	0.024 00	27.32	0.024 64	26.41	0.025 77	26.31

Source: CEPAL/IPEA: *Estructura Espacial y Productividad Industrial*, Rio de Janeiro, 1972.

Table 14.2 presents the same analytical method but refers to average industrial wages. Wages differentials (total heterogeneity) increase noticeably between 1967 and 1969. Such wage dispersion results (but with different intensities) from differences between States, between sectors and between sizes of the industrial establishments. The increase in total heterogeneity during the period amounts to 11.5 per cent, in differences between sectors 14.8 per cent, while differences between States and between sizes of plants rose by 19.1 per cent and 23.9 per cent respectively. Table 14.2 also shows clearly that differences in the average wage *between sectors* constitute the most important element in explaining total differences. What is still more pertinent is *that the differences between States, though less important than the differences between sectors, represent an explanatory element of singular importance in the total context.* Breakdown B in Table 14.2 infers that while absolute differences in wages between sectors within each State increased by 10.1 per cent, their relative importance in the total fell from 42.1 per cent to 41.6 per cent between 1967 and 1969. For example, the wage differences between São Paulo and Bahia tend to increase as the wage differences between the petrochemicals and metallurgical sectors, either in São Paulo or Bahia, tend to diminish relatively. If these differences are detected by industrial workers, it would be most interesting to compare the situation in Table 14.2 with current migration movements. Differences in spatial sensitivity between States explain approximately 40 per cent of the total wage differential, but these could be the purely random result of study at State level. Differences between spatial units show relatively stable behaviour, oscillating around approximately 35 per cent.

Table 14.3   Analysis of the differences observed in industrial productivity (Urban level) 1969

Differences of productivity	Absolute value	Relative value
Total heterogeneity	0.117 13	100.00
Breakdown A		
Between sectors	0.058 66	50.13
Between classes of urban size within each sector	0.019 19	16.43
Between sizes of establishment within sectors and urban size	0.039 28	33.44
Breakdown B		
Between classes of urban size	0.015 94	13.66
Between sectors within each class of urban size	0.061 91	52.90
Between size of establishment within each class of urban size and sector	0.039 28	33.44
Breakdown C		
Between sizes of establishments	0.016 29	13.82
Between sectors within each size of establishments	0.068 99	58 94
Between classes of urban size within each sector and size of establishment	0.031 85	27.24

Source: CEPAL/IPEA: *Estructura Espacial y Productividad Industrial*, Rio de Janeiro, 1972.

Data are given in Tables 14.3 and 14.4 for the urban level. The discrepancy between the values of the total heterogeneity in Table 14.1 and in Table 14.3 obviously results from differences in coverage between the State and urban data. Without doubt, the three breakdowns of Table 14.3 indicate that sectoral differences in productivity are substantially more significant than differences between categories of urban size and of establishments. These results confirm those of Table 14.1, which is certainly interesting, always provided the urban centres appear here classified independently of their State location. The fact that breakdown B, for instance, shows that the differences in productivity between different city sizes only explain 13.66 per cent of the total heterogeneity is perfectly consistent with the econometric study set out below. Likewise, the results of the fits between productivity by groups of sectors and size of urban centres (given below) are consistent with breakdown A, showing that the differences in productivity between cities by size for one and the same sector only explain 16.43 per cent of the total heterogeneity.

Table 14.4   Analysis of the differences observed in mean industrial wages (Urban level) 1969

Wages differences	Absolute value	Relative value
Total heterogeneity	0.068 54	100.00
Breakdown A		
Between sectors	0.037 40	54.60
Between classes of urban size within each sector	0.015 31	22.39
Between sizes of establishments within sectors and urban size	0.015 83	23.01
Breakdown B		
Between classes of urban size	0.023 52	34.37
Between sectors within each class of urban size	0.029 19	42.61
Between size of establishments within each class of urban size and sector	0.015 83	23.02
Breakdown C		
Between size of establishments	0.017 07	24.83
Between sectors within each size of establishment	0.035 02	51.12
Between classes of urban size within each sector and size of establishment	0.016 45	24.05

Source: CEPAL/IPEA: *Estructura Espacial y Productividad Industrial*, Rio de Janeiro, 1972.

Theil's analysis facilitates study of what exactly occurs within each sector, i.e. breakdown A in Table 14.3, indicates that productivity differences between urban size categories *within each sector* attain a value of 0.019 19, equivalent to 16.43 per cent of the total. The sectors for which productivity differences between urban size classes are highest include chemicals, food products, textiles, metallurgy, non-metallic minerals and engineering, in that order. The sectors for which the urban inter-class productivity differences are less important include hides and furs, plastics, paper, timber, furniture, clothing and shoes, tobacco, soft drinks, electrical and transport equipment industries.

Similarly the analysis permits a deeper examination of productivity differences between industrial sectors within each urban size class which appear in breakdown B with a total value of 0.061 91. It is inferred that, with the sole exception of cities of 500 000–1 000 000 inhabitants, the differences between sectors in each class increase in parallel fashion with the increase in city size, reaching a maximum in the city-size group of 2 000 000 inhabitants and over: in Rio de Janeiro and São Paulo the differences of productivity between sectors are much greater than in the cities of smaller size.

Table 14.4 shows that total heterogeneity of industrial wages in the urban centres included in the sample attained a value of 0.068 54 in 1969, notoriously inferior to that for the State data (Table 14.2). Logically, the differences between States are greater than the differences between urban centres since cities are grouped in size classes independently of the State to which they belong. Interestingly, too, the wage differences result from differences in the size of the urban centres reach a maximum in metallurgy, whereas plastics show the lowest value. In the case of productivity equivalent values are observed in chemicals (maximum) and in leather and furs (minimum) respectively. This and other indices of the asymmetrical behaviour of productivity and wages constitute, to some extent, expressions of the presence of monopolistic elements in industry.

Further conclusions emerge from the comparison of productivity and wages behaviour. Mean industrial productivity shows *less* heterogeneous values in 1969 than in 1967 (by 6.1 per cent) while average wages show *more* heterogeneous values in 1969 than in 1967 (by 11.5 per cent). Comparison of the three breakdowns presented in Tables 14.1 and 14.2 indicates that throughout the three-year period the *inter-sectoral* differences play completely different roles in respect of productivity and of wages. A decrease (−8.8 per cent) is noted in the differences between sectors in the case of productivity, whereas an increase (14.8 per cent) of dispersion in sectoral terms is observed in the case of wages. Although inter-State differences show an identical trend in both cases, nevertheless they register completely different values, increasing by 8.3 per cent (productivity) and 19.1 per cent (wages). Such differences rise in both cases relative to differences between industrial plant sizes: 33.4 per cent in productivity and 23.9 per cent in wages. Finally, in every year, *differences in technology were more important than any other factor in explaining differences in both productivity and wages.*

In parallel, however, it is concluded that the *spatial factor proper (i.e. the differences between States) is significantly more important in explaining wage differentials than in explaining productivity differentials.* On average, the spatial factor is 50 per cent more important for wage than for productivity differentials. Thus a policy aiming at raising and standardizing industrial wages could not be designed without due regard for the spatial aspects, whereas the same is not necessarily true regarding productivity. Any attempt to design a migration policy in Brazil would thus have to rest in no small measure on the correction of the inter-State wage differences, at least within the industrial sector.

Moreover, State differences in productivity are less sensitive than inter-State wage differences at different scales of territorial aggregation, implying that the problem of spatial differences in wages cannot be tackled without considerable loss of information using any territorial division of the country. Yet if the figures in Tables 14.1 and 14.2 represent a definite longer-term tendency, the fact that inter-State wage differentials grow faster than do the inter-State productivity differentials clearly impinges on private decisions regarding location in the industrial sector. Obviously this reflects different spatial behaviour regarding the surplus generated in the industrial sector and the capacity–use rate: in line with the economic logic of a market system, private investors tend to maximize the use of capacity.

Urban size and productivity: some empirical evidence

Most studies approach the problem of city size conceptually or empirically from a viewpoint broader than that adopted here, and discuss the possible nature of costs and benefits relating to different city sizes. Fundamental theoretical works are by Klaassen (1965) and Isard (1966), yet the most meaningful empirical work is still that of Clark (1945). Recently Neutze (1965), Harris (1971) and Alonso (1971) have made significant contributions. Few have tackled the problem in Latin America, except Geiger (1963) and Schwartzman (1969). No definitive conclusions emerge and the question of the existence or otherwise of an 'optimum size' of cities in a dynamic system appears to be losing ground as a fruitful research objective.

This does not mean city size has lost relevance. On the contrary, there are few problems that require greater research effort, especially in countries like Brazil which are experiencing rapid urbanization. To achieve success, such research demands abandonment of global, in favour of specific, studies. So here only possible empirical relationships between different city sizes (measured by population) and average levels of industrial productivity and ages are investigated for 1969. Such a study is relevant for both industrial location policy and urban development policy in Brazil today.

Efficiency in the performance of a static urban–regional system can be increased, without additional resources, through the simple transfer of activities from cities with lower, to urban centres with higher, productivity. If it can be proved that certain industrial activities or certain sizes of establishments have greater productivity in urban centres of medium size, for example, that would constitute a strong objective argument for a particular industrial location or urban development policy. But the ramifications are wider: in progressive economic development in which foreign enterprise is crucial for exporting non-traditional goods, industrial production costs (particularly in exporting industries) are converted into determinant parameters of the ability to compete internationally. Part of the direct and indirect costs of industrial production arise from inefficient urban sizes for given industries. Thus relationships between the export capacity of manufactured goods and the location of the industry in the urban system are clear.

Population constitutes a poor approximation to 'real urban size', because of obvious variations in per capita income levels, activity rates and occupational structure of the labour force. Demographic data might have been further corrected by using population density as an indirect method of accounting urban congestion. Had such corrections been possible, rank sizes would have been altered, for example, by giving a larger 'size' to Greater Rio than to Greater São Paulo (Greater Rio is a denser, more congested city and thus has inferior internal accessibility). It is not clear, though, to what extent such corrections could significantly alter the global results.

A first analytical step was to investigate whether or not an *ordinal* correlation exists between the size of all the centres selected and their average productivity levels. Kendall's ordinal correlation coefficient yielded a value of 0.083, which is not significant at 5 per cent reliability, a result reflecting sampling biases which make small centres appear to be more industrialized (and with a higher productivity level) than other centres of the same class existing in Brazil. Secondly, productivity was related to urban size by adjusting several functions. Most regressions did not yield statistically-acceptable results. Fifty-six different models were tested in all, three types of equations always being used to estimate – in each case – a lineal adjustment, a second adjustment and a logarithmic adjustment. The equations chosen combined all the urban centres and all the industrial centres first of all, making way subsequently for both sectoral and urban disaggregations.

In selecting the best among acceptable adjustments, a small set of four models was derived. These four models associate: (1) the productivity of the consumer-goods producing sectors with *large* urban centres (over 500 000 inhabitants); (2) the productivity of intermediate-goods producing sectors with large urban centres; (3) the productivity of all industry with *medium–large* urban size category centres (from 200 000 to 500 000 inhabitants); and (4) the productivity of the entire industrial sector with large centres. The last two cases are examined below.

The mean annual industrial productivity and urban size class 200 000–500 000 inhabitants are related by the expression:

$$\frac{\text{VII}}{\text{OC}} = e^{-17.064}\ \text{POP}\ \frac{1.565\ 4}{(0.556\ 4)}$$

with an $R^2 = 0.538\ 7$ (Durwin and Watson test: 2.026 87, significant at 5 per cent of reliability), where VII represents the value of industrial productivity, OC corresponds to employment and POP indicates population in the urban centres. Likewise, productivity and urban size in the group of over 500 000 inhabitants are significantly associated in the following equation:

$$\frac{\text{VII}}{\text{OC}} = e^{-1.5616}\ \text{POP}\ \frac{0.296\ 13}{(0.069\ 5)}$$

with an $R^2 = 0.698\ 9$, also significant at 5 per cent reliability (Durwin and Watson test: 1.968 31). Both curves correspond to segments of parabolas, the first of them being convex with respect to the abscissas and the second concave since the respective exponents are greater or less than unity.

The value of the exponent of variable POP in both equations is (mathematically) the constant elasticity of the dependent variable – by inference equivalent to the *elasticity of the (mean) productivity of labour in relation to urban size*. That is, as urban size increases, the productivity (of industrial labour) increases *more* than proportionately starting from cities of 200 000 inhabitants, but *less* than proportionally in cities above 500 000 inhabitants. Thus, leaving the numerical values of the above equations aside, medium–large centres display better conditions (from this particular viewpoint) for demographic and industrial growth than large-sized centres. This opinion, though, must be qualified with regard to possible differences in industrial structure of the cities included in each class.

The medium–large urban centres include San Luis, Joao Pessoa, Juiz de Fora, Maceio, Natal, Manaus, Campinas, Santos and Goiana. The substantial geographic dispersion of these cities, combined with these results, could provide solid support for a policy of 'concentrated deconcentration' of industries and for steering population migration in Brazil. Since the limits of each size class are arbitrary, the results could relate also to cities like Sorocaba (165 000 inhabitants) and Curitiba (582 000 inhabitants). Significantly, most medium–large cities show above average population growth rates within Brazil's urban system.

The urban centres in the last class (over 500 000 inhabitants) comprise Brasilia, Curutiba, Belem, Fortaleza, Salvador, Porto Alegre, Recife, Belo Horizonte, Rio de Janeiro and São Paulo. Generally urban and industrial growth in these cities would yield decreasing returns in terms of the variables studied here. Since adjustment within this class would be strongly influenced by the sizes of Rio de Janeiro and of São Paulo, the same logarithmic function was again adjusted for the same class of urban size excluding these two cities. As expected, the adjustment was still inadequate, showing a marked rise in the curve's elasticity from 0.29 to 0.42, though still below unity. This only confirms that 'increasing returns' are certainly found in a range of urban size roughly between 150 000 and 160 000 inhabitants. These broad results tend to prove that productivity rises as urban size increases and support the results of other studies. Thus Alonso (1971), in criticizing the theory of minimum costs of city size, states that increased productivity per capita is a function of rises in urban size. But Alonso did not derive precisely the type of elasticity that would link wages and productivity.

The irksome time restrictions on any research project prevented attempts to improve the adjustments in two alternative ways. One consisted in introducing dummy variables which would reflect the regional location (in terms of the five large regions) of each urban centre. The second alternative consisted in correcting the population of each city by its 'population potential' in the whole urban system: i.e. the size of each centre would be given by its own population plus the sum of the populations of the remaining urban centres, discounting the effect of distance. Both methods are thus suggested as possible extensions of this work. Nevertheless the original study (Boisier, 1973) identified certain industrial sectors with both high productivity and a high productivity growth rate which simultaneously show high geographic dispersion indices (at the urban level) and for which the importance of different urban sizes with respect to the heterogeneity of productivity is very small. Such sectors represent a potential group of activities which are exceedingly appropriate to a policy for a geographic decentralization of industrial activity.

Conclusions

This project casts serious doubts on the validity of some hypotheses which regional economic analysis has elevated almost to dogma status. The so-called 'efficiency *versus* equality conflict' is the basic weapon in the theoretical arsenal conceived to contend with the problems of regional development: Alonso (1968), Coraggio (1969) and Mera (1970) offer rigorous treatment. In its simplest form the national development viewpoint (the global perspective) is that an optimum situation should be reached in which the yield per unit of scarce resources used is maximized; for more harmonious development of the regional system (the spatial perspective), however, an optimum situation should be reached in which some measure of inter-regional dispersion is *minimized*. Both approaches involve conflicts and inconsistencies under certain conditions: the global criterion of efficiency implies a spatial allocation (or assignment) of resources which favours the most productive regions, whereas the spatial criterion of equality implies a spatial distribution of resources favouring the most backward regions. This is a typical conflict of *values* that permits only a political solution in which the role of the technical expert is reduced to stating the precise opportunity cost. The validity of the conflict between both criteria of assignment rests on accepting the hypothesis that 'more' and 'less' productive regions coexist within one and the same spatial system.

Empirical evidence proves substantively that, at least in the case of Brazilian industry, there are no regions *per se* more or less productive than others; yet there are regions with different industrial structures within which *sectors* of high and low productivity do co-exist. More important still, spatial differences in productivity at the level of all the industrial sectors are quite low whatever the spatial dimensions of analysis may be. Similarly, in several industrial sectors, productivity differences attributable to differences of urban size are negligible. It is possible to define a set of industrial sectors that register high growth rates (thus satisfying the efficiency criterion) simultaneously displaying high indices of geographic dispersion, with urban size being of slight importance in the differences of productivity (thus satisfying the equality criterion). There thus appear to be no fundamental reasons against the possibility of there being 'efficient' and 'equitable' solutions *at the same time*. Although factual evidence is insufficient to invalidate completely the conceptual basis of the 'efficiency *versus* equity' conflict, it is enough to introduce reasonable doubt as to its absolute validity.

Another facet fundamental in debate on regional development is also presented as a dichotomous option: 'place-aid *versus* people-aid'. Cumberland (1972) questions this dichotomy. But which is more efficient, State aid for *individuals* or State aid for *places*? The regional planning specialist has apparently to favour aid for places. Yet in effect all the quantitative analysis carried out here emphasizes the greater importance of *sectoral* heterogeneity over *spatial* heterogeneity, at least for industrial productivity and wages. This suggests that it might be more efficient regarding labour productivity *to regionalize sectoral policies than to design global regional policies* to solve successfully the problems caused by regional disequilibria in Brazil. The validity of this must still be tested by similar reference to capital productivity, a key parameter in this type of problem. Nevertheless, the results obtained so far introduce reasonable doubt as to the foreseeable theoretical behaviour of certain economic phenomena in a spatial context.

Differences *between sectors* always constitute the most variable element in both productivity and wages, but if it could be proven that spatial variations in wages are greater than for productivity this would indicate that the *technology* associated with the type of industrial activity is the key parameter for ascertaining the levels of productivity and wages, whereas the *economies of agglomeration* affect mainly the wage level and only secondarily the level of productivity. However logical backing from prevailing theory for this elegant hypothesis is weak. Perhaps the real reason for unequal impact of the 'space' factor on both variables lies more with social and cultural characteristics and with labour's skill level in each 'spatial unit' used in the analysis. If so, the consequences are of singular importance for the nature of regional development policy. If in effect public or private investors can locate in practically any part of the country without noticeable loss of productivity, location decision may be steered (toward the desired location) with a greater facility than that supposed and, eventually, with smaller social costs. The emphasis in regional policy, then, does not necessarily centre around the question of *creating employment opportunities* at any cost and in any location, but on *improving the supply capacity of the local labour force* through investments in human capital, i.e. health, nutrition and training. Implicitly, the modernization of some backward areas requires that State investment in production should be highly selective of sectors of activity as opposed to any global concept and should rest on a deglomeration strategy which concentrates growth in cities of medium size.

References

Alonso, W. (1968), 'Equity and its relation to efficiency in urbanization', *Working Paper* No. 78, Center for Planning and Development Research, Univ. of California.

Alonso, W. (1971), 'The economics of urban size', in: *Papers of the Regional Science Association,* **XXVI.**

Boisier, S. (1972), *Regional Disaggregation of National Plans. Some Comments on the Rotterdam and Warsaw Models,* United Nations Research Institute for Social Development, UNRISD/71/C.51/Add.1. Geneva.

Boisier, S. (1973), *Desenvolvimento Regional e Urbano. Diferenciais productividade e Salarios Industriats,* Brazilian Ministry of Planning, Brazilia.

Centro de Estudios del Desarrollo, Universidad Central de Caracas (1969), Proyecto URVEN. Caracas, *Urbanizacion en Venezuela.*

Clark, C. (1945), 'The economic function of a city in relation to its size', *Econometrica,* pp. 71–86.

Coraggio, J. L. (1969), *Elementos para una discusion sobje eficiencia, equidad y conflicto entre regiones,* Centro Interdisciplinario de Desarrollo Urbano y Regional (CIDU), Univ. of Catolica de Chile.

Cumberland, J. H. (1972), *Regional Development, Experiences and Prospects in the United States of America,* Mouton, The Hague.

De Mattos, C. (1970), *Notas sobre la planificacion regional a escala nacional,* Documento C/I, Curso de Planificacion Regional Del Desarrollo, CEPAL/ILPES/OCT, Santiago.

Geiger, P. P. (1963), *Evolucao da Rede Urbana Brasilera,* Centro Brasilero de Pesquisas Educacionals, Rio de Janeiro.

Harris, J. R. (1971), 'Urban and industrial deconcentration', *Regional and Urban Economics,* 1 (2).

Hilhorst, J. C. M. (1971), *Regional Planning,* University Press, Rotterdam.

Isard, W. (1966), *Methods of Regional Analysis,* MIT, Cambridge.

Klaassen, L. H. (1965), 'Regional policy in the Benelux countries', *Area Development Policies in Britain and in the Countries of the Common Market,* US Department of Commerce, Washington, DC.

Kuklinski, A. R. (1967), *Trends in Research on Comprehensive Regional Development,* United Nations Research Institute for Social Development, UNRISD/68/C.2, Geneva.

Kuklinski, A. R., ed. (1974), *Regional Disaggregation of National Plans and Policies,* Mouton, The Hague.

Manrique, R. (1970), *Localizacion Industrial y Proceso de Urbanizacion in Colombia,* Documento de Trabajo, 2, Centro de Investigaciones para el Desarrollo, Bogota.

Mera, K. (1970), *On the Concentration of Urbanization and Economic Efficiency,* Economic Department Working Paper, International Bank for Reconstruction and Development.

Neutze, G. M. (1965), *Economic Policy and the Size of Cities,* Australia National U.P., Canberra.

Schwartzman, S. (1969), 'Urbanizacion y Desarrollo en Brasil', *La Urbanizacion en America Latina,* Hardo, J. E. y Tobar, C., editores, Instituto T. di Tella, Buenos Aires.

Stanford Research Institute (1968), *Cost of Urban Infrastructure for Industry Related to City Size in Developing Countries,* Stanford.

Stöhr, W. (1972), *El desarrollo regional en America Latina: Experiencias y Perspectivas,* Ediciones SIAP, Buenos Aires.

Theil, H. (1967), *Economics and Information Theory,* North-Holland, The Hague.

Utria, R. (1972), *Una politica de desarrollo regional y urbano en funcion de la realidad latinomericana,* Documento presentado al IX Congreso Interamericano de Planifacaciòn, Bogota.

Index

200   *Index*

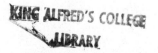